GOOD LUCK
HAVE FUN

GOOD LUCK HAVE FUN

THE RISE OF eSPORTS

ROLAND LI

Skyhorse Publishing

Copyright © 2016 by Roland Li

First paperback edition 2017

10 9 8 7 6 5 4 3 2 1

Library of Congress Cataloging-in-Publication Data is available on file.

ISBN: 978-1-5107-2590-4
Ebook ISBN: 978-1-63450-658-8

Cover design by Erin Seaward-Hiatt
Cover image: iStock

Printed in the United States of America

This book is dedicated to the eSports community.
You make this possible.

CONTENTS

Pre-Game	Why Video Games Matter	1
Chapter 1	The Evil Genius: Alexander Garfield and the Rise of North America	9
Chapter 2	The Emperor of Seoul: Boxer and Brood War	35
Chapter 3	Nuclear Launch Detected: Starcraft II Explodes	52
Chapter 4	Stream Dreams: Twitch	80
Chapter 5	A Challenger Appears: League of Legends Ascends	106
Chapter 6	Unbalanced: Women, Race, and Gaming	131
Chapter 7	Born to Win: DOTA 2 Raises the Stakes	150
Chapter 8	Capital Flood: Big Money Comes to eSports (Again)	183
Chapter 9	The Road to $18 Million: The Fifth International	200
Epilogue		223
The Players		229
Acknowledgments		235
Notes		239

Pre-Game

WHY VIDEO GAMES MATTER

On October 19, 1972, two dozen students gathered at Stanford University's Artificial Intelligence Laboratory to do battle among the stars. They piloted ships through a speck-filled void, shooting missiles and dancing against gravity in one of the world's first video games, Spacewar. First prize was a year's subscription to *Rolling Stone* magazine.

Spacewar was played on the Programmed Data Processor-1, an early computer that weighed 1,200 pounds and was limited mostly to academic centers. A group of students at the Massachusetts Institute of Technology created the game, which was primitive but joyful, sucking players in and creating a community.

"Reliably, at any nighttime moment (i.e., nonbusiness hours) in North America, hundreds of computer technicians are effectively out of their bodies, locked in life-or-death space combat computer-projected onto cathode ray tube display screens, for hours at a time, ruining their eyes, numbing their fingers in frenzied mashing of control buttons, joyously slaying their friends and wasting their employers' valuable computer time. Something basic is going on," Stewart Brand wrote in *Rolling Stone*.

Competition has always been a central part of video games. The first arcades measured skill with high scores. Top players could etch their names in three-letter combinations, showing off to subsequent players until they were knocked down. Spacewar's source code was released for free, but as video games became a commercial enterprise, developers saw the potential of formal competition as a way of attracting more customers.

In 1980, Atari created the Space Invaders Championship, where thousands of players competed. The competitive show *Starcade* was broadcast on television the next year. In the 1990s, the Nintendo World Championships were held, where kids showed off their Super Mario skills.

Games became more complex, supporting more players and richer graphics and systems. The Internet heightened competition, spawning communities that formulated and dissected strategies across the globe.

Four decades later, competitive video gaming, also known as electronic sports or eSports, has become a global phenomenon. Millions of viewers watch competitions every month, and players train full time to compete for cash prizes that reach seven figures.

The professional gamers clicking furiously and staring intently at screens would be familiar sights to those students at Stanford four decades ago, even if their branded headphones and colorful team jerseys might seem strange.

Technology's penetration into virtually every aspect of our lives has made gaming ubiquitous. Video games are played around the world, from Stockholm to Seoul to San Francisco, between players connected almost instantly by the Internet. Streaming video competitions are a click away on a computer, tablet, or phone. Broadcast costs have plummeted thanks to investments and the tenacity of some key entrepreneurs. But the most critical factor in the success of eSports is the passion, if not outright obsession, of the players, tournament organizers, investors, game developers, and, above all, the fans. They made it possible, and their flaws and struggles have made eSports an imperfect phenomenon. No one got into eSports originally to get rich, but now they can.

Passion isn't always enough. The industry is littered with the digital fragments of teams, players, and organizations that no longer exist, with a legacy of unpaid salaries and defunct websites. Companies can live and die in days, teams shuffle rosters constantly, and players quit after poor results or when "real life" intrudes. Scandals like match-fixing, unpaid prize money, and fraud abound. For all its growth, regulation is almost nonexistent. If the NBA and NFL are entering a fat and lucrative middle age, eSports is still the twenty-five-year-old who got a killer job but hasn't figured his life out yet.

The adversarial and interactive nature of video games makes them different than most other art forms, like film, television, music, and theater. The struggle against a computer or human opponent means that playing can become a craft. Many of the best games allow players to clearly differentiate themselves through skill, falling somewhere between the curated, individualized experience of traditional art and the competitive nature of sports. Games transport the player into an entirely new virtual place through sights and sounds. It's a new medium, and for some, a frightening glimpse at a future detached from reality: a waste of time.

Do video games matter? The question can be expanded. What value do athletes or actors or artists bring? Their contributions to society through competitions, movies, and artwork aren't entirely tangible, yet many are beloved more than those who provide the food, shelter, and jobs that directly sustain people.

By evoking strong emotions, professional gamers and the games they play become worthy of attention. Fans vote with their money, but also their time.

Games have grown to be a cultural force and an economic powerhouse. The research firm Newzoo projects that global video game industry revenue will exceed $100 billion by 2017. And eSports is gaining a larger chunk of that investment every day, with Deloitte projecting eSports revenue of $500 million in 2016.

The late film critic Robert Ebert claimed that video games could never be art. But there is a beauty and aesthetic to a pro gamer's movements, his or her reflexes, the coordination and sequencing of a team in harmony. Skill clearly differentiates good players from bad.

What makes a good player? First is mastery of mechanics, the physical control of play through mouse clicks and keyboard taps. In a shooting game, gun accuracy and player positioning are essential.

In other games, skilled play resembles an orchestra of feints and strikes as characters traverse the digital space, following an underlying plan that's often invisible to the casual observer. Explosions, gunshots, and fireballs are just the chrome on strategies that can resemble movements on a chessboard. Strategy arises from knowledge of games' systems, and how to maximize efficiency, and it is the second pillar of the pro gamer.

And the top games constantly evolve, so strategies shift. Successful competitive titles receive continual balance changes and even new characters, changing and challenging players to adapt and be flexible. Software updates, which adjust gameplay mechanics or stats, mean that no single strategy can remain dominant for too long. The collection of strategies and preferences that shape competition, known as the metagame, is always in motion.

The challenge is balancing this evolution without diminishing or disrupting the skills and experience that separate casual gamers from the pro players who commit their lives.

"What does it take to get really good? You have to sacrifice everything else in your life," said Frank Lantz, director of the New York University Game Center. "If that thing is going to change next week or next month, that is a tragedy.

"At the same time, you need enough flexibility that the game can evolve," said Lantz. "It's a healthy sweet spot between being stable enough that people can master it at a deep level and flexible enough that it can evolve and grow and improve."

Competitive team games, which are the most popular titles in 2016, add another layer, requiring communication and coordination, usually between five players. Beyond actually playing the game, teams have to manage emotions, finances, and focus.

Is eSports actually a sport?

The idea seems preposterous from one view. How is clicking a mouse and typing on a keyboard at all comparable to the exertions of leaping, running, or swimming through physical space? The body is not visibly engaged, aside from the fingers and the mind.

Yet is gaming all that different from NASCAR? Or chess? Or poker? All of which have been broadcast on ESPN, the American arbiter of what is a sport, or at least what resembles one enough to commit the airtime. And in the 1990s, ESPN2 broadcast competitive Magic: The Gathering, the first collectible card game, where players battle by "summoning" fantastical creatures and hurl spells like Lightning Bolt and Lava Axe at each other, all represented by cards. There's a precedent for new competitive platforms emerging. The E in ESPN stands for entertainment, and in January 2016, it launched a dedicated eSports section on its website.

Part of the unease over the growth of eSports is a fear of the new. Gaming has only been present for a few decades, compared to thousands of years of history for sports like track and field or swimming. But basketball and baseball only developed in the last century. And gaming now has decades of history to build upon.

Veterans of eSports say it's ultimately irrelevant if competitive gaming is characterized as a sport. It has all the elements of competition: high-stakes winnings, a barrier to competition that takes skill and training, the excitement of fans, and now, the technological infrastructure to back it all up.

Translating the competition inherent in games into a formalized, regulated environment has been a struggle. Leagues like the NBA and NFL are the product of many years of commercial dominance. Gaming has relatively young companies, and only a handful have been around for more than a decade. Control is complicated by the presence of the software developer, who has distinct copyright ownership over a game.

Traditional sports may have originated from one creator, but that figure is often disputed, and the rules of play are tweaked and localized throughout the world. Leagues may also adjust rules as they see fit.

A major video game, however, is a commercial product. There is usually one company responsible for its development, with the most to gain financially from a game's popularity. But a developer is not a tournament organizer or league operator, and only a few companies have sustained games as eSports.

The role of the developer is crucial as the arbiter of design and a potential enforcer of rules. Just as basketball and baseball developed from tiny fields and courts to massive stadiums with only the guidance of a business overlord, eSports has required investment and leadership to leap from bedrooms into giant arenas.

The potential scale of eSports is enormous. Like gaming, it is a global enterprise, with gamers in the heart of the American Midwest, in crowded PC cafés in South Korea, and in European cities like Moscow and Berlin.

It is still dwarfed by traditional sports, with an estimated $278 million in eSports financial activity in 2015 according to Newzoo, compared to revenue of over $10 billion for the NFL and $21 billion for European soccer leagues. Viewership for the championship of the top game League of Legends hit 32 million in 2013, compared to a peak of 120 million viewers that watched the 2015 Super Bowl.

But the pace of growth is outstripping every other major entertainment sector. Global brands like Coca-Cola, American Express, and Intel have entered a market that was laughably tiny just five years ago.

For players and fans, competition goes beyond a career. It is a passion, if not an obsession. The agony of defeat can be just as compelling as the joy of triumph. Win or lose, eSports may not change the world. But it has already changed millions of lives.

Chapter 1

THE EVIL GENIUS

ALEXANDER GARFIELD AND THE RISE OF NORTH AMERICA

Five gunmen stride through an abandoned train station. Their weapons are poised as they move in formation. Their faces are hidden by black ski masks, adding more menace to their intimidating arsenals. Suddenly, a smoke grenade flies in, obscuring their views. Shots bark out, and one of the gunman drops, his head now a bloody ruin.

The gunmen take cover. One is carrying a heavy sniper rifle, hanging back until he glimpses an enemy in his scope. One shot, one kill. His allies spring forward, using their momentum to capture more territory. Their four remaining enemies, clad in green camouflage, are slaughtered one at a time until only one remains, slinking under cover.

The gunmen stride forward and approach their goal: a valuable munitions cache in the train station. They drop an improvised bomb and it counts down to detonation: three, two, one.

"Terrorists win."

There isn't much resemblance between the digital gunmen and the five young men who controlled them and clicked their way to victory. They're dressed in jerseys with some computer company logos and jeans. They yell and high-five. One point won for the round, fifteen to go.

This isn't Afghanistan or Iraq. It's the map de_train, and the game is Counter-Strike.

Counter-Strike is a first-person shooter, or FPS, a type of game where players take a soldier's-eye view of the action, with a gun jutting out into a landscape of buildings and debris. Victory usually comes from killing opponents. The FPS is a visceral experience, a twitchy adrenaline rush where death is often accompanied by a screen-blanketing cloud of blood. The genre was conceived as early as the 1970s, but truly broke through in the 1990s with Doom, a magnet for controversy with its satanic imagery and association with the perpetrators of the Columbine High School massacre.

Counter-Strike was initially the fan creation of two college students, Minh "Gooseman" Le and Jess Cliffe, who created it as a modification, or mod, by using existing assets from Bellevue, Washington–based Valve Corporation's popular game Half-Life.

Le was a student at Simon Fraser University in British Columbia studying computer programming, and game design intrigued him. The Rainbow Six games, based on Tom Clancy's military novels, were the basis for his realistic theme for Counter-Strike. Instead of battling mutant beasts or demons, Counter-Strike pitted player-controlled terrorists and counter-terrorists against each other.

Unlike early shooter games, where players rampaged alone against computer-controlled monsters, Counter-Strike was a team game, with five humans battling five humans. Le wanted a game that was more reliant on coordination and communication than pure reflexes, so that even less skilled players could contribute.

Players earn money by getting kills, which is spent on better guns and equipment and can be shared with teammates later in the match, pushing the group concept. But Counter-Strike was never meant to be a formal competition.

"It really wasn't about eSports," said Le. "It was about playing with a bunch of strangers and having an experience that was fun."

Le did all the programming and artwork, modeling the guns after visiting a shooting range and looking at online photos. He admits now that the gun sounds were lifted from other games and edited to be distinct, because it was too hard to record real gunshots. As Le tinkered away, Cliffe worked with the community of players, which submitted their own map designs that were incorporated into the game. The game grew in popularity just by word-of-mouth, with no advertising. Valve hired Le and Cliffe and gave Counter-Strike a commercial release in 1999.

"We weren't sure if we were going to be pushed aside," said Le. He had just graduated from college. Valve added a few more programmers and ten more artists to the two-man team, but the company's flat management structure let Le maintain creative control. "I was able to grow a lot," he said.

In Counter-Strike's most popular and competitive game mode, Bomb Defusal, terrorists try to plant a bomb at specific sites on the map, while the other team of counter-terrorists try to thwart them. The idea came from the slew of real-life Middle East car bombings that occurred during the game's design, said Le.

If the bomb explodes, the terrorists win. Counter-terrorists must either defuse the bomb or survive the one-minute-and-forty-five-second round without an explosion. An alternative way to win is to completely slaughter the other team. The first team that wins sixteen out of thirty rounds is the ultimate victor.

Counter-Strike has clear objectives and a scoring system that makes fast-paced competitive play possible. And unlike other shooters, where players were reincarnated and can return to fights after dying, dead players are eliminated for the remainder of the round and their team has to play at a disadvantage. The game has a steep learning curve, and crisp control differentiates newcomers from veterans. The guns simulate recoil, adding realism, and the effect differs between guns, potentially throwing off players' aim. Players have to learn to shoot straight by aiming with a mouse while simultaneously using the W, A, S, and D keys for movement.

Counter-Strike drew in players like Alexander Garfield, who grew up in the suburbs of Philadelphia. He subscribed to *Nintendo Power* and got his own PC around 2000. Two years later, he discovered Counter-Strike.

Garfield first played the game after dragging his computer to a friend's LAN, or local area network, where gamers play in the same room with their machines physically wired together to do battle. LANs are considered the purest form of competition because players are in the same location, and slowdowns due to distance, known as lag, usually aren't an issue. For casual gamers, LANs create a fun atmosphere with a social intimacy that's sometimes missing online.

In Garfield's first game, he had zero kills and thirteen deaths. "I thought it was insanely frustrating because bullets wouldn't go where I was pointing the gun, and I got completely destroyed," said Garfield. "I started playing at home, and I was totally hooked."

Gaming was a competitive outlet for Garfield, who didn't have the bulk to conquer the lacrosse fields or basketball courts, despite being a big fan of Philadelphia's sports teams. "It really hit something that I was looking for," he said. After a player grasped the basics, the next level was learning tactics, coordination, and communication.

Garfield's play took him beyond the suburbs to opponents around the country. California was well known for its local leagues, and Texas was another hotbed for gaming. He made online friends beyond his town, and he also began writing for the website GotFrag, which covered Counter-Strike with the scrutiny of a daily newspaper.

His parents were tolerant of gaming, as long as Garfield remained a diligent student and did other activities.

Garfield's family came from humble roots but had achieved affluence through education. Garfield's dad, Eugene Garfield, was born in 1925 in the Bronx. Eugene had a taste of labor at an early age.

"I grew up working. When I was nine, I was delivering orders in a grocery store and worked in a laundry for hours just to earn a quarter. Later, I went to work for my uncles. I delivered orders in my Uncle Lou's liquor store. Then I worked in the garment district after school and summers," Eugene told the *Chemical Intelligencer* in October 1999.

Eugene would study science and invent the "impact factor," which measures how many citations an academic journal receives on average in the past two years, which can be a way of ranking its influence. It became an arbiter of power in the scientific world, and Eugene made a fortune and eventually sold his company, the Institute for Scientific Information, to Thomson Reuters. But money was never Eugene's primary motive.

"Too often, people are afraid of failure. They worry that they cannot manage financially. Money never drove me; it came to me. Nevertheless, if I had worried about money, I might never have achieved financial success," he said.

Garfield's mom, Catherine, grew up as one of eleven siblings on a farm outside Philadelphia. She worked at Eugene's company and met him there.

When Garfield was applying to college, his mom encouraged him to write about his gaming passion in his applications. He recoiled. "She thought I should write about it for my college essay, and I was like, 'Absolutely not. You are out of your mind, Mom.' Because I thought no one would ever take it seriously," he remembers.

Garfield was waitlisted at Ivy League schools and chose Pomona College near Los Angeles over liberal arts schools on the East Coast. "It was more of a laid-back atmosphere," he said. In 2013, Pomona would feature an essay about Garfield's gaming career in its alumni magazine.

Shortly after arriving at school, Garfield recalls playing one versus eight classmates in a Counter-Strike match and beating them all. Then he quit gaming to focus on classes and a new girlfriend.

Garfield considered becoming an aerospace engineer, because of his affinity for numbers. "I never liked writing papers as much as I liked taking tests," he said. But part of him wanted something different. Garfield didn't want his identity to be an extension of his family's scientific legacy, and he didn't want to follow a standard degree to success. His dad could probably have landed him a job, but he didn't want any handouts. "I wanted to do my own thing, on my own path," said Garfield.

During Garfield's first semester, in January 2004, four students stole an eleven-foot iron cross that a student had built for an art class at nearby Claremont College and set it on fire. There were disagreements—should it be classified as a hate crime or freedom of expression? Students were suspended instead of expelled.

"It ignited this whole semester of tension," said Garfield, and it influenced his choice of studies. Following the events, he went on to major in sociology and minor in classics and African American Studies. He could decide on a career later. For now, it was more important to learn.

At the end of 2004, Garfield was home over Christmas break and realized he missed gaming. "It wasn't the scene itself that drew me in. It was the competition. And I think that aspect more than anything else has kept me here," he said. He tried out as a player for a smaller Counter-Strike team, but he got nervous and couldn't handle the pressure of playing. Instead, he began writing for the website of Evil Geniuses, a Counter-Strike team from Western Canada founded in 1999.

A competitive gaming team aspires to be like a traditional sports team, but in the early days of eSports, there was only a loosely organized tournament system, without the regularity of a season that culminated in an ultimate championship, like the NFL or NBA. Events were sporadic and held in various regions. Gamers were closer to tennis players or golfers, playing in one-off tournaments with their own prize pools.

The first major US video game tournament was the Cyber-athlete Professional League (CPL), founded in 1997 by Angel Munoz.

Munoz, who grew up in Puerto Rico, worked as a stockbroker and investment banker. He founded a technology-focused investment firm in Dallas, Texas, called New World Investments, Inc. Five years later, Munoz sold the firm to a company from the United Kingdom. With no immediate career plans, Munoz started playing video games and got hooked.

Serendipitously, Dallas was a shooting game haven, thanks to the presence of id Software, the game developer that made the classic titles Wolfenstein 3D, Doom, and Quake and also organized some early events.

Munoz saw financial potential and launched the CPL with funding from computer parts manufacturers Logitech, Intel, and Nvidia. The CPL grew to become the premier North American eSports event, hosting a variety of shooter games, with Counter-Strike emerging as the primary title. It would eventually pay out millions of dollars in prize money over the next decade.

The early days were lean, but competitors from Europe and North America flocked to the Hyatt Regency Hotel in Dallas to battle for a few thousand dollars, lugging their giant computer towers. Most of them lost money after paying for flights and lodging, but the thrill of competition drew them back throughout the year. Players sat at creaky chairs and tables, with fans and defeated foes looking over their shoulders while they shot and strafed.

Some newcomers tried to replicate the CPL's model, but there was often a knowledge gap in running a successful tournament. The Cyber X Games were held in January 2004, seizing its name from the X Games—which focused on "extreme sports" like skateboarding and motorbiking—despite no formal affiliation. Held in Las Vegas, it boasted a $600,000 prize pool. But infrastructure issues and network failures crippled the event. With only a few matches played, tournament organizer Joe Hill cancelled it.

Money was scarce. Event organizers grabbed the modest revenues from broadcasts and ticket sales. Players took home the prize money. The teams themselves were more like agents, handling the logistics of transporting players to events and connecting them with actual sources of money: sponsors. Managers sought to attract funding from companies, usually in exchange for putting their logos on team jerseys and perhaps having the team appear in promotional videos. Sometimes sponsors would give teams free equipment, which players would use or the team would sell.

Evil Geniuses' manager was named Mohammad Ocean, or "a tall guy named Mo," as Garfield puts it. The team had gotten sponsorship commitments from two computer companies, Abit and ATI Technologies, worth a total of around $36,000 a year, a solid amount for a young team. The money funded regular trips to the CPL and the other big competition: the World Cyber Games, or WCG. South Korea's Samsung Electronics sponsored the event, which was envisioned as the Olympics of video gaming, with teams grouped by nationality, fighting for bronze, silver, and gold medals.

In the fall of 2004, Evil Geniuses represented Canada in the WCG finals in San Francisco. Garfield remembered the first signs of the team's unraveling. Some team staff had to buy their own plane tickets, and Ocean became more difficult to reach. He had been going through some personal issues and had some disagreements with sponsors, according to the team's players.

After the team was eliminated early, Ocean disappeared. The team was going to disband, and the players were ready to take their chances with other teams. But Garfield wanted to preserve Evil Geniuses, and not for business reasons.

"They were my friends," said Garfield. "They were special because of who they were, not because they finished first, second, or third."

He offered to find sponsors, and the players laughed but agreed to give him a chance. First, he tried to mend the relationships with the team's previous sponsors. But the salespeople were angry and confused that Ocean had stopped returning their calls, too. One demanded that Garfield return sponsorship money that had previously been paid. It was a dead end, and Garfield began cold-calling other companies that had any potential ties to gaming. He thinks his greatest asset was persistence. "The first couple of deals I got, I was constantly on the phone and I just wouldn't leave people alone," said Garfield. "ESports was still totally new to them."

Garfield got a few hundred dollars for the team, and the friends agreed to stick together. An early backer was the Danish company SteelSeries, a gaming mouse and keyboard manufacturer that began investing in eSports in 2001 and still sponsored Evil Geniuses in 2016. "There are very few areas that so beautifully marry cutting-edge technology with creativity and art and fantasy," said Ehtisham Rabbani, CEO of SteelSeries. "I think that's what makes gaming so beautiful."

Garfield even managed to get the online computer merchant Newegg as a temporary sponsor, even though they didn't ship to Evil Geniuses' home of Canada. He highlighted the team's American fan base and its charisma. The team was diligent in thanking sponsors during interviews. Evil Geniuses also got around $500 from Zboard, a specialty gaming keyboard company that was later sold to SteelSeries, and the team's nationality led to a sponsorship from Intel Canada.

"I focused on what I thought was special about the team, which was its personalities," said Garfield. "I think the reason that my sales pitch worked was that I really believed in what I was selling."

His age may have been a barrier initially, but Garfield turned out to be an effective salesman. He was soft-spoken, with a mop-top haircut and a slim stature. He didn't command the room, but he had passion and a compelling PowerPoint presentation. "I was very genuine. I was an example of my culture," he said. "I guess there was always this part of me that wanted that responsibility and was able to deliver it."

The money wasn't always reliable. Garfield would go to the Wells Fargo bank in Claremont near his college and get into fights with the tellers because checks for him wouldn't transfer fast enough. He had to book flights for his entire team on his college debit card for competitions that were sometimes days away. He almost broke into tears. He borrowed $3,000 from his mom to fund plane tickets, and his dad lent him money too. He eventually paid them back.

Most of Evil Geniuses' players were students and balanced part-time jobs with training for Counter-Strike. They lived in different cities, which limited the amount of time the team could train together in the same room. Most practice sessions were held online, which was less effective.

Robert "blackpanther" Tyndale joined Evil Geniuses in 2003 and recalls that the team's lack of practice led to little mistakes, which led to major losses. Team morale was also a factor. When facing a big deficit or losing a lead, players would blame teammates or ignore advice. Having an in-game leader, known as the captain or shot-caller, was crucial for maintaining morale and dictating strategies and assigning players to roles that suited them. "You have to have a real insider's perspective on players' skills," said Tyndale, who was captain for part of his career.

Evil Geniuses' breakout tournament was the CPL Summer 2005. The Canadians beat the European juggernaut SK Gaming's Swedish division in the semifinals in overtime and clinched a spot in the finals. But like many eSports tournaments, the format was double-elimination, and SK Gaming came roaring back from the lower bracket and played Evil Geniuses in a rematch for the championship.

In the finals against SK Gaming, little mistakes "ate away at us," remembers Tyndale. Evil Geniuses' opponents were better able to handle the pressure, as the most successful team in CPL history with seven championships, and they were unfazed by the earlier loss. SK triumphed, and the Canadians ended up second, surpassing expectations but still falling short. It was a highlight for Garfield, who owned a mouse pad emblazoned with SK's curving logo, but it was still disappointing.

Evil Geniuses was established as a contender, but it still wasn't the top team in North America. A 2004 documentary on the team was titled *About Average.* They never seemed able to get that breakthrough victory. "There was quite a lot of heartbreak. But it was still an amazing group of people," said Garfield. As a life-long fan of Philadelphia sports teams, he was used to rooting for the underdog.

Sometimes, the team was thwarted by freak accidents. In 2005, at a tournament in South Korea near the height of Evil Geniuses' skill, Tyndale accidentally threw a flash grenade at a box on the map de_nuke, which led to a known game error, or bug, that blinded the entire enemy team. The tournament rules meant that they had to forfeit the game because of the mistake, and they were later eliminated.

And while their friendship was essential for keeping the team together through turmoil, it may have held some players back from bigger victories with other squads. Evil Geniuses' best player was Matt "bl00dsh0t" Stevenson, who was nicknamed "The Sword" for his stunning plays. He would face off against four gun-wielding opponents and somehow triumph with just a knife. At one tournament, Tyndale remembers he shot blindly through a wall and scored a kill. Many teams tried to poach him from the team, but he remained committed to Evil Geniuses because of friendship. "He would never have as much fun" on another team, said Tyndale.

Tyndale's fondest memories with Evil Geniuses weren't from battling at tournaments. He remembers just hanging out with his teammates in new cities, like when they drank wine in Italy during his teammate Pasha "LaRi" Lari's birthday. He got to travel the world with airplane tickets and hotel rooms paid for by the team's sponsors (and sometimes Garfield's mom). It was a pretty sweet career, and well worth the hours of practice each week.

But Evil Geniuses still struggled to win, and many of their defeats came at the hands of America's top two teams: Team 3D and compLexity.

Craig "Torbull" Levine, 3D's founder, is regarded as the godfather of American eSports. As a student at New York University's Stern School of Business, Levine began working at an East Village Internet cafe called web2zone. In 2002, a business developer from Samsung, the cafe's owner, visited and told him that the South Korean conglomerate would sponsor Levine if he made a team that could qualify for the World Cyber Games.

Levine called up some of the top players he had previously played with who were free agents, and Team 3D was born, named for its three principles: desire, discipline, and dedication. The team began dominating American competition and qualified for the WCG, but the Samsung contact proved to be unreliable and a deal never happened. The team managed to secure sponsorships from Intel, the giant semiconductor maker; graphics card specialist Nvidia; and the computer store CompUSA. Unlike Garfield, Levine was willing to cut players and poach others, which kept 3D atop the standings. The team became a legitimate business and had some of the most intricate playbooks in eSports, preparing ten to twenty strategies for each tournament. The level

21

of professionalism surprised some of its players. "I never went into it with the idea that I was going to be a pro gamer. I just kept wanting to compete," said Sal "Volcano" Garozzo, a former Team 3D player. "It just naturally happened."

Jason Lake's compLexity was a comparable upstart. Lake had never played Counter-Strike until meeting his roommate at Emory Law School in Atlanta, Georgia. He founded compLexity with hundreds of thousands of dollars of his own money, and signed the best US players who weren't already playing for other teams. They were paid $1,000 a month and made their debut in a CPL event in December 2004, placing fifth.

"I really thought this was the sport of the future," said Lake, who had been a linebacker on his high school football team. Unlike the majority of players and managers, who were no older than their twenties, Lake was thirty-two when he started the team and was running a law firm and raising two young children. He became a father figure to his team, ready with fiery inspiration both before and during matches, where he paced behind his seated players. Lake developed a set of spontaneous catchphrases. When his team gained an early lead, he would yell, "Welcome to the show!" On the verge of victory, he would exhort his players to close out matches, roaring, "Backbreaker!"

Team 3D and compLexity got so good that they were beating the Europeans, the most dominant region in Counter-Strike. In July 2005, the same week Evil Geniuses came up short against SK Gaming's Swedish division, compLexity became the first US team to win a championship on European soil at the Electronic Sports World Cup, beating SK's Danish team and winning $40,000.

It was a sign of progress for North America, which lagged behind Europe and Asia because of weaker infrastructure, including both slower Internet and a lack of sponsorship money. There was also a cultural barrier. Video games were always considered a fringe activity in America, with the stereotype of the obese nerd in his parents' basement, swigging Mountain Dew and eating Cheetos. It didn't matter that Counter-Strike pros were mostly physically fit and their success was highly dependent on working and communicating with other people.

North America could only look at European countries like Sweden with envy. The country's speedy Internet and cold climate encouraged the youth to play computer games indoors. Stockholm was home to the gaming festival DreamHack, started in 1994 in a school cafeteria. It's grown to fill arenas and holds the Guinness world record for the world's largest LAN party, with over twenty-two thousand participants.

With 3D, compLexity, and Evil Geniuses, the North American teams proved that they could compete. But by the mid-2000s, the American Counter-Strike's tournament circuit was stagnating. Angel Munoz realized that he preferred being an entrepreneur and not a manager of the CPL's growing logistical needs, and the tournament's quality started deteriorating. Some players claimed that Munoz stopped paying prize money. In 2006, a competing tournament called the World Series of Video Games launched and stole the CPL's biggest sponsor, Intel, and took over some of the CPL's events.

Lake was still struggling to get outside investment and was pumping in thousands of his own dollars to keep the team afloat. Team 3D's star player, Kyle "Ksharp" Miller, quit competitive gaming for the steady income of a technology job just a few months after he was profiled in the *Washington Post*. And

Garfield's Evil Geniuses still couldn't manage to get its first big tournament win.

Television was the clear path to a bigger audience and mainstream money. It could do for gaming what it did for skateboarding or grunge music: it could make it cool. MTV had run a documentary in 2005 on eSports and highlighted the CPL, but network executives declined to commit to regular broadcasts. Competitive gaming needed a believer if it was going to become a legitimate industry with real careers.

Fortuitously, David Hill, the president of entertainment at News Corp's DirecTV, had become obsessed with the shooter game Medal of Honor. The Australian native would pretend to work in his home office to avoid his wife, and play for hours. He also saw his grandchildren gaming, and there was also the recent success of the World Series of Poker on ESPN. He believed the same spectacle could be created in gaming.

Hill pushed DirecTV to create its own gaming league. But he needed someone who knew the industry but wasn't already working for rival tournaments like the CPL. He found Team 3D's Craig Levine, who was eager to bring gaming to a new audience. Of course Team 3D would be a star of the new league, and Craig painted the team as the perennial champion, with its slick leader David "Moto" Geffen as its camera-ready spokesman. It already had a rival in compLexity, which Levine described as the scrappy underdog, a team of overlooked kids trying to prove themselves. It wasn't entirely accurate—compLexity had already won a number of tournaments—but it made for good television.

In the summer of 2006, DirecTV filmed the Championship Gaming Invitational, a test run for a full-scale tournament, at Treasure Island, the decommissioned naval base off the northeast coast of San Francisco. The elaborate stage was bathed in flashing lights in front of a roaring crowd, although the "fans" were assigned to root for the two teams without having any real loyalty. CompLexity triumphed over 3D and won $50,000 and a glowing green Mountain Dew trophy.

In 2007, DirecTV gave approval for a full-scale tournament called the Championship Gaming Series, or CGS, which was broadcast from July to December. The first setback came almost immediately. In March 2007, Hill returned to Fox after News Corp's stake in DirecTV was sold to Liberty Media. The CGS had lost its architect.

But DirecTV gained two big media partners: Britain's BSkyB and China's STAR TV. It secured sponsorships from Mountain Dew and Alienware, the gaming division of computer maker Dell, which had previously hesitated in investing heavily in eSports. Andy Reif, who had worked at the AVP Pro Beach Volleyball Tour and Paramount Pictures, became the league's CEO and commissioner. Reif was not a gamer, but he understood entertainment. Producers who had worked on the Olympics and NBA Finals were hired. They were committed to making eSports a big-budget spectacle. Gaming was going to be beamed into millions of homes around the world.

But what would they watch? Reif and his team had to decide what games to feature, and it was tricky to balance accessibility and depth. The CGS tried to get exclusive broadcasting rights for the games, and the cooperation of game publishers factored into what games were selected. Modern graphics were also a selling point. The CGS picked the fighting game Dead or Alive 4, soccer simulator FIFA 07, and Project Gotham Racing 3. "Dead or Alive was picked for being cinematic and easy to follow," said Reif, despite fighting games like Street Fighter being bigger competitive titles.

The CGS debated whether to feature Counter-Strike. It was a violent and potentially disorienting experience for new viewers, with its first-person perspective. But Levine convinced them that in order to have legitimacy, they had to feature the premier competitive game.

Tweaks were made for television. Counter-Strike's sequel, Source, was chosen over the venerable original title because of its more modern graphics, despite being widely criticized by players as inferior for competitive play after changes in physics and targeting. Round times were cut down to create tension and to fit into the time constraints of television. Player's avatars were modified to wear sports jerseys so teams were more easily distinguishable.

Reif said in retrospect that trying to appeal to a broad audience was difficult. The league had to educate viewers who had no background or knowledge of the games, in contrast to the hardcore fans who were already going to Counter-Strike events. "This was for mainstream television, not just followers of one game," said Reif. "Trying to pick games for a general audience—we were hamstrung."

Like the failed Cyber X Games, CGS planners looked at ESPN's X Games and tried to emulate its marketing strategy by focusing on the struggles and hopes of the players. The CGS sought to dispel the negative stereotypes of gamers, highlighting their energy and passion, and trying to get the audience invested. "You wanted to tell a story," said Reif.

DirecTV set aside $50 million for the league for five years. A major expense was salaries. One of the biggest was for Johnathan "Fatal1ty" Wendel, the first Western eSports superstar.

Fatal1ty grew up in Kansas City, Kansas. As he tells it, he spent the last $500 in his bank account in 2005 to travel to Texas and play at the CPL. He placed third and won $4,000. Then he went on one of the most dominant stretches in eSports history, winning nearly half a million dollars at various events. He played an array of single-player shooters: Quake, Unreal, and Painkiller, which centered the glory on him, rather than a team. His career culminated with a $150,000 championship at the CPL's 2005 World Tour, where he vanquished his Dutch rival Sander "Vo0" Kaasjager.

Fatal1ty became one of the first non-Asian competitive gamers to stick to a practice regime rather than relying on raw talent. And he built a personal brand that didn't require outside sponsors, but made Fatal1ty its own brand, with its own T-shirts and computer equipment.

Fatal1ty was no longer competing regularly, but the CGS hired him as a commentator for a reported $300,000 a season, despite the fact that he hadn't played Counter-Strike professionally. "You have to pay if you want the best," said Reif. "He was the only mainstream name in gaming."

The CGS was also a boon to the players. The CGS only filmed for a few months each year, but players had to be available full time during that period. They had to commit to the league by signing an exclusivity agreement. Players in the American division were paid $2,500 a month, compared to the $1,000 they were making on teams like compLexity. "There's no way I could ask my players to stay," said Lake. The league also paid for housing in Marina Del Rey by the beach, near where games were filmed at the Barker Hanger in Santa Monica, and gave the gamers a food stipend of $50 per day.

To get a job of his own at the CGS, Lake had to sell himself. He channeled his persona, with his signature white dress shirt and red tie, the roaring epitome of the fiery coach. He got the job to manage compLexity. Levine stepped away from 3D because he believed he could do more as a tournament organizer and became a general consultant for the league. Levine's protégé, David "Moto" Geffen, retired as a player and became 3D's manager.

The CGS's first season draft for its six American teams was held at the Playboy Mansion in Los Angeles. Another ten teams played in other regions around the world. As part of its emulation of real sports, the teams got home cities, even if the players had no geographic ties. Team 3D became the New York 3D, and compLexity was based in Los Angeles. Evil Geniuses shed its Canadian roots and became the Chicago Chimera. The name wasn't the only thing the team ditched.

Evil Geniuses' former captain, Tyndale, had been on a gaming hiatus but was promised a spot at the CGS by his former teammates. For Tyndale, gaming had led to another passion. His global travels for competition exposed him to new clothing styles, from Seoul, South Korea, to Monza, Italy. He realized that his college campus at the University of Alberta in Edmonton didn't have that variety, and he began running a local clothing store, which cut into his gaming time.

But his former teammates picked other players for the CGS, and Tyndale found himself with no team and no CGS spot. But his time spent competing was still valuable. His experience working on advertising campaigns for his team's sponsors made him aware of the marketing that fed the industry, and Tyndale became an entrepreneur and brand consultant in the fashion industry. "I loved the idea that this was all fueled by marketing," said Tyndale. "Empowering people to represent your brand—it just makes sense."

Tyndale doesn't have too many regrets. He put "pro gamer" on his resume, which was always a source of conversation at job interviews, and he still has a heavy bronze medal to show off from WCG Singapore, where Evil Geniuses placed third.

Alexander Garfield, who was in his fourth year of college, was happy that his players had gained spots in the league, and he had applied for one of the open CGS general manager positions with the hope that he could continue working with his friends. He had no major tournament wins and a restrained personality, a terrible fit for television. He was rejected and felt ready to leave eSports. "I was going to quit the whole thing," said Garfield. "It was a very dark summer."

But his mom—the person who thought he should write about gaming for his college essay, the person who had lent him $3,000 to fly to events when his team was close to breaking apart—convinced him that he had built something that would outlive the loss of five players.

"You put too much time into this to not get anything out of it," she told him. With the players rebranding as the Chicago Chimera, Garfield still had the naming rights to Evil Geniuses. "That's when it really became mine," he said. Garfield began to rebuild. He picked up the second-tier American talent that had been overlooked by the CGS, including high school students since the top talent was now taken.

The Chicago Chimera ended up winning the first-season CGS championship and $500,000. But glory still eluded Garfield.

He didn't get completely left out. Lake was still running his law business in Georgia and had two young children. He needed help. "It's a young man's game," said Lake. "You have to be available 24/7 when the eSports mistress calls." Lake ended up hiring Garfield as an assistant manager for compLexity. Although Garfield wasn't an official employee of the league, he got experience while still running Evil Geniuses and finishing college. Garfield had always been skilled at getting sponsorships, and now he learned how to manage new personalities. "He did a great job," said Lake, who calls Garfield a "super smart guy."

Lake was initially optimistic about the CGS. But after he saw the production, his confidence plunged. He recalls one stunt where a player was dressed up as a ninja and was filmed running across a rooftop. "I was incredibly disheartened," he said. "They should have just focused on the pure competition and the true personalities involved, rather than trying to make it into something ridiculous." But Lake was committed to eSports, and in May 2008, he sold his law firm in Georgia and moved with his wife and two young children to Los Angeles, near where the CGS was filmed.

The CGS's first season drew a reported fifty million viewers, with 90 percent of them in Asia. DirecTV was broadcast in around twenty million households at the time, which was too small to get Nielsen ratings, said Reif, the CGS commissioner.

In retrospect, Reif believes the CGS overextended by starting off in multiple continents with teams throughout the United States, Asia, and Europe. "The model was way too aggressive," said Reif. But with three major media companies involved in DirecTV, no partner wanted to sit back, so the league went global immediately. Regional finals were held in Los Angeles, London, and Kuala Lumpur, and the World Championships were held in Los Angeles.

The CGS expanded again in 2008 for its second season, starting teams in Kuala Lumpur and Dubai. It also sought to acquire established European teams like SK Gaming and Fnatic, but they were too expensive and remained independent. The huge growth ate away most of DirecTV's $50 million commitment. The timing was also terrible, as the economy was hurtling toward the worst recession in decades, fueled by the subprime mortgage catastrophe, lack of regulation, and greed.

Gaming tournaments started to collapse. The World Series of Video Games closed in September 2007, despite signing a deal months before with CBS. Angel Munoz's Cyberathlete Professional League shuttered in March 2008.

And in November 2008, with the economy in free fall, the CGS announced it was closing after only two years. "Profitability was too far in the future for us to sustain operations in the interim," a spokeswoman said.

Reif believes that the CGS had created excitement and had potential, but two seasons wasn't enough time to establish a real fan base. After all, the X Games took about a decade to succeed. "It was a super-ambitious undertaking," said Reif. "It was just too big an idea."

Reif now works for IP Global Group, which markets the surf and water sports brand Body Glove. He still recognizes the allure of eSports, but he hopes that future gamers have a backup plan, like he did. "Pursue your passion, but have a plan that's really viable for how to spend the rest of your life," said Reif. "It's not a dream for many. It's a dream for a few."

In the wake of the CGS, North American eSports—and the global economy—was in shambles, and there was a new wariness for corporate investment. The seemingly endless money that the CGS had invested meant that it had expected a huge return. "When you invest a lot in something, you expect to get a lot back," said Garfield.

But North America's eSports pioneers weren't giving up, wounded as they were.

Craig Levine reacquired the 3D brand but never restarted the team. He went on to focus on his website E-Sports Entertainment Association, or ESEA, a matchmaking service for Counter-Strike players that also offered coaching lessons and amateur tournaments. Years later, he joined the Electronic Sports League, or ESL, one of the few survivors of the 2008 meltdown.

Jason Lake of compLexity went from running a law firm and one of America's top teams to becoming unemployed for the first time in his adult life, and he had just moved his family across the country. He considered abandoning the industry. But he couldn't. "I always viewed compLexity as my third child. To see it lying there in the dust was not acceptable," said Lake.

Lake bought back the brand for $1,000 from DirecTV, which had no more plans for gaming. The team had no staff and no website, but Lake recruited a few friends and managed to get the sponsor Sound Blaster on board. He was ready to rebuild, and the natural move was to re-sign his Counter-Strike team, whose core roster had been together for four years.

But in December 2008, four of compLexity's long-time players—Danny "fRoD" Montaner, Tyler "Storm" Wood, Matt "Warden" Dickens, and Corey "hanes" Hanes—announced that they had joined a new squad: Garfield's Evil Geniuses.

"We hope that the team's rich history with Jason Lake and compLexity is always preserved in the minds of eSports fans around the world, as Jason is one of the true eSports pioneers and deserves only the highest level of respect. But we're equally excited for these players to begin writing a new chapter as members of Team EG," Garfield said in a press release on the team's website.

The reality wasn't so rosy. "They wanted out. They weren't happy there," said Garfield of the players.

"It was so hard for them. All of us really cared about Jason," he said. "They were afraid to tell him." Lake was the ultimate alpha personality, both on stage and in negotiations, and he wouldn't take no for an answer. Garfield and the players drafted a resignation letter and signed it together.

Lake was enraged. "A traitor is a traitor. Alex, you are a traitor. There's no eloquence that can cover factual truth. The knife in our back will not be forgotten, nor ignored. Vultures thrive on the misfortune of others. They never succeed and never redefine evolution," he wrote online.

Garfield was taken aback and didn't respond. He said he was "naively honest" and didn't think strategically about public relations. What he had done was reasonable, given Evil Geniuses' economic strength. Lake's former players could have financial security and an established brand, instead of a gutted team that had to restart from nothing. And there were no regulations against signing players who had been with other teams, a trend that is largely true a decade later. "The industry is inherently competitive, not only in terms of the actual matches that are being played but also in terms of how cutthroat and unregulated things can be behind the scenes," said Garfield.

Seven years later, Lake is more forgiving. "When I was down and out and vulnerable, I felt that was a knife in my back," he said. But he now acknowledges that for the players, it was "probably the wise thing for them to do."

It was the first power play in Garfield's young career. "He's intelligent. He has the guts to make the moves that people might consider controversial," said Lake. "There are lines that are crossed and people are hurt. But at the end of the day, he's done an amazing job with the brand."

With the CGS consolidating all the major American Counter-Strike teams and wiping them out financially, Evil Geniuses stood to become the strongest squad in North America. Garfield went from being a CGS reject to one of the most powerful players in the brave new world. "The biggest winner was the girl who wasn't invited to the prom," said Lake.

Garfield bristles at that narrative. "Plenty of people said that: 'I got super lucky. I was left there with no competitors,'" said Garfield. "Because they passed on me, they deserve credit for the motivation I got—it's a very warped piece of logic."

But it's undeniable that Garfield had an advantage compared to the rivals who had committed to the CGS, including 3D and compLexity, teams that Evil Geniuses had never been able to catch. And he capitalized, despite his business training being limited to two-thirds of the book *The Lean Startup* and "every Dilbert comic that you can possibly get your hands on," which gave him distaste for bosses.

With its new Counter-Strike team, Evil Geniuses finally became champions, winning four major tournaments in 2009 and over $50,000 for the year. They became an economic powerhouse, getting some of the industry's first mainstream sponsors, like the drink maker Monster Energy. The team began getting comparisons to the New York Yankees, whose exorbitant salaries make headlines, but not always championships. And Garfield remained an enigma, with fans still imagining him as an older businessman in a suit, an eSports George Steinbrenner, and not the fun-loving musician who fell in love with Counter-Strike.

"People viewed us as having this really big war chest," said Garfield. "I think when people are not given information and they have to fill in the gaps themselves, they fill it with something negative . . . especially with an allegedly powerful figure."

But for Evil Geniuses to become a truly global brand, it would have to look to the East.

Chapter 2

THE EMPEROR OF SEOUL

BOXER AND BROOD WAR

South Korea has the fastest Internet on the planet. After the country was battered by the Asian financial crisis in 1997, the government looked to information technology as its economic savior. Between 1998 and 2002, the government invested $11 billion to modernize the country's network infrastructure. South Korea evolved from an economy dependent on the chemicals and industrial sectors to a "knowledge-based society" centered on technology.

Competition among service providers led to falling Internet fees for South Korean consumers, from around $40 per month in 1999 to less than $20 by 2006, when US customers were still paying $50. South Koreans began looking for cheap entertainment options amid the recession, and video games were ideal. Animosity toward Japan, which had ruled Korea as a colony until 1945, meant the personal computer became the preferred platform over gaming systems from Nintendo and Sony.

Workers who were laid off during the recession began establishing "PC bangs," or Internet cafes that provided cheap access to gaming computers. For South Koreans, gaming was a social activity, in contrast to the Westerners, who saw it as a solitary hobby, an inauthentic, artificial experience compared to more laudable physical sports.

South Korea's most popular competitive title was StarCraft, a real-time strategy game, or RTS, released in 1998 by Blizzard Entertainment of Irvine, California. Real-time strategy games have two major elements: macro, short for macromanagement, the building of a war economy of workers and production buildings; and micro, or micromanagement, the aspect of controlling an army to move and destroy the opponent. Macro and micro are the yin and yang of competition, and top players excel at both. Although players can play in teams, most competitive RTS games like StarCraft are played one versus one.

Players view the map from an aerial perspective, making the game particularly friendly for spectators. Workers collect resources—food, stone, wood, gold—that are distributed in clusters throughout the game's various maps and create tactically significant locations. Workers deposit the resources in central buildings such as Town Halls or Command Centers, which must be protected to continue a flow of revenue.

Resources are spent to create buildings, such as a Barracks, which train a variety of fighting units for an additional cost. As the game progresses, players can build more advanced and powerful units by creating prerequisite structures, a system known as a tech tree.

Perhaps the most precious resource is time. As the name implies, real-time strategy games have constant action without pauses or turns. And every action—building a unit, moving across the map, researching a technology—takes a varying amount of time. Each order must be given manually, with a keyboard and mouse. A typical StarCraft match can end in around twenty minutes, but it may stretch onward for over an hour or more if no decisive battles occur and a player is continuously in motion.

Playing StarCraft well is like mastering a piano concerto. The sheer physical requirements are daunting. Players have a growing list of tasks, lest they fall behind: Produce units! Scout! Build another base! Keep scouting! Keep producing! Attack! Top players are a whirlwind, with hundreds of actions per minute, or APM, measured by each keystroke and mouse click. Speed is not enough. Top players also need precision and strategy, the fruit of thousands of hours of practice.

StarCraft was initially conceived as a science-fiction reskin of Blizzard's popular medieval fantasy-themed Warcraft franchise. Warcraft I and II have two opposing factions, Orcs and Humans, which have the same units based on statistics, though they differ in appearance and have a handful of different abilities. (Orcs have a powerful spell called Bloodlust that turns their troops into angry killing machines with faster attacks, so most competitive players chose Orc.) StarCraft's breakthrough came when the designers decided to make three factions that were not simply mirrors of each other.

Terrans are humans of the near future, with industrial grit and a space-cowboy demeanor. They have infantry, tanks, and spaceships. The Zerg are a voracious, bug-like swarm of killers, with nasty claws, acid sprays, and teeth. They rely more on packs of weaker units, which are cheaper to build compared to the other races. The Protoss are an enigmatic, psionic alien race with futuristic lasers and energy beams. Their armor is a distinctive golden chrome and their units are powerful but slower to amass.

Despite dozens of different abilities and creatures, the three factions became close to evenly matched after multiple game updates, known as balance patches. The competitive beauty of StarCraft was a happy accident. It was further refined by the game's expansion pack, StarCraft: Brood War, which added additional units, including the iconic Medic, a Terran healer clad in a white spacesuit; and the Lurker, a Zerg subterranean beast that impales foes with devastating spikes.

Like real war, vision of the enemy in an RTS game is limited by a mechanic known as Fog of War. Players can only see areas of the map where they have units or buildings, so their opponents' early moves are hidden. Players generally will use one of their early workers to move across the map and seek out the enemy to see what path he or she has chosen, but some trickery is still possible, such as placing buildings outside the main base, into the hidden nooks of the map.

The economy of the game creates a flow, with games starting with small skirmishes with weaker troops. Players build additional bases across the map, which can change from game to game, and then combat culminates with a huge clash that determines victory or defeat. But strategic decisions can make a game much longer or much shorter.

A hyperaggressive opening can potentially lead to a swift victory, such as the famous "Zerg rush," which involves quickly pumping out a swarm of Zerglings, ravenous little creatures that hatch two-per-egg at a cheap cost and quickly slash and devour enemy workers, but fall easily to more powerful units. But such an opening requires resources to be spent on military production rather than constantly producing more workers, so if damage is not inflicted upon the enemy, the aggressor can find him or herself in the equivalent of invading Russia in winter, bloodthirsty but famished for resources while his or her opponent amasses greater numbers.

Rush strategies are sometimes derided as "cheese," defined as attacks whose success generally depends on surprise and the opponent not being prepared. The Zerg rush is the epitome of cheese, with virtually no recovery if significant damage isn't inflicted.

The rush was a turnoff for casual players, who complained about imbalance, but it could be stopped if it was scouted and the defender quickly prepared defenses. The rush often became a critical element for a competitive game by providing multiple paths to victory. "Rush strategies are important because they add another axis to how you can play the game," said Rob Pardo, Blizzard's former chief creative officer and the balance architect of StarCraft, on a podcast. "Players hate getting killed in the first two minutes and they complain."

Other strategies are the middle ground, or "standard" opening that balances economic and military production. The other extreme is the "greedy" opening of a fast expansion, when a player builds a tiny military force in the early game and invests the large amount of minerals required to establish a second base. If a player can protect two bases and survive, his income will eventually double as he produces more and more workers.

StarCraft's intricate depth became an escape from the real world for players like Lim Yo-Hwan. He grew up in South Korea playing soccer and gaming in the arcades of Seoul. He had two working parents, which gave him a lot of free time. He wasn't a very good student, and as he prepared to graduate, he felt emptiness.

"My high school years were like a dark tunnel. They were times when I wandered in the darkness, not knowing where the exit was," Lim wrote in a translation of his 2004 autobiography, *Crazy as Me*. "I could not find my path by myself, and I did not share my parent's expectations and hopes. Not given any other choice but to enter college, my school life was in itself a dark tunnel.

"In this way, I spent my high school life miserably. They were the times when I did not love myself, and I confined myself in the dark tunnel and endured day after day. But even in the dark tunnel, I was searching for something. I felt as though my life's treasure was hidden somewhere," he wrote. "Then one day, I discovered my life's treasure."

In 1998, as he was entering his final year of high school, he tried to get tutoring from his friend Jinsuk. He was eager to study, but instead Jinsuk introduced him to StarCraft. Lim was fascinated. His family didn't own a computer, which his parents considered another arcade machine, another distraction from his studies.

StarCraft's deep strategy was more compelling than dreary classrooms and academics. Lim began playing against a computer opponent, learning the basics of the game, before going to the local PC bang and meeting new opponents. Then he discovered Battle.net, Blizzard's online matchmaking service, which opened his world to thousands of rivals, and he played constantly until he was ranked second overall (the top-ranked player was a cheater, he wrote in his memoir).

"That summer, while my friends were grinding themselves with their text and reference books, I sat in front of the computer and said good-bye to the world that I had lived in—the school fields, the neighborhood arcades—and stepped into an entirely new world. A new space, with more friends, and the door that led me to a world that I had never experienced was the exit of the dark tunnel that I had searched for so long," wrote Lim.

This single-minded focus is reminiscent of another, vilified status: video game addiction.

There are horror stories of broken finances, weight loss, shattered relationships, and even death. A South Korean couple neglected their newborn daughter, who reportedly died of starvation, while nurturing their virtual child in the roleplaying game Prius Online. A Taiwanese gamer went into cardiac arrest and died after a marathon gaming session. But these examples are extremes, and some gaming advocates argue that gaming is just an outlet for underlying psychological issues, and not the root of dependency in the same way drugs or alcohol become physically addictive.

But in response, the South Korean and Chinese governments have enacted gaming restrictions for minors, such as having curfews for Internet cafés. The *Diagnostic and Statistical Manual of Mental Disorders*, which provides guidelines for US psychiatrists, is reviewing research on whether to include Internet gaming dependency as a disorder.

Perhaps the key difference between a successful pro player and a gaming addict is that a pro has purpose. The hours of practice are a path to success. The goal is to win tournaments. An addict is often escaping the responsibilities of life by inhabiting the digital world. He or she is adrift, suppressing obligations and emotions with gameplay. But the line between professional player and addict is blurry, and the ability to make money is perhaps the only clear distinction.

For Lim, relentless focus would eventually pay off. In 2001, the head of the technology company Sinabro approached Lim while he was gaming at the PC bang. Was he interested in becoming a professional gamer with sponsorships? Of course! His parents, who had supported him financially, wondered initially if he was being conned. But he insisted that gaming was his passion, and he would soon go only by his gamer ID, BoxeR.

Although he learned the game as Protoss, BoxeR soon switched to Terran, because humans were always the heroes in the science-fiction movies that he watched. In May 2001, Terran was considered the weakest race, but he battled to the finals of the prestigious Hanbitsoft OSL Tournament. His play was broadcast on OnGameNet, one of South Korea's television networks dedicated to gaming, along with rival network MBC Game.

He faced Jang "JinNam" Jin Nam, a more famous Zerg player in the finals at a theater hall. BoxeR, wearing a silvery jacket, used relentless aggression, surgically gutting his opponent's weak areas with flying transport units known as Dropships, ferrying lethal groups of Marines and Medics to wreak havoc in the weak worker lines of his opponent. He won the first game, then the second. Facing elimination, JinNam crashed waves of Hydralisks, slithering, spike-spitting Zerg beasts, into BoxeR's Marines and Siege Tanks but the Terrans held the line.

JinNam typed "gg," for "Good Game," the respectful term for surrender. Four blasts of flame shot up above his booth. The announcer bellowed "Lim Yo-Hwan." BoxeR had won his first championship.

He became the Hope of Terran. He was an innovator, using the shunned Vulture, a speedy but fragile motorbike that could bury Spider Mines on the map, which would scuttle into enemies who got close and explode. He had a high-tempo, aggressive playing style, pumping out Marines in risky, all-in offenses in the game's opening minutes.

Four months later, BoxeR would win the next OSL, sponsored by Coca-Cola, and then became the first champion in the inaugural World Cyber Games at the end of 2001. He was the most successful and popular pro gamer in South Korea, and arguably in the world. He got a new nickname: the Emperor.

BoxeR's fan club swelled to over a half million members. He was recognized on the street. He had to quit playing basketball to protect his valuable fingers. Fans would hold signs with his name and face at matches. But some would hide their own faces from the camera, supposedly to ensure that they weren't seen skipping school or work to attend. BoxeR signed a contract with the team SK Telecom T1, backed by the telecommunications conglomerate of the same name, for $180,000.

In 2006, BoxeR joined the Korean Air Force to complete his mandatory two years of military service, required for all South Korean males. He joined the Air Force ACE StarCraft team, made up of former pro gamers who were also enlisted, and still commanded huge crowds. A military video game had surpassed the country's real military in cultural influence.

But BoxeR and the StarCraft superstars that followed, like Lee "NaDa" Yoon Yeol, Kim "Bisu" Taek Yong, Lee "Flash" Young Ho, and Lee "Jaedong" Jae Dong, were anomalies. They were the exalted few, playing in arenas and introduced with dramatic videos and strobe lights, resembling rock stars or actors. But most pro gamers toiled for meager salaries, sacrificing their educations and social lives for a chance at glory. The cutthroat environment of winner-take-all reflected the Asian approach to education. Even in elementary schools, students are graded based on their performance relative to peers, rather than individual grades. And rankings are public.

"Korea is a society driven by competition," said John Park, who worked at the StarCraft broadcaster GOMTV. "An athlete who has won a silver medal would often hang their face in shame and apologize to the public for not achieving gold. Koreans just love to make rankings and compare, and if you are not first, you are nothing."

And even the Emperor had to abdicate the throne eventually. By the time he left the air force, BoxeR's skills had deteriorated, and he never recaptured the glory of his early career. Faster, hungrier stars replaced him.

Dal Yong Jin, a communications professor at Simon Fraser University, describes a process of "commodification" for pro gamers and fans that turns the experience into a product meant to enhance the brands of Korea's huge conglomerates, known as *chaebol* (a word that combines "wealth" and "clan"). Company logos from SK Telecom, CJ Group, and Samsung were affixed to player uniforms and tournament banners, associating companies with the emotional excitement of competitive gaming. But aside from the superstars, players were commodities with little value. They could be tossed aside and replaced with another hopeful gamer, with few fans noticing.

Still, in the early 2000s, South Korea had more opportunities for StarCraft pro gamers than anywhere else. In the West, independent team managers tried to obtain sponsorships from companies that were often unfamiliar with eSports. In South Korea, companies invested directly into the teams, providing an infrastructure and management structure that was unparalleled.

South Korea popularized the team houses, where players would train for ten or more hours a day, practicing shoulder-to-shoulder with their teammates. Meals and bunk beds were provided, so players wouldn't have to worry about sustaining themselves. They could discuss strategy face-to-face and make in-game decisions in the same room. The team house was cited as a big step toward professionalization and was replicated, with some success, by Western teams. But Korean players had to sacrifice a social life, the freedom of hanging out and going to the gym, having romantic relationships, and, perhaps most crucially, getting an education. It was more work than play.

The government also endorsed gaming, with the Ministry of Culture, Sports and Tourism forming the Korean e-Sports Association, or KeSPA, in 2000, as a way of promoting and regulating competitive gaming. Amateurs had to battle through the Courage Tournament, where only the winner would receive a pro-gaming license, which allowed them to play in KeSPA-sanctioned matches. KeSPA's board is now made up of eleven corporations, including top teams owned by SK Telecom, Samsung, and CJ Group, as well as broadcasters OnGameNet and GOMTV.

In America, there wasn't much work to be found. StarCraft was a popular game, but the competitive scene was on the fringe, with fewer tournaments compared to Counter-Strike. Despite the lack of prize money, the country's top players were devoted.

In New Hampshire, Dan "Artosis" Stemkoski befriended the only Korean boy in town, who introduced him to StarCraft. He initially preferred in-line skating and basketball, but after breaking his ankle in freshman year of high school and being bound to a chair, the easiest thing was to play StarCraft. "When I find something I like, I become really obsessed and do it nonstop," said Artosis. "Anything I get into, I super get into."

His parents were divorced, and his mom would try to hide his keyboard or monitor to prevent him from playing through the night, but he had spare equipment and gamed on. The next day, he slept through his classes. "If you have two strong parental figures in your house, you're probably not going to be allowed to play StarCraft all day," said Artosis, but he was able to outsmart one.

After finishing high school, Artosis struggled to find a viable career. He dropped out of college multiple times and worked at local retailers like Christmas Tree Shops, but every year he would quit to train in StarCraft to qualify for the World Cyber Games, the only significant tournament in the United States. He used his savings to pay for plane tickets to qualifiers, which were never held in remote New Hampshire. One year, he flew to Dallas and played in a CompUSA parking lot, even though the qualifier in Atlanta was closer, because he knew the local competition there was better. And he picked Terran as his race, because he thought it was the hardest to play.

"2004 is the year I decided that I couldn't live if I didn't become a StarCraft pro," said Artosis. "There was no choice in it. It was just kind of like realizing and accepting that I had never cared about or loved anything as much as StarCraft."

Artosis played over a dozen hours every day, putting aside friendships. He won the WCG US finals in 2004 without dropping a match and got a free flight across the country to the world finals in San Francisco. He lost early in the group stages to the eventual runner-up in the tournament, but he had accomplished his goal of reaching the big stage.

The next year, Artosis was even better. "I had reached completely new levels in my play. I was so confident, and I was like, 'I'm going to make it to the World Championships. I'm going to go deep this year,'" he said.

He easily qualified for the US championship at the WCG 2005, held in the Hammerstein Ballroom in New York City. One more tournament and he would represent his country at the global championship in Singapore. Artosis had trained more than almost all his opponents, and he had another edge: he was an ace at the Terran-versus-Terran matchup, and the bulk of American players also played Terran. But when he saw the tournament bracket, he was uneasy. There were two open spots for the world championships, and instead of having a double-elimination format where players would be eliminated only after losing two rounds, the players were split into two groups, and if they lost a round, they were out of the tournament.

In another strange decision, the matchups were determined alphabetically by last name rather than past performance, and almost all the Terran players weren't in Artosis's group. He would have to defeat Protoss and Zerg players if he wanted to move on.

Two other players were also unhappy about the alphabetical placement the first round: brothers Nick "Tasteless" Plott and Sean "Day[9]" Plott, who trained together in the suburbs of Kansas City, Kansas, and would now have to play each other in the first round. Like Artosis, they grew up mostly with their mom, a single parent, who failed to prevent them from gaming all day.

Tasteless wore a pink T-shirt and the sides of his hair were dyed blue. He had a deep voice and a swagger, telling a filmmaker at the event that he and his brother were basically playing the finals, even though it was just round one. "Whoever wins this is winning the whole thing, man," he said.

Day[9] beat Tasteless, who was crushed by the fratricide and disappointed that he didn't even get a chance to face a new opponent. "He was better than me at the time. I really just wanted to compete in a tournament with someone obviously that I didn't play with in my house," said Tasteless.

Day[9]'s next opponent was Artosis. They were arguably the two best players at the tournament, but because of the alphabetical seeding, one of them was going home in the second round. Day[9] puked in the bathroom in between rounds, battling nerves. In the end, it was Artosis who couldn't control his anxiety, and he was defeated.

"I was panicking. He just wrecked me," said Artosis. "When he slapped me down when I was at the peak of my skill, that kind of forced me into a situation where I had nerves, where I was like, 'Oh God, even if I make a goal, I might not reach it.'" It would be a few months before Artosis could bear to compete again.

Tasteless and Artosis were both despondent, and they also noticed that the tournament's commentator was clueless about StarCraft. As he was struggling to describe what was happening in the game, the tournament staff asked if any of the defeated players would help commentate. Artosis was thinking it over, but Tasteless jumped at the opportunity and went on stage. He impressed the crowd with his knowledge of the game and his clear delivery, thanks to his experience on the debate team in college. Ultimately, Day[9] won his group and was one of two American players who went to play in Singapore. Tasteless ended up going as well, not as a player but as a commentator.

The commentator, or caster, is an essential component of the eSports experience. Top broadcasters can become as well known as star players, just as John Madden became one of the most famous names in football in the broadcast booth. A commentator is able to create a narrative from the game and give meaning to the action on screen. A combination of gameplay knowledge, familiarity with players, and energy is essential. As with traditional sports commentary, eSports often employs a duo of play-by-play and analyst or color commentator.

The play-by-play announcer provides a rapid flow of the action happening on-screen. During huge fights, it can turn into a controlled frenzy of yelling. The analyst offers insight into deeper strategy or cites statistics, but instead of batting average or free-throw percentages, data includes a player's win percentage versus Zerg or the number of times they build a fast expansion. Games have also started having dedicated observers, who move the camera for the audience's viewpoint and have to prioritize what action to show on screen.

"To be a good caster, I think you have to be very comfortable with yourself," said Tasteless, who equates a typical event with five hours of unscripted live television.

Early eSports commentating was primitive. Players would record audio and bundle them with game replays in zip files. For live games, they would sometimes have to join games as a neutral third player and hide their units in order to observe the entire map. Technology improved, and eventually developers added features that allowed commentators to broadcast within the game without extra programs.

After Tasteless went on to study philosophy in college, he stayed involved and flew around the world to StarCraft events. He wasn't paid, but he got his travel expenses reimbursed. In 2008, with just one semester left in college, Tasteless received an offer to cast for Arirang TV in Seoul. Moving across the world was less daunting for him because he had been to Hong Kong and Thailand, where his father had worked. And with his passion burning for StarCraft, Tasteless took the plunge after just a few days of deliberation.

He met an enclave of Western StarCraft players in Seoul, who were known as foreigners because they weren't Korean. Despite modest success in gaming, some made a fortune playing online poker and living in upscale apartments in the Gangnam neighborhood. Some Western players eventually switched to poker full-time because it was far more lucrative. Their rapid decision-making skills and ability to multitask made them fearsome at it, too. "They'd open ten tables at once. You can pretty much follow a basic algorithm. It was a bunch of Brood War players versus degenerates," said Tasteless. "People were making millions of dollars."

Tasteless stayed with his Western friends for a month before moving into a closet-sized apartment near the Nambu Bus Terminal. For the next couple years, he learned the culture and the language. With ten million people, Seoul has three times as many people as the entire state of Kansas. But the hyperdensity appealed to him. Being able to walk to restaurants and entertainment was much more exciting than his small-town life in Kansas City, where he had to drive everywhere.

"I think surburbia is actually much more suffocating," said Tasteless. "I come here, and everything makes more sense to me." Now, he feels more at home in South Korea than America.

Tasteless was the first English-language StarCraft commentator in the country and soon joined GOMTV, run by Gretech Corp., maker of the Gretech Online Movie Player, one of the most popular video streaming programs in South Korea.

For hours and hours, Tasteless screamed about Marines and Zerglings. He would lose his voice for a few days, but he didn't care because he was only casting one day a week. Fans would speculate that he was smoking too many cigarettes. "I just sound like a chain-smoking, horrible emphysema guy. Even though it's just the screaming," said Tasteless. He eventually developed callus-like growths called nodules on his vocal chords and would be speechless for weeks.

He learned how to manage his voice after casting with Jason Lee, a prominent South Korean voice actor and StarCraft commentator, and learning techniques from the veteran commentator Marcus "djWHEAT" Graham and a roommate from college who did voice acting.

Artosis was still stuck in the United States, and he was disappointed that all his American competitors were toiling so hard with no recognition. He decided to start running his own online tournament to elevate the local scene, which he commentated. Soon, Artosis was offered a job at a new website called SCForAll, run by South Korean broadcaster SpoTV, but on the condition he move to Seoul. He jumped at the opportunity and became the second English-language commentator in South Korea. He ate frugally and slept at friends' apartments, struggling to make a living. But soon, his fortunes would change.

Chapter 3

NUCLEAR LAUNCH DETECTED

STARCRAFT II EXPLODES

In May 2007, StarCraft's creator, Blizzard Entertainment, held its Worldwide Invitational Tournament in Seoul. During the opening ceremony, Blizzard CEO Mike Morhaime unveiled one the developer's trademark computer-animated videos. A chained brute of a man stepped into a futuristic chamber. Motors whirled and he was encased in a blue metal shell, the music swelling as flesh became one with machine. A digital screen said "TERRAN MARINE MILITARY STATUS: ACTIVE" in Korean, drawing a cheer from the crowd. Chomping on a cigar, the man, now ready for battle, snarled, "Hell, it's about time." The logo for StarCraft II blasted across the screen as the audience freaked out. The future had arrived.

While the original StarCraft's almost perfect balance and fiercely fought gameplay was mostly an accident, StarCraft II was designed from the start to be competitive. Dustin Browder, the game's lead designer, was hired at Blizzard in 2005. He was taken aback when he was told the game would be designed as an eSport. "Really? That weird thing in Korea?" he recalled thinking during a presentation at the 2011 Game Developers Conference. "This is going to be insanely hard. You're going to have to invent Basketball II," his fellow designers told him.

The design principles for StarCraft II were clarity, uncertainty, and skill.

Clarity meant that the game had to be watchable. The audience could see the screen from a distance and be able to tell what was going on. The Zerg Ultralisk, for example, was "300 tons of rage, muscle, and hate" in the game's storyline and would tower above dozens of man-sized units, but it had to be scaled down to a more manageable size so it didn't block the view of other units. The Protoss High Templar's Psionic Storm, a vortex of lightning that enveloped a certain area, could have been rendered as a huge cinematic blast that took up the entire screen. But StarCraft II was meant to be a serious competition, so the effects were scaled down to the precise area of damage. The focus wasn't to impress, but to create an experience that was clear to both players and viewers. Browder compared the appearance of military units to football jerseys.

Clarity also came in the form of distinct units with clear roles. Browder had designed games like Command & Conquer: Red Alert 2 and other real-time strategy games with over one hundred units. More units meant more options, which meant more gameplay, which meant more fun, he thought. StarCraft II reversed that concept, with about forty-five units total spread among the three races, and some units were repeats from the original game. Browder would suggest extra features and units that he thought were cool, but they would be rejected in the name of competitive balance. Some of the ideas were used in the single-player campaign, where the player battled against the computer. But for multiplayer, limiting choices eliminated redundancies and gave units more defined roles. Restrictions bred competitiveness, said Browder, who became a distinct presence in the StarCraft community with his beard and bald head. When he commentated replays, Browder created a catchphrase for bloody fights: "Terrible, terrible damage!"

Next, uncertainty meant that there would be degrees of success—abilities could miss, hit, or be partially effective, creating drama and tension. A game could end in five minutes or an hour, in contrast to the structured time limits of traditional sports.

Finally, if StarCraft II was a game of skill, there had to be a clear delineation between good and bad players, in contrast with most big-budget games, which often cast the player in an all-powerful role and seek to attract as many players as possible. "We were not trying to separate the haves and have-nots. We were trying to bring them together," said Browder of previous games he designed.

But StarCraft II's steep learning curve was a potential hurdle for casual players. "The best have to be the best, by far," said Browder. "We were afraid that would cost a customer for us."

A big part of the challenge was managing all of the tasks of building, scouting, and fighting. Some gamers dismissed the game as being purely about clicking really fast, and the designer didn't dispute that the game had a high mechanical barrier to entry. But there was also a daunting amount of decision making and knowledge required.

"It's about clicking really fast, while doing seventeen other things, and getting in your opponent's head and know how he's going to click really fast and where he's going to click," said Browder.

To make games more enjoyable and make all players aspiring champions, Blizzard created a system of tiers: Bronze, Silver, Gold, Platinum, Diamond, and eventually Masters and Grandmaster, with the latter reserved for the top two hundred players in each region. After a number of placement games, players would be assigned a tier and only face players of a similar skill level. If they won enough games, they would get promoted.

But the gameplay was always tense and made some players nervous to play games, known as "ladder anxiety" after trying to climb a "ladder" into the next tier. For some, losing felt like personal failing, a negative judgment on their competence and intelligence. Others would sweat or their hands would shake from the pressure. By making StarCraft II hypercompetitive, Blizzard pushed all players to act like aspiring professional players, with all the anxiety that came with it.

"We joke about how StarCraft is bad for you in some ways. It actually is a very discouraging thing to play a twenty-minute game where you're really taxing your brain and juggling a bunch of tasks, and then you fail at that," said Tasteless. "I think people who play RTS games probably are more willing to be stressed out or upset than most people who play games."

When StarCraft II's beta period, the testing period before the game was officially released, began in the spring of 2010, Artosis had his friend who worked at Blizzard text him. It was three in the morning, and he played seventy-three games in a row before taking a break. He was ranked number one in the world for a week. He realized that Zerg had the highest skill cap and switched over.

But hardcore gamers who played the original StarCraft were afraid that StarCraft II would be dumbed down. There were some modernizations that cut down on the sheer amount of actions that were needed because of the original game's engine limitations. For example, multiple buildings could be selected at once and told to produce the same unit with one keystroke, simplifying production, and workers could be set to automatically go harvest minerals and gas instead of requiring a manual order each time they were produced.

Tasteless still prefers the original StarCraft for its demanding mechanics. "I think the fact that as you had a bigger army, or more bases, you were given more tasks to juggle is what made the game actually so perfect," said Tasteless. Although StarCraft II gets more complex as the game develops, players can select an unlimited number of units at once, as opposed to the original game's limit of twelve at a time, making larger army control easier.

Artosis believes that StarCraft II has more strategic depth, with more varied army compositions and possible build paths, while the original StarCraft is more dependent on mechanics. Thus, the player with better mechanics will typically win in the original game, but the sequel let players with weaker mechanics and more clever strategies win more easily.

The tension between living up to its predecessor while still doing something new was a challenge that StarCraft II never entirely overcame. But when the game was finally released in July 2010, it was a blockbuster, selling over 1.5 million copies in the first two days, a new record for a strategy game.

In South Korea, the question was when and if the elite Starcraft I players would switch over to the sequel. This transition was complicated by a copyright dispute between Blizzard, the game's developer, and KeSPA, the South Korean governing body for eSports.

Blizzard wanted royalties and recognition that it was the sole rights holder of the game. KeSPA argued that StarCraft was more like a sport with no copyright protections, and because the original game could be played offline through LAN without control from Blizzard, they could broadcast it freely.

There were rumors that Blizzard required StarCraft II to be played online on its Battle.net servers in part so it could control the way that broadcasters and tournament operators used the game commercially. It also could block KeSPA from broadcasting the games online until the copyright dispute was resolved. But the system meant that competitive StarCraft risked disruption from Internet outages and other technical issues that didn't affect LAN games, the digital equivalent of a rain delay.

Negotiations stalled with KeSPA, and Blizzard ended up partnering with GOMTV as its new South Korean broadcaster of choice, because it was willing to recognize the game developer's rights. In August 2010, GOM announced the first season of the GOMeXP Global StarCraft II League (GSL), the first major StarCraft II event in Seoul, with a prize pool of $170,000. The commentators would be Tasteless and Artosis. They had gone from sleeping on friends' couches to casting one of the biggest eSports events in the world.

"It was extraordinary to see something we conceived in our head come to realization," said John Park, who was known as "John the translator" for his work with player interviews in the early GSL seasons.

GOMTV opened up qualifiers to anyone, and almost two thousand players battled for one of the sixty-four spots in the main tournament, from casual amateurs to veteran pro gamers, although mostly those with mediocre accomplishments. The original game's stars, like Jaedong and Flash, continued to play StarCraft I, which was still broadcast on television. A few non-Korean players participated, including Western students who were studying in Seoul. Artosis both commentated the tournament and qualified to compete, playing Zerg, thanks to his earlier skills and endless practicing, but was eliminated early.

In the end, it was the Zerg player Kim "FruitDealer" Won Ki who won the tournament with innovative strategies like using floating transports called Overlords to drop Banelings, suicidal sacks of acid that explode in a green splash, directly on his enemies' heads. It was a triumph for a player who had previously been forced to give up gaming. His name was a reference to his work at his family's fruit stand to care for his ailing father, a menial job that most South Koreans looked down on. He sometimes displayed a few pieces of fruit in his player booth while competing as a memento. He won $85,000 and became StarCraft II's first champion, but his dominance was short-lived, and he was replaced by stronger, faster players in subsequent seasons.

In contrast to the original insular StarCraft scene, which was dominated by South Koreans and had no superstar Western players, GOMTV made an effort to globalize. The league gave direct invites to Western players and eventually sent Koreans to compete abroad. "We didn't want the StarCraft II pro scene to become Korean-exclusive," he said.

The influx of foreigners led to some memorable moments. Payam "TT1" Toghyan of Canada got lost one day and had to call Park from a police station. Aleksey "White-Ra" Krupnyk also gave him a big bottle of vodka, a "really stereotypical Ukrainian thing to do," said Park, who was touched and amused.

"I never told White-Ra, but I was never able to finish that bottle. I only drank half of it, and kept the rest in my refrigerator, but after a year it started to smell like kimchi and I was forced to throw it away," he said.

StarCraft II also invigorated a Western eSports scene that had never before reached the heights of South Korea. It would firmly establish eSports in America. Improvements in technology also played a big factor. The ease of uploading videos on the Internet led to a significant expansion in the online American audience for eSports. On YouTube, Alex "HD" Do and Mike "Husky" Lamond were two commentators who provided energetic play-by-plays and analyses of professional matches, racking up hundreds of thousands of views even during Starcraft II's beta.

Tasteless's brother, Day[9], became one of the most beloved eSports figures after creating the Day[9] Daily, an online video show that broadcast four days a week and gained thousands of loyal viewers. He was still a student at Harvey Mudd College at the time, but in StarCraft, he was the teacher, reviewing replays and preaching the virtues of proper keyboard mechanics and giving tips on how to deal with playing with anxiety. He also invited viewers to send in their own replays by email, and he would review them. Thanks to the power of the Internet, he could interact with any of his distant fans.

As the scene grew, StarCraft players, commentators, and public figures began facing the scrutiny and hate that athletes and celebrities often encounter on social networks like Twitter, Reddit, and TeamLiquid.net, a popular fan site and news hub that also had its own StarCraft squad. But for the most part, the new eSports personalities didn't have the protection of publicists, the barriers of league management, or the media training to prevent missteps. Insults would hit them directly.

It was a cycle that could be both virtuous and toxic. Players and broadcasters and tournaments all relied on fans to boost their visibility and revenue. They had to interact with the community, and many figures were celebrated. But those who ran afoul of fans could see their feelings smashed and sometimes their careers snuffed out. It was a swift rise to the top, but often an even faster plunge.

Fans criticized Tasteless if his voice sounded fatigued or he wasn't as knowledgeable about cutting-edge strategies. Tasteless eventually completely withdrew from participating in all social networks. "There's something just very unhealthy reading people talk about you all the time. These are just strangers talking on the Internet," said Tasteless. "The Internet is a pretty awful place."

To improve, he watched commentators of different sports rather than getting feedback from his audience. He also had the luxury of working at the station with standard hours and not being subject to the whim of online fans. "I know there are people who don't like it. My attitude is they should just not watch my shit and go away," he said.

As the GSL continued beyond its successful first season, Tasteless and Artosis were exhausted. They were a hit, effortlessly blending sharp analysis, energetic battle narration, and nerdy humor. But they were casting as often as six days a week. GOM needed more commentators and picked relative unknowns who were suddenly thrust into the spotlight without the same reputation and experience as the veteran duo. And they were thrown quickly into a maelstrom of Internet feedback.

No caster was as abused as Kelly "kellyMILKIES" Ong, who cast lesser matches in the GSL's Code A tournament, a second-tier league whose best-performing players would qualify for the premier tournament, known as Code S. There was immediate backlash. Ong is from Singapore and had an accent that viewers found hard to understand, and immediately there were calls to fire her. In retrospect, part of the bad fit was that GOMTV didn't understand the nuances of English accents. Tasteless recalls, "All they know is that people from Singapore speak English so it's probably fine."

And as a woman, Ong was also seen an outsider, despite spending years in gaming. She had played Counter-Strike competitively starting in 2005, but the audience shunned her. "They view women as the other," said Tasteless.

The interactions went beyond simple trash talk. "People were emailing her Photoshopped photos of her nude, being raped and killed," said Tasteless. "It was really horrible. It really took a toll on her emotionally."

After one month at GOMTV, Ong stopped casting and returned to Singapore.

Although fans were free to use slurs when they insulted eSports personalities, if public figures said something offensive, it could destroy their careers. Jake "orb" Sklarew was a top player during the early days of StarCraft II and dropped out of college and worked at a restaurant to save money before entering eSports full time. But he had a weakness. He was color-blind, which didn't greatly handicap his play, except for one crucial aspect: Terran nuclear missiles, which land after a brief delay on a spot marked by a red dot and can devastate an army by themselves. Sklarew found them almost impossible to see, particularly on green backgrounds, and he was knocked out of six tournaments in a row when he tried to return to pro gaming. So he switched to focus on commentating.

It was a positive switch for him, removing the anger that came from losses. He had overwhelmingly positive feedback from his audience, a shift from his playing days. He got his big break in the spring of 2012, when Evil Geniuses hired him to commentate games for the team, which had expanded into hosting its own tournaments.

But in March, a thread on Reddit linked to screenshots of him calling opponents from his practice games "nigger" and "faggot" on multiple occasions. The thread erupted. Sklarew awoke to the drama and called it a "witch hunt" and "slander." He claimed that he shared the account with other friends and it wasn't him. But more screenshots popped up, including one where he was playing with a webcam. Reddit users even analyzed how he grouped up his units in order to tie the language to him. They staged a campaign to complain to Evil Geniuses' sponsors. Sklarew eventually apologized. He explained that he would get enraged when he lost, and his opponents would goad him with their own abusive language. He would lash out. It was a mistake, he said.

Alexander Garfield, who had minored in African American studies, remembered back in 2003 when a team of white and Asian Counter-Strike players pretended to be black. When they were discovered, the community was mostly amused. Garfield was disappointed. Now, Sklarew was in a similar position. And while Garfield didn't think he was actually racist, or a "bad guy," having the visibility of commentating a tournament with corporate sponsors meant he had to be held to a higher standard. The principles of professionalism had been violated.

Garfield fired Sklarew, effectively ending his eSports career as other tournaments shunned him. Garfield implored fans to write positive messages about how Evil Geniuses handled the situation to sponsors like Monster Energy to offset the negative comments. In order for eSports to grow, the fan base had to be more stable. Going directly to sponsors during controversial moments, especially when the team was preparing a response, should be a last resort, he said. "If the organization has a good moral compass, it can act," he said.

Evil Geniuses had long known that StarCraft was the future. In 2009, it signed a younger generation of top North American Starcraft I players to prepare for the game's sequel, including Geoff "iNcontroL" Robinson.

Evil Geniuses initially offered StarCraft players $200 a month, along with paying for travel costs and some free equipment. It was less than top Counter-Strike players, but iNcontroL jumped at the chance since StarCraft was so small in the West. "Nobody thought $200 was going to get them out of their mom's basement," said iNcontroL. "But they thought it was a damn good deal compared to something that they would probably be doing for free.

"The thought of being a full-time pro gamer didn't exist in our minds. We're getting paid to play a fun hobby. I still can't name a pro who set out to make money. It was from passion."

The move was prescient. StarCraft II attracted the attention of Major League Gaming, or MLG, one of the few American eSports tournament survivors of the early 2000s. The company's founders, Sundance DiGiovanni and Mike Sepso, met at a party in New York and bonded over gaming. They began creating tournaments for console games like Halo, Call of Duty, and Super Smash Bros. MLG's logo was a deliberate throwback to the white silhouette on a red-and-blue field of the MLB and NBA, but with a controller instead of an athlete.

MLG launched its first StarCraft II tournament in Raleigh, North Carolina, in 2010, with a modest prize pool of $7,000. For one of the first times, American fans wouldn't have to stay up late to watch top competitors playing in South Korea. Like the GSL, MLG had an open bracket that was open to anyone who wanted to try to play, and novice and pros alike fought to make the cut.

The winner of the first MLG was a newcomer named Chris "HuK" Loranger, who overcame a turbulent childhood and a stint in juvenile prison before he was sixteen. Gaming was a salvation for him. HuK soon joined Team Liquid, which had grown from the main American StarCraft website into its own team and became one of the game's most popular players.

The first MLG that iNcontroL remembers attending had a single viewing bench. By 2011, there was a sea of thousands of people watching each game live at convention centers. Players were idolized. "There were girls throwing themselves at players. There were guys bringing laptops to get signed, shaking and crying," said iNcontroL. "They were the heroes standing up to the Koreans."

Online viewership boomed. MLG's annual online viewership doubled from 1.8 million in 2010 to over 3.5 million in 2011, and then tripled to 11.7 million viewers in 2012. GOMTV and MLG eventually partnered to allow Korean pro players to compete in the United States for one of the first times. Since the original StarCraft had no major tournaments in the United States aside from the WCG, Koreans had rarely had a reason to travel to the country to compete, until now.

The best result for iNcontroL was a top-four placement at MLG Dallas in 2011, but his results fell off after the Koreans arrived and dominated. But by this point Evil Geniuses was paying its players $3,000 per month, enough to survive on. Gaming professionally was now a viable career for a handful of top players. "That's when it became a reality," said iNcontroL.

Evil Genius' rise as a StarCraft powerhouse was clinched with the September 2010 signing of the most dominant non-Korean StarCraft player: Greg "IdrA" Fields. IdrA, named after "Indrajit," a warrior prince in Hindu mythology, grew up in Kalamazoo, Michigan, and New Jersey. Although he never owned a video game console, he became obsessed with golf and chess and would play until he burned out. StarCraft sated his competitive urge. By the sixth grade, IdrA was playing seriously, picking Terran and emulating South Korean players. "I hated losing and instead of just not playing I had to keep practicing," he said.

He competed in some smaller events, but like his peers, he was nervous at LANs and would throw up before matches. By

2007, like some of his peers, IdrA was on the verge of quitting to play poker, which was more lucrative and had easier competition.

In the middle of his senior year of high school, IdrA entered the eSTRO SuperStars Tournament. It was an online event, and he stayed up past midnight on a Sunday to compete. First place was a spot on eSTRO's StarCraft team in Seoul. The stakes may have been higher for his opponents, who were prepared to move across the world. For IdrA, it seemed like an unrealistic dream, and his nerves were manageable. He defeated top American players and, in the finals, he faced his friend and training partner Alex "Skew" Brola, who couldn't handle the pressure and, in the end, IdrA had an offer to go to South Korea.

"Toward the end of my career it flipped and I was way better under pressure because it sharpened me. Looking back I kinda see a hint of that in my play there. I knew everyone's play style well and instead of just trying to sit back and play my game, I played around their styles," said IdrA. "I just became a much more mature player for a night."

IdrA had a potentially life-changing offer. He had already earned a scholarship to study physics at Rensselaer Polytechnic Institute in New York, but he didn't care about academics. "I was that stereotypical underachiever," said IdrA. "So I just felt no desire at all to go to college, whereas Korea was a really cool, unique thing. And I already spent all the time I could playing the game. It seemed like the logical extension of that."

His parents, who were chemists with years of academic training, were alarmed by his choice. "My dad in particular just thought a nonstandard path through life was a massive risk," said IdrA. But he was determined to move, and his mom eventually helped him make the transition. His dad remained hostile to gaming.

IdrA soon adjusted to a rigorous ten hours of StarCraft practice a day, seven days a week. He now realizes that the training house was "inhumane," but he was young and he didn't mind gaming all day. "At the time I was a complete shut-in nerdy little kid," he said. "I was one of the least outgoing people you'd ever meet. I was happy to just sit there playing the game. Stuff just kind of didn't bother me even though I was aware it was objectively pretty crappy conditions. I don't have a great explanation for it." Eight years later, he still isn't sure how he endured. IdrA later joined the B team of the powerhouse CJ Entus.

Unlike Tasteless, IdrA didn't embrace the foreign culture of Seoul. He barely saw the actual city, preferring the pixelated world of StarCraft. It was only after he became better friends with Artosis and Tasteless that he experienced the city and socialized.

IdrA only played one major televised game in South Korea and had no noteworthy results, but he became a perennial champion at foreigner events. Competing with the top Koreans wasn't realistic. "It was cutthroat in the best of conditions and I was always going to be a bit of an outsider," said IdrA. But he hung on for StarCraft II. Finally, his thousands of hours of practice would be rewarded financially.

Although he anticipated success in the game, StarCraft II never impressed IdrA as much as the original game. The skill barrier was lower, he felt, and mediocre players who wouldn't have stood a chance in the original StarCraft were somehow successful pros in the sequel. But he was confident that he would be strong.

After his CJ Entus contract ended, IdrA planned to sign with a Western team and picked Evil Geniuses over Team Liquid, because he felt it was a more established business.

IdrA was one of the few foreigners playing in South Korea's GSL tournament, and Evil Geniuses broke into the Asian market for the first time, which led to some culture shock. Alexander Garfield relied on Tasteless, who was briefly signed to the team, for help. Garfield remembers having to pay a huge security deposit of around $20,000 for a Seoul apartment up front, a common practice in the city. "I thought Nick was taking me for a ride. I was thinking, *am I going to get this back?*" said Garfield. He eventually did.

At his peak, IdrA was untouchable in the Western scene. He was known for a passive style that eschewed early aggression, which had some roots in his early days of playing custom StarCraft maps like Big Game Hunters and Fastest Map Ever, which had abundant resources and a social code that discouraged early attacks.

IdrA's fearsome economic management translated early-game greed into overwhelming numbers later on. Artosis persuaded him to switch from Terran to Zerg, which had a defensive-minded style that was focused on securing additional bases around the map, a strategy that let IdrA demonstrate his superior multitasking. But his weakness to early aggression and unconventional pressure became well known. If he was able to play a relatively passive early game where his opponent gave him space to build up his economy, IdrA usually had the advantage. So his opponents would try to catch him by surprise.

In his most successful run at the GSL January 2011 tournament, IdrA faced Team Liquid's Jonathan "Jinro" Walsh, a Swedish player who was also having a breakout tournament. They were playing to advance to the semifinals, which would be the best result ever for a non-Korean player in Seoul.

In the second game of the best-of-five set, IdrA faced Jinro and opened with the relatively safe build of early Zerglings and a speed upgrade, rather than grabbing a quick second base. At three minutes and thirty seconds, Jinro sent two workers to the entrance to IdrA's base and began building bunkers, a defensive structure that Marines can enter and shoot from. The strategy would blockade IdrA and starve him of a critical second base and more resources. IdrA charged at Jinro's defenses with worker Drones and exploding Banelings, but only damaged the bunkers to a sliver of health before his forces were wiped out. He quit. Four minutes and three seconds had passed. IdrA would lose the series, and he failed to make it to a GSL quarterfinals again. Jinro lost in the next round to the South Korean player MarineKing.

IdrA would later say that he didn't have a chance.

"It's not like not caring about the game or getting frustrated or anything like that. It's just really, really easy for Zerg to get into an unwinnable situation. It's not a comeback race. You don't make things happen. If your macro is twice as good as your opponent, then yeah, you can have a comeback," he later told Artosis.

"But Jinro's a solid player. He had a huge advantage. I wasn't going to come back from that," IdrA said. "It was an unwinnable situation. It just wasn't worth it to play it out."

GOMTV would eventually change maps so buildings couldn't block base entrances, perhaps in an acknowledgment that such "bunker rush" strategies were unfair.

Beyond that single loss, IdrA's amazing economic skills made him seem like a machine operating at maximum efficiency when he was winning. But he also seemed almost robotic when he fell behind. He assumed that his opponent would play perfectly and a comeback was impossible, so he would quit when a more determined player might have stolen a win.

That mentality spread to games where he had the advantage. Against Team Liquid's HuK, he was fooled by a Protoss ability called Hallucination, which creates illusions of units that deal no damage. HuK was on the verge of losing a game against IdrA. HuK conjured a fleet of fake Void Rays, laser-blasting Protoss aircraft, and engaged. IdrA likely would have won the fight, but he quit before it was even finished because he thought HuK had the upper hand.

At the start of the next game, they had a now infamous exchange of broken grammar in chat:

Liquid.HuK: u realize

Liquid.HuK: most of that army

EG.IdrA: fuck off

Liquid.HuK: was halluc

Liquid.HuK: LOL

Liquid.HuK: just saying

Liquid.HuK: u werent loss

IdrA would come back in the series and defeat HuK, four games to two. It was his only happy moment during his career. "I was a little happy there. Otherwise I just hated everything," he said.

After strong results through 2011, IdrA was slumping and, perhaps more critically, losing his passion for competition. He left South Korea to live in Evil Geniuses' new team house in Arizona, a new effort that adopted the Asian model of structured practice. The team provided food and shelter, letting the players focus on gaming. The proximity meant that players would practice side by side, share strategies, and improve together. It also became a multimedia hub with promotional videos. Alexander Garfield continued to live in Los Angeles but picked Arizona for the team house because housing prices were cheap in the wake of the subprime mortgage crash, and his chief operating officer, Scott "SirScoots" Smith, lived there and could provide guidance.

Living in Arizona was isolating for the players, who had no outside friends and limited access to nightlife. StarCraft players were generally introverted, and it was hard to get them to function as a team. The house provided a setting to film video content for sponsors, but the team's weaker players continued to have lackluster results, and its stars were falling behind the South Koreans.

IdrA began seeing a sports therapist, but he couldn't seem to control his emotions. He would lash out at opponents in non-tournament games. He seemed to have a particular and brittle concept of how to properly play StarCraft, and anyone who diverged from that idea was awful. Garfield was sympathetic to IdrA's struggles.

"I saw a lot of myself in him," said Garfield. "Maybe not my current self, but my former self in the way he thought about competition and success and failure."

Garfield started playing classical violin when he was five. When he was twelve, he picked a strict teacher from Australia who would scream at him if he didn't play properly. It wasn't his parents' choice. It was what he needed to do if he wanted to improve. "My mom really didn't want me to study with that teacher," said Garfield. "I wanted to study with the guy because I knew he would scare the shit out of me into being great. I wanted to be great so bad."

He improved, but it was also traumatic and warped his personality. "You tend to motivate yourself with negative thoughts rather than positive thoughts. In a competitive environment that can cause you to spiral down very quickly," said Garfield.

IdrA's harsh training conditions in South Korea and his personality had created a similar dynamic. "Something would happen that Greg felt was unfair and out of his control, but rather than shrugging it off and moving on from it, his mind couldn't let go of the fact that there was some sort of failure on his part, and he would punish himself for that," said Garfield. "I feel like he almost wanted to lose to prove how broken the game was. He created a self-fulfilling prophecy for himself in that way."

Winning wasn't even satisfying for IdrA, but a hatred of losing drove him to compete. It was an unsustainable motivation, and he contemplated retirement. But Garfield wasn't ready to give up on his top player, and he knew that IdrA could win again. And IdrA's blunt personality and dramatic failings had made him one of the most popular players, which made him invaluable to the team. Garfield offered IdrA a six-figure salary, along with other incentives for broadcasting his practice games and selling merchandise. He kept playing.

Garfield continued expanding Evil Geniuses' ranks. In July 2011, it became one of the first Western teams to sign a South Korean pro player, but at a cost. Garfield had been preparing his budget for a year for the deal. He met Lee "PuMa" Ho Joon, a promising Terran player, after he won the first North American Star League Tournament. Garfield gave him a business card in front of a crowd of around twenty people at the event's afterparty. His interest was clear.

At the time, PuMa wasn't signed to a contract and had no salary, but he had been practicing at the team house of the Korean squad Team SCV Life, or TSL, for ten months. Garfield said that he told PuMa to first speak to his coach, Lee Woon Jae, to get approval before a formal offer was made. Lee went public and claimed that Garfield had wronged him by not notifying him first. PuMa wasn't an official player, but Lee considered him part of the team.

"It's not just TSL, but most StarCraft II teams right now run on trust and faith instead of contracts," Coach Lee wrote in a translated post. "It's really disturbing. It feels like the player I raised was just stolen away from me. . . . There needs to be a system to stop foreign teams from stealing Korean players like this."

It was an echo of Jason Lake's accusations of betrayal in 2008. Again, Garfield was being accused of being a predator, when he was trying to be an eSports trailblazer, trying to legitimize and grow the industry and, above all, give a player the resources to compete comfortably. He was on the defensive again, even though he had communicated his interest to PuMa and Coach Lee before finalizing any deal.

This time, he tried a media appearance, appearing on a podcast to defend the signing. But his tone wasn't effective. "I definitely sounded combative and aggressive," Garfield recalled.

He followed up with a nearly three-thousand-word post on TeamLiquid.net to try to explain himself.

Perhaps the cultural barrier exacerbated things, but the controversy reflected how disorganized the eSports labor model is. There is no draft like the American sports leagues. Deals are made over instant messages and Skype calls. A player's worth isn't mandated by a league's salary regulations, and a young player like PuMa has limited bargaining power when it comes to picking a team.

"The industry model is broken, because the player has no agent," said Garfield. "The player has to have the right to advocate for himself."

Ultimately, Garfield paid a buyout of a few thousand dollars to Coach Lee, even though Puma didn't have a formal contract with his previous team. A few months later, Lee was involved in more controversy and accused of not paying salaries by two of his players, although the accusations were later deemed false. Team SCV Life disbanded under financial pressure in 2013.

PuMa won multiple tournaments, and the deal was a harbringer of more South Koreans signing to Western teams.

Garfield wasn't done. A couple months after PuMa's signing and weeks of rumors, Evil Geniuses signed the beloved HuK away from Team Liquid in August 2011 for a six-figure salary. Although HuK wanted to stay with Liquid for less money, Garfield's offer was "potentially life-changing" and he couldn't walk away from the deal without regrets. Five years later, he is still signed to Evil Geniuses.

The deal sealed Evil Geniuses' reputation as the eSports New York Yankees, a team known for its exorbitant salaries and early 2000s championship dynasties. But the Yankees are also known for buying superstars who lose their luster, and the team has been in a World Series drought since 2009.

Garfield was determined to make HuK win. He was going to be pampered, with every need attended to, so he could focus on winning. HuK could be a diva, and he was willing to walk away if he wasn't getting what he wanted. The demands drove his manager at Evil Geniuses, Cody Conners, to take a temporary leave of absence.

But Evil Geniuses now had a good chance to become the best StarCraft team in the world.

There were also signs of hope for IdrA. On the flight to the Intel Extreme Masters Tournament in October 2011 in Guangzhou, China, IdrA read *Mindgym,* a book about achieving mental toughness in competition.

At the tournament, IdrA beat his new teammate PuMa on his way to his first championship in months. His face was expressionless after he won, and a smile only flashed across his face for a moment when a staff member came over to congratulate him.

Garfield was elated. IdrA seemed to have overcome a barrier. But there was another reason for the win: "eSports felt like perpetually up and down, and the worse my personal life was going the better my competitive life was going. When I broke up with a girl or something I would retreat into the game and go back to practicing twelve hours a day," he said. He believes that the isolation from the fallout of a relationship led to his win in Guangzhou, rather than a change in mentality.

At the MLG Orlando tournament just two weeks later, Evil Geniuses looked poised to dominate. IdrA went up three games to none against the Terran legend BoxeR, but his lead disappeared under a flurry of aggressive Marine openings in the next three games. Garfield couldn't take it anymore. He went into IdrA's player booth to talk to him directly, freaking out Adam Apicella, an executive vice president at MLG. There was a rule prohibiting teams from entering the booth in between games, but Garfield claimed that BoxeR's wife and manager, Kim "Jessica" Ga Yeon, had already violated that rule repeatedly by going into his booth.

Garfield could see the turmoil in IdrA's eyes. "Do you believe you can win?" said Garfield, trying to pump him up.

IdrA said no. Garfield told him he wouldn't leave until he heard yes, so IdrA said yes, but Garfield didn't believe him. "This really isn't helping. Can you leave?" IdrA finally said.

Maybe it had helped. IdrA came back and took the series, but he was still mad at himself. In IdrA's mind, BoxeR was someone who should have had no chance of beating him, despite his legendary status in StarCraft's early days. He shouldn't have been a threat at all. The next round, IdrA lost to the dominant Korean Protoss player Jang "MC" Min Chul, who went on to play HuK, Evil Geniuses' newest player, in the finals.

Protoss-versus-Protoss was a swift, aggressive matchup, heavily dependent on timing attacks to obliterate the opponent, rather than focusing on gaining a stronger economy. HuK showed off his army control with a flourish, and he became the first two-time champion of MLG's StarCraft events. Garfield exulted in the crowd. Both of his parents were watching the stream. He calls the win one of the highlights of his career. It broke the impression that "EG is where good players go to die," he said.

As HuK won, IdrA disintegrated. He had always had blunt disdain for opponents, but his language began intensifying. In March 2013, as his base was being destroyed in a ladder game, he wrote to his opponent, "i genuinely hope something bad happens to you like you get cancer or something."

In another game, he wrote "david kim should be raped with a tire iron I can't believe how terrible this game is," referring to the Blizzard employee who was in charge of StarCraft's competitive balance.

His Protoss-playing opponent agreed—"hate this lategame ye"—but the community was outraged.

In his mind, IdrA was making vicious remarks that were so over the top that people shouldn't take them seriously. But it backfired.

This behavior, friends say, was not a true reflection of the intelligent, friendly, and calm Greg Fields that they knew. But gaming was an emotional investment, a digital value judgment of players' worth. Defeat wasn't just fuel for lashing out. In IdrA's mind the entire balance of the game was broken. Blizzard had taken something beautiful in the original StarCraft and made a sequel that he thought sucked.

"The game just made me really angry and I said stupid shit when I was angry. I like never even get mad at pretty much anything since retiring. It's kinda bizarre really. Anyone who knows me now and doesn't know my history would be shocked.

I'm not a nice fuzzy person but the game just made me different," said IdrA.

Two months after his cancer remark, and assurances from Garfield that it wouldn't happen again, IdrA clicked on a forum post on TeamLiquid.net that praised Evil Geniuses for its marketing strategy, which focused on player personalities and not just results.

IdrA commented on the post that some of the most successful South Korean players didn't have the most fans and acknowledged that a player's personality could be more important than skill. "Winning is at best tangentially related to making money in this industry solely because of what you and the rest of this community chooses to watch. We work in an entertainment industry," he wrote.

A commentator followed with a snarky post about IdrA: "I am sure he is a nice fellow, who is pained and crying inside by his enforced facade for entertainment whenever he streams."

IdrA lashed back, "nope you're all a bunch of fucks it just so happens i get paid to treat you like it. it's fucking awesome."

He had gone too far. Garfield tolerated, even encouraged, trash talk and bluntness against opponents as a natural part of competition. But insulting the community, the basis of IdrA's livelihood—and Evil Geniuses' survival—was too much. And fans were once again gathering to complain to Evil Geniuses' sponsors directly.

On May 9, 2013, Garfield made his own post on Team Liquid's forums.

"As most of you are already aware, we let our players be themselves. We believe that our industry's diverse assortment of vibrant personalities plays a huge part in helping make eSports so much fun—for ourselves, and for the viewers. No great novel is without great characters, and we like to let our players find their own roles within the eSports storyline by showcasing the personalities they were born with. We have strict guidelines that regulate certain kinds of more extreme speech, and we take disciplinary action when those guidelines are violated, but for the most part, we stay out of the way," Garfield wrote.

"This is why it was never really an issue for us that Greg can be rude to his opponents in games, or that he usually speaks his mind very bluntly and directly. But, to us, there's a very big difference between a player being disrespectful to an opponent in a ladder match, and a player being disrespectful to the entire community of people who, via their own enthusiasm and passion for the entertainment product he creates, actually make his profession possible."

Evil Geniuses fired IdrA, but Garfield offered to pay his rent for the rest of the year. He had moved to Emeryville, a small city across the bay from San Francisco, to train near Evil Geniuses' new headquarters. And Garfield would be his agent to find some new sponsors if he wanted. But IdrA refused, partly out of pride, but also because he knew that he didn't want to compete anymore.

After commanding one of the highest salaries in Western eSports, IdrA was unemployed. He was also relieved. "On some level, he enjoyed it, but that was not worth the amount of anxiety and stress doing something that he hated," said iNcontroL, who was visibly emotional after his teammate's departure. "He knew if he was pushing buttons hard, he would get fired, but he didn't care."

IdrA had already been talking to Evil Geniuses about transitioning to a commentator role, and he had already been praised for his deep game knowledge and analysis. But it was a far cry from a six-figure salary. He received a couple thousand dollars for a weekend working at a tournament, but such events happened only about once a month. In February 2014, he announced he was leaving the game and returning to school. "If I wanted to continue to scrape out a living I probably could, by lowering standards, accepting donations, and whatever else. But I've never liked the game and I don't see that changing anytime soon so I see no reason to scrape by with no future just for the sake of staying with it," said IdrA in his farewell post, also on Team Liquid.

Being a public figure on a different part of the tournament stage wasn't appealing either. "I think I would've ended up horribly unhappy that way. I am not an entertainer at heart, regardless of how things looked during my career. And I don't think I'd be particularly adept at moving into the business side of eSports. So it was a messy exit but I think it needed to happen," he said.

In 2014, IdrA briefly rejoined Evil Geniuses to compete in a new Blizzard game called Heroes of the Storm. He hadn't expected to ever compete again, but he found the five-versus-five gameplay fun, and having teammates shielded him from anger. But finding the right team dynamic and designating a leader was challenging. Although IdrA had a dominant personality, he wasn't an effective leader. The game's growth was slower than expected, and he decided to retire again.

The student who had passed up a college scholarship to move to South Korea returned to academics. In 2015, IdrA took an introduction to theoretical physics class at a community college and now plans to transfer to a larger school in the fall of 2016. Life is slower, but the course is satisfying. "It's interesting and I'm good at it. I'm not really passionate about anything," said IdrA. "I'm just not wired like that as a person. Any kind of extreme emotional reaction I get is usually on the negative end of things and I don't tend to be emotional in general, despite what the rageyness would seem to indicate."

He doesn't have regrets when it comes to his StarCraft career. He's earned enough money to pay for college, and while he never triumphed over the top South Korean players, he'll always be a memorable part of the game's history. He just couldn't overcome his mental hurdles. "I definitely expected a lot of myself and got down on myself for not living up to that, but hard on myself in terms of genuinely reflecting and trying to improve myself—I coulda done a lot more of that," he said.

IdrA doesn't miss competition. He misses his friends from Evil Geniuses, and he's lost touch now that he lives in a suburb west of Chicago. The constant traveling, training, and competing has given way to a calmer existence as he prepares to go to college.

He doesn't miss his fans, who would chant his name and ask for his signature after games. He wasn't trying to insult them in his forum post; he was just trying to target the haters, the ones who wanted drama instead of really caring about eSports. But he knew he had to get out of the public eye. "I'm very antisocial. I was always nice as I could be to them but it was very draining," said IdrA.

Chapter 4

STREAM DREAMS

TWITCH

In April 2005, Justin Kan and Emmett Shear, two seniors on the verge of graduating from Yale University, took the train from New Haven, Connecticut, to Boston to sell an idea.

Kan and Shear met in second grade at the Evergreen School, a private school in their hometown of Seattle. They had both learned how to code and headed off to Yale together, where Shear studied computer science. Kan studied physics because his mom wanted him to learn something quantitative. The subject was difficult, so he did a combined double major with philosophy and was able to skip the hardest physics classes.

It was a few weeks before graduation, and Shear was set to start a job at Microsoft. Kan was going to become a junior analyst focusing on electricity deregulation at the Washington, DC, firm Dean & Co. The job had nothing to do with his major, but it was the only job he had been able to get.

But another path emerged. After Google released Gmail, Kan and Shear became enthusiastic users, but they wished that they could sync their emails with their calendars. They came up with an idea for a service that they named Kiko, a digital calendar that would partner with email and generate revenue by advertising events.

Entrepreneurship was in their veins. Kan's grandfather had operated a rock quarry and bicycle factory in Malaysia and China. His mother had been an engineer and later started her own real estate brokerage. Shear's dad had also founded a startup focusing on information discovery.

Serendipitously, a friend had sent Shear an email advertising a new company called Y Combinator in Cambridge, Massachusetts, which would mentor and fund new tech startups. The deadline was the next day, and Kan and Shear stayed up late to apply along with another college friend, Matthew Fong, who soon left Kiko to work at Goldman Sachs because he needed a visa and preferred working in finance.

Y Combinator's founders were tech veterans who had sold Viaweb, one of the first web applications, to Yahoo for $49 million in stock in 1998. The sale made three partners, Paul Graham, Trevor Blackwell, and Robert Morris, into sources of wisdom and cash for the next wave of entrepreneurs.

Graham was initially reluctant to become an angel investor, but after meeting with Harvard students who aspired to found their own companies, he realized that he could be a valuable mentor. On a walk home from dinner with his future wife and Y Combinator's fourth partner, Jessica Livingston, they decided to start the company and launched in March 2005. In coding, a Y combinator is a program that runs other programs. Y Combinator would be a company that started other companies.

In exchange for around 7 percent equity in the company, Y Combinator would give founders a few thousand dollars and look to mentor the next Bill Gates or Steve Jobs. Livingston, a former investment banker, played a key role. She had an unerring ability to judge a founder's character at interviews, and she became an oracle when it came to picking the right people. She was nicknamed "Social Radar."

In their application, Kan and Shear listed their credentials and some bragging rights to prove that they were exceptional. "Emmett only learned to program when he was sixteen and picked up a C++ [programming language] tutorial. He did nothing but program, sleep, and eat for the next six days. Justin once played a forty-five-minute half of a rugby match before realizing he had a nosebleed from being struck in the face," they wrote in their application.

The Y Combinator founders were skeptical of the calendar idea, but intrigued by the two young men. The program focused on the potential of the applicants, rather than just the feasibility of their idea, which could be modified. Kiko was a "company with a bad idea and good founders." So Kan and Shear were invited to a meeting at Y Combinator's office.

They booked a cheap hotel in Somerville, Massachusetts, which seemed to be near their meeting, based on MapQuest. They stayed up until three in the morning working on the site's demo and had to rush to the meeting in a cab, making it with five minutes to spare. Kan's memories of the meeting are hazy, but he remembers being nervous and letting Shear do most of the talking. After about forty minutes, they finished and walked around Cambridge, eventually making their way to a comic store. Then, Shear got a call.

Despite some misgivings over the calendar idea, Y Combinator believed in the two men. They would invest $12,000 in Kiko, enough for Kan and Shear to rent a home in Boston and feed themselves for a few months, for 4 percent of the company.

Their idea was worth $300,000 on paper, and they became two of Y Combinator's first class of fifteen founders.

The duo had independence. They were free from the daily cubicle grind, free from bosses. But they also lacked the stability of a salary. The funding was hopefully the beginning of big user growth, culminating in a big sale, known as an exit, or if they truly became massive enough, an initial public offering that would make them millionaires. The latest tech boom was just beginning. Facebook had only launched the year before.

For three months, Kan and Shear lived in Boston, coding and brainstorming with their mentors. The future seemed bright, but there was that one risk that they had listed in their application: "Google might crush us like ants by releasing a superior product tomorrow, supported by their vastly superior backend systems."

Less than a year later, in April 2006, Google Calendar was released. Kiko was immediately crippled. It was time to move on, and Kan had the idea of selling the company and its assets on eBay, mimicking what another startup called Jux2 had done the year before. Kan created an auction with an opening bid of $49,999.99, in hopes of paying back their investors. They posted a link on the social network website Reddit, another Y Combinator startup, where it jumped to the front page. With the help of the tech press, the auction got sustained buzz.

Kan watched the final day of the auction in his underwear at his friend's apartment amid a scorching New York summer. Elliot Noss, CEO of Toronto-based Internet domain management company Tucows, ended up buying the company for $258,100. Kan and Shear were ecstatic. The $300,000 valuation that Y Combinator had bestowed Kiko wasn't that far off, even if the company had no hope of competing with Google.

And failure would prove to be valuable exposure. The idea of liquidating a startup through eBay was a novel idea, and the press was eager to talk to the upstarts. Their next project would "change the way people think about the Internet," Kan boasted to reporters.

After one Y Combinator dinner, Shear and Kan were discussing the future when Kan imagined how a live audio feed of their discussion would be interesting and valuable for fellow entrepreneurs. That idea evolved into a video feed, which evolved into the idea of broadcasting Kan's life for twenty-four hours a day, seven days a week. It wasn't a business idea so much as taking reality television to a bandwidth-enabled extreme.

They had a meeting with Y Combinator's Paul Graham and Robert Morris to pitch new ideas, and Kan said the one thing that came to mind, a perfect, if immodest, name for the website: Justin.tv. Again, the idea wasn't as important as Kan and Shear's expertise and passion. "I'll fund that just to see you make a fool of yourself," said Morris, who gave them a check for $50,000.

Kan and Shear wanted to create the new company outside of Boston and its miserable winters. They considered New York, but San Francisco, the land of tech and venture capital, beckoned. They also convinced Michael Seibel, another Yale friend, to come along on vacation. Seibel had majored in political science and had just finished working as finance director for the senate campaign of Kweisi Mfume in Baltimore. He had never been to the West Coast.

In October 2006, Kan, Shear, and Seibel piled into a Honda Civic and drove across the country. It was a beautiful, warm arrival. The Navy's Blue Angels planes soared in formation across the sky.

It quickly became apparent that Seibel was indispensable as he took charge in their search for an apartment, which would also be Justin.tv's first office. They ended up at the Crystal Tower apartments in the North Beach neighborhood, which was nicknamed the "Yscraper," after the five other Y Combinator–funded startups that also lived there. Seibel had no aspirations of working in tech, but his friends convinced him to be CEO of the new company. "This is a once-in-a-lifetime opportunity. Campaigns are every four years," Seibel remembers thinking. He also became the house chef for the tech community in the building because he was the only one who knew how to cook with something more sophisticated than a microwave.

Justin.tv needed one more partner: someone who could actually build the camera-to-computer connection that would make an endless livestream possible. They emailed the Massachusetts Institute of Technology and got in touch with a student named Kyle Vogt, who was a hardware expert. Vogt visited San Francisco the following January during his monthlong break, and he never returned to school.

The night before the stream of his life was about to go live, Kan was anxious. He had been a shy as a kid, but he put himself in uncomfortable situations so he could grow. "I wanted to do things that forced me to get out there, have new experiences and meet new people," he said. It wasn't the first time Kan had been an exhibitionist. In college, he posed for a calendar in the nude aside from a few strategic clouds of whipped cream. Starring in a never-ending reality show was just another adventure, and no one else was willing to do it, so it was up to him.

On March 19, 2007, Kan strapped a camera to his head. For months, he would record every moment of his life, only turning away from the camera when he went to bathroom. He ate, went on dates, and stared at a computer. A third of the time, Kan sprawled on his bed, asleep, as fans impatiently waited and urged his coworkers to wake him up using the site's chat room. He even posted his cell phone number so fans could text message him. Justin.tv became an almost immediate sensation. Technology blogs covered the site, and two weeks after the launch, the *San Francisco Chronicle* published a front-page story on Kan.

A key appeal was the site's community and the ability to interact with Kan. Viewers pulled pranks like reporting a stabbing at their apartment. Kan was recorded on stream, his hands up as police arrived, trying to explain what was happening. "Uh, tech company," he said as an officer walked in with a flashlight. The next day, someone falsely reported a fire. The authorities would eventually call to confirm incidents after a slew of hoaxes. Years later, the practice of calling the police with fake reports became known as "swatting" and would terrorize video streamers. Another time, fans ordered a huge amount of pizza to be sent to the apartment.

Kan soon appeared on the *Today Show* with his camera attached to his head. "Is it about being understood? Or that you see that there's a need out there for something honest and real?" asked host Ann Curry.

"We're trying to create a new genre of media," Kan told Curry. "I'm only the beginning of something that could be really popular."

"Fame, I have to tell you, Justin, has a price," said Curry. "Good luck and keep your shirt on, buddy."

Kan later told the *Yale Daily News* that Curry was a "bitch."

Kan had a fan base, as well as critics who called the site narcissistic, pointless, ridiculous, fame-grubbing, and embarrassing. But Justin.tv had to find a way to convert publicity into an actual business model. Y Combinator tells its startups to launch fast and make changes after, to "iterate" in tech lingo, while a more dramatic shift is called a "pivot."

Thankfully, the community that had gathered around the site gave the founders a clear path forward. "Our traffic's not growing. We're not very interesting. But a lot of people asked to create their own streams. It was a no-brainer," said Kan.

After a few months of development, Justin.tv became a platform that allowed any user to create a channel and broadcast whatever they wanted. Justine Ezarik, known as iJustine, became the channel's second star in May 2007, which made her a pop culture icon, although she soon switched to YouTube. Most users expanded beyond reality TV. They performed music, illicitly rebroadcast sporting events, or played video games. Content became eclectic. The site gained momentum, and by July 2008, it had passed one million registered users, without any marketing.

One of the site's first challenges was working with the Jonas Brothers band, which was just beginning its career. The trio of Joe, Kevin, and Nick had recently signed to Hollywood Records and appeared on the Disney channel, and they agreed to stream some performances on Justin.tv. The first broadcast had some hiccups, but it went well enough that the band and its managers agreed to another session, which they promoted heavily. Viewership surged to six digits, the most ever for one channel.

"A hundred thousand girls would be refreshing and it would bring down the site without fail. It was our first real scalability test," said Kan. The band's managers called to complain about the site crashing, and Kan and Seibel passed the phone between each other, not sure what to say. The broadcast was delayed by about twenty-five minutes until the stream was restored, and Hollywood Records abandoned Justin.tv for a competitor, Ustream, for future productions.

Another time, the site crashed when Vogt was on vacation by Lake Tahoe. His coworkers knew where he was staying but he wasn't answering his phone. They had the idea of calling a pizza deliveryman to knock on his door to tell him, "The website is down."

"What type of pizza do you want?" the deliveryman asked. "I don't want a pizza. I'll pay you, just go now!" they responded. The deliveryman found Vogt, who had been napping, and he fixed the site in two minutes. Then he called the office and asked them, "Why didn't you send the pizza? I'm hungry."

Kan eventually stopped streaming his life to focus on managing and coding. Justin.tv's landlord pushed them out of its North Beach apartment for illegally running a business in a residential building. The company ended up leasing an industrial space at 47 Lusk Street in San Francisco's South of Market neighborhood, which has become the planet's premier home for technology startups. A blue "Justin.tv" sign was installed at the entrance.

By 2008, the company needed more cash, and Seibel, who was handling the bulk of marketing, was stressed. One late night, he was watching *The West Wing*, a reminder of his days running political campaigns in Washington, DC. A character on the show, Matt Santos, was struggling to manage a campaign alone. Seibel realized he needed help, too. "Who's the smartest person who could help us with this stuff?" he wondered, and settled on Kevin Lin, another friend from Yale.

It was 4:00 a.m., so Seibel stayed up a few more hours and then reached out to Lin, who was running a distribution warehouse for a San Francisco beverage company called Fizzy Lizzy, where he had recently prepared an investment pitch. Lin was flattered, but with a background in event planning and a childhood dream of becoming a veterinarian, he wasn't familiar with live streaming. "There were thousands of people with more intimate knowledge of . . . all things Internet," Lin said.

Lin also wasn't convinced that Seibel was dedicated enough. "In college, we called him 'Same Day Seibel' because he was such a procrastinator," said Lin. He made a deal with Seibel: wake up at 7:00 a.m., and Lin would help before going to his actual job. Seibel obliged, and they brainstormed and studied monetization strategies, coming up with revenue projections for a potential investor. Then Lin wished them good luck and went on his way.

Ultimately, the investors never materialized and the projections were way off. But a few days later, the Justin.tv founders and Lin went to eat at Louisiana Fried Chicken, a couple blocks from the office and next to AT&T Ballpark, home of the San Francisco Giants.

"Before I could even take a bite, Justin looked me square in the eye and said, 'You should join us,'" said Lin. Again, Lin thought that thousands of other people were more qualified, but he considered the offer. The beverage company where he was working was going through its death throes, and joining Justin.tv meant he could stay in San Francisco.

In June 2008, Lin became the company's chief operating officer and Justin.tv's seventh employee. He joined Bill Morrier, the company's first engineer, and product designer Jacob Woodsey, who used to play soccer with Kan and Shear when they were growing up in Seattle.

Kan believes his biggest strength was convincing others to believe in what they were building. "I'm an okay web developer. I'm a shitty programmer. I'm a mediocre manager," said Kan. "But I'm really good at convincing people to get excited about things that I'm excited about. I have true passion about building startups."

Initially, Justin.tv had no advertising strategy. They eventually signed on some small brands, but the question was how to scale. "We were just trying to figure out what to do," said Lin. "Online video was still nascent."

In 2007, Justin.tv raised a Series A funding round of $8 million, the company's first significant investment, from Alsop Louie Partners and Felicis Ventures. "These are four fearless kids who are doing something crazy," said Seibel. "People were investing in the team."

But online streaming rivals were getting bigger. Livestream raised $10 million in July 2008 and focused on broadcasting events for corporations, in contrast to Justin.tv's bedroom streamers. Ustream raised a $46.6 million round of funding in February 2010. "Every time we walk into a meeting with Sony, Warner Bros., you name it, Ustream either just left the building or is walking right in," said Lin. "Oh my God, we're screwed," he remembers thinking.

"Ustream was kicking our ass," said Seibel. "We were seen as more of a copyright violator, even though they were equally guilty."

In December 2009, Seibel testified in front of Congress on a panel on copyright infringement for sports broadcasting. Lorenzo Fertitta, CEO of the Ultimate Fighting Championship, accused the company of promoting piracy to increase viewership, which Seibel denied. The UFC sued Justin.tv in January 2011, claiming that over fifty thousand viewers had illegally watched uploaded copyright content. The site hadn't done enough over two years to address the problem, the UFC claimed. They later settled.

Competition from Ustream led Justin.tv to strive for more efficiency. "We don't know if we can compete with these guys, so let's focus on what we know. Let's focus on tech," said Lin.

Justin.tv built out its own data center infrastructure and content delivery network, and it hired Jonathan Shipman away from YouTube to be its director of operations. They kept lowering the cost and speed of streaming, and self-sufficiency would be valuable as the site kept growing. They wouldn't have to pay third-party providers for bandwidth, which could costs tens of thousands of dollars for a few hours. "If we're really going to survive, we have to build it ourselves," said Lin. "Third-party companies couldn't scale. It turned out to be a very wise decision."

The company kept expanding, taking an adjacent space at 36 Clyde Street and cramming fifty employees into around 4,500 square feet. A storage closet doubled as a conference room. Meetings were often held outside. The office needed swamp coolers in the summer and space heaters in the winter. During a video tour for a tech website, a visitor opened the office refrigerator, and "all we had was twelve jars of mustard," said Lin.

"It was so sad. We were like, no one's going to work here," said Lin. "We tried to be as cheap as possible. We were always really, really frugal."

For the first two years, the founders were working seven days a week. Sometimes they would sleep in the office. Seibel remembers waking up one morning, showering at the office, and changing into new clothes. When he emerged at the workspace, he pretended that he had just arrived from home.

Kan thought about quitting all the time. "Startups are so stressful. It doesn't always feel like it's going well," he said. He would be coding in the dark during the summer as friends were posting beach and vacation photos on Facebook.

But the bond between his friends kept him going. "Hopefully when you're feeling bad, someone else is feeling decent," he said. "It kind of balances it out."

Because of the close quarters, everyone could hear Lin's calls pitching broadcasters to join the site. "We got super close because of it," said Lin. "Everyone's kind of got this nervous tension: 'Are we going to convince these guys to move over?'"

By mid-2010, it had become harder to raise money and the company was burning through its cash reserves. The team resolved to become profitable. They got better at serving ads and cutting costs and finally made money. The following March, the entire company went on a trip to Hawaii to celebrate.

By 2011, Justin.tv had grown to about $10 million in revenue a year, but growth had slowed, an ominous sign. "If something's not growing on the Internet, it's about to be shrinking," said Kan.

And the employees also wanted more. "We were internally just bored. That's when we forked the business," said Lin.

Seibel thought about what else he could do in online video and gathered a few colleagues to launch a new product. They created a mobile streaming application called Socialcam and ultimately sold it to the software company Autodesk for around $60 million in 2012.

Another team started thinking more seriously about gaming. Justin.tv had a nascent gaming community from the beginning, both inside the company and among users. Tia Marie, the former community director, was a big gaming advocate and gaming shows like *4Player Podcast* built a fan base. But the fate of eSports was uncertain, as the industry was still licking its wounds from DirecTV's CGS collapse, so the site held off on focusing on promoting gaming. "We felt it was too early," said Lin. "The scene was sort of figuring itself out."

Then, the StarCraft II beta came out, and the Justin.tv office played for hours and hours. As they watched early commentators racking up hundreds of thousands of views, they realized how powerful gaming really was. Gaming was only about 3 percent of the site's traffic, or about a million viewers a month, but there was potential.

"A lot of what kicked it off was our obsession with StarCraft II," said Lin. "We were playing all night." The company started its own LAN tournament, called Startupcraft, inviting friends from Dropbox, Twitter, and Facebook to compete.

On June 6, 2011, to coincide with the major video game industry gathering E3, a gaming-centric version of Justin.tv was officially spun off as a separate brand and domain name. Justin.tv cofounder Emmett Shear became CEO and Lin became COO of the new site. They first considered naming the site Xarth.com, but eventually settled on Twitch, a reference to the quick reflexes needed to play at a high level. The site would eventually pick a rich purple logo, in contrast to the colder colors of its competitors, a deliberate move to differentiate itself.

They began talking to more and more gamers, who had a simple message: "You guys are idiots. Your platform is terrible," said Lin. In response to feedback, they worked to reduce latency, created a broadcaster dashboard with stats, and began a partnership program similar to YouTube, which let broadcasters split advertising revenue with the company. Also, instead of showing ads only when a viewer first loaded a stream, broadcaster partners could choose to show ads whenever they wanted, usually during breaks in between matches. "Our first innovation in live video was the commercial break," said Lin. Fans could also subscribe to broadcasters for $5 a month and receive benefits like custom emoticons and no ads, but all streams were free and paying was voluntary. The streamer reportedly gets $2, and Twitch gets $3 per month.

As Twitch began directing more and more resources into video game live streaming, it fast became a leader. It was free for viewers, accessible with a click, and, thanks to years of work, could now support millions of viewers across the site. It was revolutionary for both million-dollar tournaments and individuals playing in their bedrooms. The proliferation of personal computers and broadband Internet meant that streaming games required no extra costs, although serious streamers can buy microphones, webcams, and even lighting rigs. Twitch democratized the live broadcasting and consumption of gaming.

"Twitch represented the ideas, the philosophy, and the message of what live streaming is about and what it represents," said Marcus "djWHEAT" Graham, director of programming at Twitch, who has worked in eSports since 1999 as a commentator and broadcaster.

Before Twitch, the cost of broadcasting online severely limited the reach of early gaming competitions. "We got bills for $18,000. We were eating these costs," said Graham, but Twitch's free service and advertising model made streaming a potential profit generator. "Suddenly, we had the ability to use this platform and not only not spend money, but make money."

The site began focusing on the world's biggest video game tournaments, instead of just bedroom streamers. Twitch convinced tournament organizers like ESL and the North American Star League to use the site, promising that the company was committed to gaming. "We understand the space. We'll build features," Lin remembers telling them.

One of the site's first big events was DreamHack, the Swedish gaming festival, and it was nearly a disaster as the site crashed the day before the event started.

Shear tore through the underlying code and brought Twitch back to life with a few hours to spare. Over one hundred thousand concurrent viewers watched, and unlike the earlier debacle with the Jonas Brothers, the website held strong. Other tournament organizers began ditching their own broadcast platforms to move over to Twitch. "Those great moments happen almost every day now," said Graham.

Next, the site had to convince game developers to become partners. Twitch initially didn't have broadcast rights for games, which are owned exclusively by the developers, and it had to hope it wouldn't get sued. Fortunately, developers are in the software business, not the event business, unlike the litigious UFC. Most saw their games streaming on Twitch and realized the benefit of free exposure and marketing.

Mike Morhaime, CEO of Blizzard, and other gaming executives noticed how big the site was getting and met with Twitch staff to figure out how they could partner. "That was really validating," said Lin. Twitch now has proper licenses and also mutes copyrighted music in recorded videos.

Although it got its start in PC gaming, Twitch expanded to consoles in 2013 and was integrated into Sony's PlayStation 4 and Microsoft's Xbox One gaming systems. Gamers could stream from their console by pushing a single button on their controllers.

The personal Twitch streams of professional players are akin to watching the practice regime of great athletes through their own eyes. Viewers can see the precise shooting in Counter-Strike or the furious multitasking of StarCraft, and they can also share in the triumphs and defeats of their favorite player.

The idea of watching someone else play a game, the core of eSports, befuddles many outsiders. But if you're passionate about something, expertise has universal appeal. Watching someone who's really good at gaming is compelling just as watching someone who's really good at basketball, or cooking, or sewing can be compelling.

"Thank goodness this is here, I don't even have television anymore. I just watch Twitch all day," fans tell Lin. "This is a new form of entertainment."

Justin.tv's viewership had flatlined, but Twitch exploded, growing to twenty-eight million unique visitors a month by March 2013, and then forty-five million by the end of the year. Users were also sticking around on the site, watching an average of 106 minutes of video a day in 2013. By February 2014, Twitch was fourth in peak US Internet traffic, behind Netflix, Google, and Apple, but ahead of Hulu and Facebook, according to the *Wall Street Journal*. Twitch's share was still small, at 1.8 percent, in contrast to Netflix's monstrous 32 percent and Google (and YouTube)'s 22 percent, but those sites had a variety of programming genres. Twitch was all about gaming. In January 2015, Twitch surpassed one hundred million monthly viewers.

This data would be a valuable metric for eSports teams like Evil Geniuses as they sought to court sponsors. The exposure from having an Intel or a SteelSeries logo on a player's jersey was previously impossible to determine, but thanks to Twitch viewer data and tracking affiliate marketing links, sponsoring a video game team now had substantive value.

Twitch is also about much more than eSports. Popular streamers can be of average or even mediocre skill, but if they connect with an audience, Twitch can become their day job. A streamer's appeal can come from cracking jokes or being attentive to responding to their stream chat's questions. Streamers like Jayson

Love of Billings, Montana, who runs the channel MANvsGAME, make a living by broadcasting their adventures in single-player games.

Love was working dead-end retail jobs when he was inspired to stream his journey by beating tough single-player video games on Justin.tv. In November 2013, he was featured in the *Wall Street Journal* as the face of the new streaming generation, and perhaps the most compelling part of the story for the business-minded audience: he was making over $100,000 a year by playing video games in his bedroom. That's more than most pro gamers, and double America's average household income.

The rise of the bedroom streamer has also happened on YouTube, where Felix "PewDiePie" Kjellberg of Sweden has the most popular channel on the entire website with forty million subscribers for his "Let's Play" recordings of his gameplay and reactions. He is not a professional gamer, but rather a personality, looking to "sharing gaming moments on YouTube with my bros." PewDiePie's passion for gaming and unguarded reactions provide something young viewers crave: authenticity.

Love and Kjellberg are outliers, bolstered by their years of experience and their personalities. Spectacular earnings are still limited to the few superstar streamers, but a few thousand people now make minimum wage streaming on Twitch and creating their own smaller communities, said Lin. Having a successful channel is a big commitment. Full-time streamers may stream for over ten hours, seven days a week, equivalent to how long professional gamers practice.

Love's marathon broadcasts, which included streaming for as much as eighty-two hours straight, also took a toll. On a December 2015 broadcast, he admitted using drugs to fuel his marathon gaming sessions over the past year. "Every single time you've seen me, I've been pretty much saturated with speed. With amphetamines, like Adderall," he said on stream.

"A lot of people out there, you think you know me," Love said. "You'll never know me. I know what's so great about the platform, with the interaction and all of that, it feels like we're very close sometimes. There's this whole side of my life—the majority of my life, the majority of me as a person—that you have no idea what's going on."

The gateway that connects broadcaster and viewer is Twitch chat, the scrolling box of text and emoticons to the right of the video feed that was available the first day Justin.tv launched. Viewers can say anything to the broadcaster, from innocuous gameplay questions to disgusting harassment over appearance, race, and gender.

Twitch chat has been called the id of eSports, a cesspool of the darkest thoughts of a virtual stadium crowd. Quality begins to degenerate as viewership rises and moderation tools like deleting messages and banning users struggle to keep up. At a few thousands viewers, any semblance of intelligible discussion usually gives way to repetitive messages (known as "copypasta") and spamming of the site's emoticons, which have become the site's biggest cultural memes.

Twitch's iconic emoticon is Kappa, which viewers can summon by typing "Kappa" in the chat box, converting it into the grayscale portrait of a smug-looking former Justin.tv employee Josh DeSeno. He has a slight smile that suggests mischief, a cheeky Mona Lisa for the digital age. He appears to be barely holding back a laugh. Kappa has become shorthand for trolling and sarcasm. It is spammed roughly two hundred times per minute across the site.

Other faces, many featuring broadcasters, signify other emotions: Kreygasm features streamer Kreyg throwing his head back in pleasure or amazement, and viewers post it in reaction to an amazing play. BibleThump is a weeping cartoon baby from the indie game Binding of Isaac and demonstrates sadness. ResidentSleeper is a snoozing reaction for boredom. It is its own language, a system of emojis for gamers. "Twitch chat is its own animal," said Lin. "You kind of have to let it be what it wants to be."

One of the company's darkest moments came when Twitch was still Justin.tv. In November 2008, Abraham Biggs, a Florida college student, was going through emotional turmoil, chronicled by his posts on the bodybuilding.com forum. "The hate that rages within me, rages not for those I love so dearly or those who have crossed my path. This hate rages full force towards me and only me," he wrote. He bought a cocktail of drugs and started streaming on the site from his room.

Viewers watched and typed in chat. Some pushed Biggs to swallow the drugs, others pleaded with him not to, but he did. Someone called the police. Biggs was wearing a gray T-shirt and white shorts and was sprawled on his bed when a police officer entered the video frame, gun drawn. The officer covered the screen. All turned black. Biggs was nineteen.

The incident highlighted the challenges of regulating such a huge platform. "We tried to put in more ways for the community to flag content and bring it to our attention," said Kan. "We had, even then, like over a thousand live streams going on at one time. You can't observe them at all times. There's no image recognition for what suicide looks like."

No major tragedies have happened since, although some viewers have dealt with repeated raids from police from prank calls reporting crimes in their homes, mirroring what Kan personally experienced a few days after starting Justin.tv. Twitch's problems with anonymity and toxicity are also part of a broader Internet problem, and part of a broader statement on humanity. Twitch, like much of the Internet, can be a tough place for women. Women are instantly judged based on their appearance, whether they are an obscure gamer playing from home or a polished presenter at a tournament. "Fap fap fap" is one of the milder reactions, a reference to masturbation. Women have even been given a bastardized term, "grill" instead of "girl."

Racism and homophobia still appear in crowded chats, despite Twitch's ban on hate speech. When moderators step in to delete spam or ban users from chatting, they are sometimes called Nazis. The concept of "freedom of speech" is twisted into freedom to offend, to harass, or to mock.

Freedom can mean authenticity and genuine connections. But it can also be an unfiltered look into the ugliness of humanity, from casual bigotry to quick insults to a parroting incessancy, a preference for idiocy over real conversation, all exacerbated by the echo chamber and unwieldiness of thousands of viewers. But it can also lead to a frenzy of excitement and hype over eSports events, and for all its communication flaws, Twitch has done nothing but grow.

In 2013, Twitch moved its office to the sixth floor of the old Standard Oil Building at 225 Bush Street, with two more floors to grow into. It's a hub of Internet culture and art, with meetings rooms named after mythical game locales like Bioshock's Rapture and the Legend of Zelda's Hyrule. Murals with Twitch faces and video game characters abound.

Twitch opened an office in London in 2014 and has salespeople in New York and Los Angeles, with more growth planned in Asia and Europe. The site now has twenty-two server data centers around the world.

As it got bigger, the founding team began drifting apart. On February 10, 2014, Justin.tv, Inc., was renamed Twitch Interactive, Inc., an acknowledgment that gaming now trumped the original general-interest site. Justin.tv was shut down in August, wiping out seven years of memories. Justin Kan had moved on, too. He had another idea: Exec, an errand service that connected labor with customers, which he later sold to Handybook, a company that books cleaning and household services.

Seibel left Socialcam after it was sold and is now also a full-time partner at Y Combinator, where he focuses on recruiting and diversity. Vogt became CEO of Cruise, a startup working on self-piloting cars, where Kan's brother Daniel is COO, which was later acquired by General Motors. Shear and Lin remain the leaders of Twitch. Although their old partners moved on, the original team remains close, hanging out and taking trips together when time permits. "Going through Justin.tv was the experience of a lifetime. I was lucky to do it with such amazing partners," said Kan.

In 2014, rumors boiled that Twitch was going to be sold to Google. The Internet giant had killed off Kan and Shear's first company, Kiko, and now it might absorb their second one. But Amazon.com emerged as the winning bidder, paying $970 million for Twitch in August 2014.

The online retail giant gives Twitch more firepower, more servers and resources to keep growing. It won't need money from investors anymore. And the original founders remain in charge and are still passionate about gaming. The site has also expanded to allow channels to broadcast musical performances and painting and drawing, but gaming will always be the focus, said Lin.

"I think what's great is, we're the same people," said Lin. "They help us move faster but they're leaving us alone."

With Amazon's cash, there are concerns that one entity has too much power over eSports. "There's an awful lot of influence, power, and money in one office in San Francisco," said Jason Lake of the gaming team compLexity. But Lin argues that Justin.tv and Twitch began through passion, and its founders remain committed to creating a quality platform and fostering community, not a cash grab.

Now, Twitch looks at Google as a competitor. The search giant, rebuffed in its attempt to acquire Twitch, launched YouTube Gaming in August 2015, a year and a day after Amazon bought Twitch. Gaming content was already one of the most popular verticals on the site, and YouTube seeks to make livestreaming, rather than just recorded videos, a centerpiece of the page. Twitch, meanwhile, is adding video uploads and video playlists in 2016, bringing it more into direct competition with YouTube.

Another rival is the tournament organizer MLG, which broadcasts tournaments on its own video platform and lured popular streamers with cash. It convinced Call of Duty star Matt "NaDeSHoT" Haag of the team OpTic Gaming, who has millions of fans, to switch to MLG, though he later expressed regret over leaving Twitch and returned in March 2016. Other sites like Azubu and Hitbox have also sprung up to challenge Twitch.

Twitch has also had a hard time cracking one of the world's biggest markets: China, where local pros can command hundreds of thousands of viewers on Chinese streaming sites like Douyu.tv, although there are rumors that viewer counts are faked and inflated. "Twitch has basically zero headway in China—their streams lag if they load at all, and similarly anyone trying to stream on Twitch from China will not be able to do so smoothly," said Josh "Autumnwindz" Lee, a Chinese translator for eSports events.

There is also the question of the role of conventional television in eSports' future. South Korea established around-the-clock gaming channels like OnGameNet that had a big role in establishing StarCraft in South Korea. But many games do not conform to the thirty-minute chunks of traditional programming. Almost all conventional sports have an established time frame, with drawn-out overtimes being a rarity. But aside from Counter-Strike's timed rounds, most competitive games are more open-ended. A game can be a twenty-minute stomp or occasionally an eighty-minute marathon. And there is no good way to cut to commercials.

But the biggest brand in sports recently tried broadcasting video games on television. On April 26, 2015, ESPN2 enraged many sports fans by broadcasting Blizzard's new five-on-five game Heroes of the Storm. The University of California Berkeley battled Arizona State University, with Cal's Golden Bears winning and receiving free college tuition for four years.

It was the first time that the network had broadcast a live competitive gaming match. Social media freaked out, as the event trended worldwide on Twitter. Many viewers expressed confusion, or outright disgust, that video games were being featured on ESPN.

John Skipper, president of ESPN, had previously said that he considered gaming to be a competition, not a sport. "Mostly, I'm interested in doing real sports," he said shortly after Twitch was sold to Amazon. But the growth of eSports was undeniable, and ESPN continued covering gaming events on its shows and published an issue of its monthly magazine focusing on the industry. In January 2016, it launched a dedicated eSports section on its website. A month later, Skipper admitted to Re/code that he was now a believer, and going to a video game tournament convinced him that ESPN had to cover eSports. "Those were young, predominately male consumers, and that's what matters to us, so we entered the business," he said.

Other networks have followed. In 2016, Turner Broadcasting plans to show two ten-week tournaments of Counter-Strike: Global Offensive, the sequel to Valve's original shooter, on TBS. It's the heaviest eSports commitment for cable television since DirecTV's short-lived Championship Gaming Series, which featured Counter-Strike: Source.

But does eSports need television anymore? Twitch's Marcus Graham, who commentated at the CGS, is skeptical. The thirty-minute format is too rigid, and regional restrictions can also lock out thousands of potential viewers. "I think TV is actually a step backward," said Graham. TV is also missing an important ingredient of Twitch's success: chat.

Twitch was built for the community, and the community is what made it so massive, not corporate cash. In September 2015, Twitch's first ever convention, TwitchCon, took over Moscone Center West in San Francisco for two days, flooding the convention hall with twenty thousand fans in purple T-shirts and hoodies. It was a physical affirmation of the site's digital power. The event kicked off with speeches from Shear, Graham, and Lin. Near the entrance to the event, a band played tunes from Super Mario. A second TwitchCon is planned in San Diego in 2016.

If you visit Twitch today, you'll see an ecosystem of big and small communities, orbiting around personalities and brands. Some are reprehensible. Others are inspiring. Events happen daily, from 'modest charity marathons to blockbuster million-dollar tournaments. The site is a heartbeat for the video game industry.

In 2014, Justin Kan joined Y Combinator as a partner, becoming an arbiter in selecting the next wave of startup founders who get funding and guidance from the now-prestigious program. Kan is still creating more companies, most recently the Artist Union, a set of social media tools for musicians. But sometimes, when he has free time, he watches Twitch.

Chapter 5

A CHALLENGER APPEARS

LEAGUE OF LEGENDS ASCENDS

Before StarCraft II reshaped eSports, Blizzard Entertainment released another real-time strategy game called Warcraft III in 2003. The game had its own competitive scene and was popular in China and Europe, though it didn't have the same draw in the United States. Player salaries became bloated, with top player Jae Ho "Moon" Jang making nearly $500,000 over three years. His salary was a bet that the game would keep growing, but Warcraft III soon stagnated with infrequent updates as Blizzard focused on other titles.

Warcraft III's real eSports legacy would be a design choice: the game fused the real-time strategy elements of StarCraft with the role-playing genre through the addition of heroes.

The hero designs were based on many fantasy tropes, such as a holy Paladin with protective spells, the Orc's Samurai-esque Blademaster, and the Night Elf's druidic Keeper of the Grove. Heroes gained new powers by earning experience from kills and could single-handedly win battles. Gameplay was based more around micro-level individual unit control with smaller army sizes, compared to the macro-level production and economic focus of StarCraft.

Heroes formed the basis of many of Warcraft III's custom games, which fans created with a map editor that came bundled with the base game. Just as Counter-Strike was born from Minh Le and Jess Cliffe tinkering with Half-Life, the creativity of fans of Warcraft III led to the creation of its most popular custom game, Defense of the Ancients, or DOTA.

A creator known only as Eul made DOTA, which was also inspired by an earlier fan-made StarCraft map called Aeon of Strife. A series of map designers updated the game by adding new characters, culminating in 2005 with the stewardship of Ice-Frog, a mysterious developer whose real name has never been revealed. DOTA would plant the seeds of an entirely new genre, known as the multiplayer online battle arena, or MOBA, that would take eSports to new heights.

DOTA eliminated Warcraft's base-building and armies to focus players' control entirely on one hero. Ten players were divided into two teams, just like Counter-Strike, and they roamed and battled across a square map that has largely remained the same over a decade of play.

There are three "lanes," or paths to the enemy. Two sweep across the top and bottom sides of the map, and a third lane slices diagonally through the middle. Every thirty seconds, computer-controlled troops, known as creeps, appear for each team and march toward the enemy base until they collide and battle with each other. Players become more powerful from killing computer- and human-controlled foes, gaining experience and leveling up to gain new abilities. They also use gold to purchase items that augment their heroes' powers. The goal is to demolish buildings that guard each side's territory, with the ultimate target of the Ancient, a massive structure deep inside each team's base that must be destroyed for victory.

Changing the focus from the individual competition of Warcraft to a team game introduced more complexity and variance. Mechanics like casting spells effectively and targeting the right foe are important, but communication and coordination with your team is a huge part of winning. The social element draws players in, but it can also repulse them—insults and "rage" directed at teammates is common when players feel their allies haven't played well.

Just as a basketball team requires different elements to be successful—a shorter but more agile point guard and a towering and strong center—DOTA teams excel when they have a balance of characters that fulfill different roles. Variety and versatility are prized, and synergy between two or more heroes is even better, while one-dimensional teams generally have crippling weaknesses that can be exploited. Just as in traditional roleplaying games, a mass of hulking melee fighters can be dealt with by ranged firepower, while a team of squishy spellcasters would crumble if the opponent can close the gap. Some heroes are deadly in the early game with powerful spells, while others only hit their lethal potential after gaining additional levels and items. Variety creates potential; synergy is strength.

The key mechanical skill in DOTA is known as "last hitting," which requires the player to time an attack to deliver the killing to creeps. Killing players is flashier and more dramatic, but getting gold from the creeps is the backbone of becoming more powerful. (If players die, they are revived after a number of seconds, a duration that increases as they level up.)

Last hitting is one of DOTA's beautiful systems, said Frank Lantz, director of New York University's Game Center, who teaches video game design. It is a melody of anticipation, a dance, a rhythm arising from keystrokes. Players have to focus on the steadily depleting health bars of the computer minions to time their final attack while remaining wary of the opposing player, who is trying to do the same thing. DOTA players can also kill or "deny" their own minions to prevent their opponents from getting the last hit.

Like StarCraft's mining of resources, DOTA's last hitting is a way to tie economic progression to the passage of time and create a flow to the game through economy.

Almost every element of DOTA is meant to enrapture the player. You guide your avatar through a sweeping terrain of trees, roads, and water. The computer-controlled minions march ceaselessly, crashing into each other. Your opponents dance around the conflict, ready to gut you if given an opening. Towers crumble, enemies are slain, the Ancient explodes.

Getting the first kill, known as first blood, is a rush. Executing abilities effectively provides a tactile satisfaction, and multiple kills earn the praise of the deep-throated announcer. The game is a drug.

But as a fan-made map attached to an aging game in Warcraft III, DOTA's competitive future was always going to be constrained. To reach its full potential, DOTA needed a fresh start. It was an opportunity that would be seized by Brandon Beck and Marc Merrill.

Beck and Merrill met at the University of Southern California in Los Angeles and bonded over their love of video games. They snuck into the E3 video game convention by getting press passes through Beck's college radio station gig and met their game design heroes.

After graduating, they got real jobs. Beck worked at Bain & Company, the Boston-based consulting firm led at one point by presidential candidate Mitt Romney. Merrill worked briefly at US Bank and then handled public relations for Advanstar Communications, an events company.

But their passion was always gaming, and near the end of 2005, they moved in together into an apartment in Los Angeles, armed with two computers and an idea. They wanted to create a game that was worthy to be considered DOTA's spiritual sequel.

Merrill and Beck named their company Riot Games and they called the game League of Legends. They acknowledged that their game wasn't an original concept, advertising it as a new title from "the original creators of DOTA." Riot hired Steve "Guinsoo" Feak, one of DOTA's original designers, along with other staff from Blizzard. Another early Riot employee was Steve "Pendragon" Mescon, the operator of a big fan site called DotA-Allstars.com. Mescon shut down the website after he joined Riot, igniting a firestorm and creating an almost immediate rift between the League of Legends and DOTA community.

Riot wanted to retain the depth of the original DOTA but lower the barriers to entry. They began removing mechanics that they saw as unnecessary, such as the ability to "deny" friendly units. Gameplay was also less harsh compared to DOTA. Dying would no longer subtract gold from a victim, and mana, the resource needed to cast spells, was more abundant.

Unlike DOTA, which had heroes heavily inspired by Warcraft units, League of Legends had all new Champions, with only tangential references to past games. Champions were like superheroes, each with incredible abilities and a clear theme, inspired by fantasy and pop culture motifs. Yasuo was a samurai whose slashes summoned whirlwinds. Leona was a sun-blessed warrior with powerful defenses. Orianna was a robotic, feminine machine that manipulated a metal ball.

The founders also created their own in-game alter egos. Beck was nicknamed Ryze, a blue wizard crackling with arcane energy, and Merrill was Tryndamere, a sword-wielding barbarian who uses rage to fuel his attacks. Merrill's wife, Ashley, was the namesake of the frost archer Ashe.

Like Justin.tv, Riot had to attract venture funding to pay for the cost of developing the game. The first ten venture capitalists they approached all turned them down. But they kept pushing, armed with the belief in their game. "I was a twenty-six-year-old CEO with no CEO experience," said Beck during a 2011 commencement speech at his alma mater, the USC Marshall School of Business. "Because we made our passion our work, coping with the grueling demands of a startup became a lot easier."

Riot attracted the attention of a Chinese behemoth, Tencent, which owns QQ, the most popular Internet portal in China, and WeChat, the most popular messaging service, with over six hundred million active users. Tencent, headquartered in Shenzhen, just to the north of Hong Kong, wanted to invest in a Western video game company and considered two: Riot and Zynga, maker of the Facebook-based Farmville.

Riot and Zynga both based their nascent games around the free-to-play model. Instead of the established video game industry standard of shipping a $60 game and then moving on to the next title, both League of Legends and Farmville didn't cost players anything to try. Revenue would instead come from in-game purchases, and players would be enticed by a constant flow of new features.

Tencent already had success distributing free-to-play games in China like Dungeon Fighter Online and the shooter Crossfire with in-game payments for items or other powers, a practice known as microtransactions. Even its name, Tencent, could be seen as a reference to small amounts of money accumulating to become huge profits. Riot's business model was similar, and Tencent bought a stake, even though Zynga had already launched Farmville and League of Legends was still in its early alpha stage.

In 2008, Tencent and venture capital firms Benchmark and FirstMark invested $8 million in Riot, partly because of Merrill and Beck's leadership. "The way we structured it was to really empower the founding team," said Brad Bao, the former general manager of Tencent's US branch, who oversaw the transaction. "They're very smart and very persistent on values."

There was also a second funding round from Tencent that wasn't disclosed, which valued Riot in the "low millions," said Bao. In early 2011, Tencent increased its stake in Riot to over 92 percent for $231 million, according to a financial report, and bought the remainder of the company at the end of 2015.

Riot Games grew out of Merrill and Beck's apartment, leasing an office in an industrial park in West Los Angeles. It had a leaking ceiling, and a fire escape stairwell with a whiteboard served as a conference room—worse conditions than Justin.tv's early years.

For Merrill and Beck, it was important to have positive player experience first, rather than maximizing revenue. The game's business model had to complement the gameplay, not corrupt it.

Since Champions were the game's core asset, Riot decided that new players would have access to only ten of them for free on a rotating basis. But to permanently unlock champions, players would have to spend one of two currencies: Influence Points, which could be gained by playing games, with bonuses for winning; and Riot Points, which had to be purchased with real money.

Riot Points could also be spent on Champion "skins," which are visual costumes that have no impact on gameplay beyond

Competitors at the World Cyber Games in San Francisco in October 2004. ("WCG 2004 Auditorium" by Peter Kaminski. Licensed under Creative Commons BY 2.0.)

Bryce "Machine" Bates practices at the IGN ProLeague Season 3 tournament in Atlantic City in October 2011. (Photo by the author.)

Alex "HDStarcraft" Do and Taylor "PainUser" Parsons commentate at the IGN ProLeague Season 3. (Photo by the author.)

Starcraft II at DreamHack 2012 in Sweden. ("dreamhack-100" by Andrew Bell. Licensed under Creative Commons BY 2.0.)

Daniel "Artosis" Stemkoski and Nick "Tasteless" Plott commentate at a GSL StarCraft II tournament in South Korea. (Photo by Tara Stemkoski.)

Justin.tv founders Justin Kan, Kyle Vogt, Emmett Shear, and Michael Seibel. ("the justin.tv team" by Karen. Licensed under Creative Commons BY 2.0.)

Heather "sapphiRe" Garozzo competes at a Counter-Strike tournament. (Photo by HLTV.org.)

Players compete side by side at EVO 2009. ("Evo 2009 day 2" by Chris Ainsworth. Licensed under Creative Commons BY 2.0.)

SKT Telecom T1 celebrate with the Summoner's Cup after winning the League of Legends Season 3 World Championship in Los Angeles. Riot cofounders Marc Merrill and Brandon Beck are also on stage. (Photo © AP Images.)

The crowd is bathed in lights at the League of Legends All-Star tournament in Paris in May 2014. (Photo © AP Images.)

Confetti rains down at the International 2014 in Seattle. ("IMG_7682" by Jakob Wells. Licensed under Creative Commons BY 2.0.)

Team Secret compete at ESL One New York in November 2014. (Photo by the author.)

Kurtis "Aui_2000" Ling plays with Cloud 9 at the International 2014. ("Cloud 9 takes on Vici Gaming" by Dota 2 The International. Licensed under Creative Commons BY 2.0.)

Danil "Dendi" Ishutin prior to the main event at the International 2015 in Seattle. (Photo by the author.)

The crowd reacts after Evil Geniuses win the International 2015. (Photo by the author.)

cosmetic changes. The economic model dodged the "pay to win" style, where players are essentially forced to pay for more powerful effects in order to be competitive, which is death to legitimate competition.

Riot's triumph was convincing players that they weren't obligated to spend money, but that they wanted to. They were making their characters look cool. They were supporting a game they loved. And they felt obliged to keep playing after investing time and money to unlock features, as well as because of the social bonds they made with teammates and friends.

Although the items are just bits of digital data with no real-world presence, they have tangible value just like Instagram photos or Twitter posts have value. Most of the items could be had for a few dollars, with more elaborate sets selling for around $25.

League of Legends took around $18 million to develop, Merrill told the *New York Times*. Within a few months of its October 2009 release, about twenty thousand people were playing, and they kept coming back. "Our game and most games as a service really live or die based on the replayability and stickiness factor of the game," Merrill said at the 2010 Game Developers Conference.

Riot added new Champions every couple weeks, so players constantly had something new to buy or earn through playing more games. The company lacked funds to invest in expanding game design, so the focus was on fun gameplay and clear abilities rather than spectacular graphics. "Gameplay trumps art needs," said Merrill. "Having that instant, visceral feedback is key to being effective."

The game had personality and humor, and it didn't take itself too seriously. The visuals were cartoony compared to the photorealistic console games of the era, which resembled

Hollywood productions. "We wanted to build the Honda, not the Rolls-Royce," said Merrill. The game could run smoothly on older systems, widening its appeal.

A big deficiency for the original DOTA was that, as a custom map for Warcraft III, it didn't have any sort of organized competition within the program. Players could create game lobbies that could host up to ten players, but the range in skill was enormous. A professional player could potentially compete against someone who was playing for the first time.

Riot's answer was creating a matchmaking system in an early game update, similar to the one that StarCraft II used. Riot created a system of tiers ranging from Bronze to Challenger, the highest level.

The early client was, by Riot's own admission, lacking for viewers of competitive games. Spectating games was messy, and the game still doesn't have a formal replay system for past games. Six years after it launched, Riot has said that it was no longer a priority to add a replay system because it would require extensive work.

But the popularity of the League of Legends in eSports would be undeniable, and it soon began appearing as the undercard in tournaments featuring StarCraft II. In the summer of 2011, over 1.6 million people watched the first League of Legends World Championships at DreamHack in Sweden. Europe's Fnatic won first and took home $50,000.

One of League of Legends' first partners in the United States was David Ting. Adulthood hadn't dulled Ting's love of gaming, particularly StarCraft. He and his wife bonded over the game, and his kids started playing when they were four years old.

When StarCraft II was released, Ting was vice president of engineering at IGN, a top video game news site and a unit of

News Corp. He was impressed by the game's growth and after talking to pro players and other event operators, he had the idea of IGN expanding to become a tournament organizer. "We fell in love with the people," he said. "I felt like I could commercialize it."

In June 2011, he became the general manager of the company's new eSports division, the IGN Pro League, or IPL. At the time, he wasn't aware of News Corp's previous failed eSports venture with a three-letter acronym, the CGS.

Ting described pumping money into StarCraft as an altruistic move. Pro players sacrificed their educations and social lives to train, and by eliminating financial pressure, Ting felt he could directly improve players' lives. "When you don't worry about where the food is coming from, you can sustain it," said Ting. It was a natural idea to expand into other games.

In October 2011, the IPL held its first live tournament in Atlantic City, New Jersey, with a $100,000 prize pool for StarCraft. It took over event spaces at the Caesars and Bally's casinos. As a side event, there was a League of Legends tournament with a modest $20,000 prize pool. Team Dignitas, an established United Kingdom squad, beat North America's Epik Gamer and won $10,000. Two new American teams battled for third place, with Counter Logic Gaming besting Team SoloMid.

There was strong enough interest that the IPL decided to hire someone to manage League of Legends tournaments full-time. The opening interested Nick Allen, who grew up in Sacramento, California, and organized fighting game tournaments. He was studying to be a social worker and was a year from getting a master's degree when he applied for the job. His skills in conflict resolution and relationship management would prove to be valuable as he interacted with young players and team owners in the coming years. Allen got an interview at IGN, though he was more interested in StarCraft II.

Allen didn't really want to play League of Legends, but the opportunity was too good to pass up. In the week prior to his interview he played about thirty-five hours to gain a basic understanding. "It was just miserable. I just did not like it," he said. "This is just not good." But he told himself, "It's OK. I'll get there, I'll show them that I'm amazing, and then I'll move to the main product, which is StarCraft."

Allen got the job and started in January 2012, and then something unexpected happened. About seven thousand viewers tuned in to the first online tournament that he worked on, just shy of StarCraft's eight thousand viewers at the same event. The staff was puzzled. League of Legends was just a few years old, while StarCraft had over a decade of competitive history. At the next tournament, the gap closed even further, and by the end of 2012, League of Legends was soaring in viewers, up to thirty thousand, as StarCraft dwindled down to a few thousand. "Things were changing, and not for the better" for StarCraft, said Allen.

In the fall of 2012, the underdog Taipei Assassins of Taiwan dominated in the League Season 2 World Championships, surprising their opponents with an aggressive style and winning the championship over South Korea's Azubu Frost. The event drew 8.2 million viewers, a new record for eSports. Asia, the perennial victor in StarCraft, was rising to become the dominant force in a new game.

Allen's impressions of League of Legends also shifted. He played on a team with his coworkers and began enjoying the game more. At night, he found he no longer wanted to grind on the StarCraft ladder, alone. League of Legends was more fun, less stressful, and more social. For the next three years, it would become his game of choice.

At the beginning of 2013, everything changed. Riot announced that it would take over tournament operations in Europe and the United States. "Riot's always had a hard time working with third parties," said Travis Gafford, a journalist who covers League of Legends for Yahoo. "They felt they could do a better show themselves."

It was an unprecedented move for a game developer, which usually focuses on making games and marketing them. Running a global tournament was a whole new territory, and shunning third-party organizers who had been doing events for years was unprecedented. League of Legends also would shift to a seasonal schedule, with two days of games per week for each region, which would eventually determine seeding for playoffs. It was similar to the NFL's model, but a departure for eSports, which are typically separated between smaller online matches played from players' bedrooms and huge LAN events that only happen every few weeks or months.

"You're cutting yourself out of the industry," Gafford remembers critics saying. "I don't know if people want to watch these things every week. They want big events."

All of the top teams like Team SoloMid and Counter Logic Gaming would be enlisted in the new tournament, leaving leagues like the IPL without stars. Allen and his team were scrambling to figure out their next step, but their efforts suddenly became irrelevant.

In February 2013, News Corp sold IGN to the media company Ziff Davis, which shut down the IPL. The events, which had budgets of around $1.5 million, had never been profitable, though they were close to breaking even, according to Ting.

"From a monetary standpoint, I didn't do well. It was still the greatest time of my life," said Ting. "I helped the ecosystem. I made a lot of friends. I actually made people's lives better."

In April 2013, Blizzard, StarCraft's developer, purchased the IPL's assets and hired some of its staff, forming a new eSports group in San Francisco. Ting became head of online publishing at Blizzard, and Allen also received a job offer. It looked like he would get to work on StarCraft after all.

But then Allen got a call from Riot Games. He visited the company's office in Los Angeles and enjoyed meeting the staff, and he got a competing job offer. Allen's wife was a nutritionist, and Southern California would be a good fit for her career, too. He took the job in April 2013 and became director of North American league operations. In the eSports tradition of three-letter acronyms, the new tournament would be called the LCS, or the League of Legends Championship Series.

The LCS's two hallmarks would be stability and control. Riot hired its own commentators and production staff and rented out gaming venues in Los Angeles and Berlin. In Asia, the leagues had different names and slightly different structures, with Riot outsourcing some of the production in South Korea to the long-time eSports broadcaster OnGameNet and KeSPA, and Tencent led the league in China. But Riot set the standards and also ran the World Championship at the end of each year.

Matches take place each week in the various regions, each of which has around ten teams. Twice a year, the bottom few teams are dropped into relegations. There, they fight a batch of hungry young teams, who are fighting for entry into the league after qualifying for the promotions through a tournament called the Challenger Series. "We were worried about an old boys' club, which is why we thought the relegation system was so important," said Allen.

Unlike other games, the ten North American and ten European League of Legends teams who qualify for the LCS don't have to depend on the uncertainty of prize money to survive. Riot's players and teams have the most professional support out of any game. Riot pays the teams directly for a housing stipend, coaches, and other support staff including designated analysts, regardless of results. Riot spends roughly $3 million for the North America and Europe regions, or around $200,000 per team each year, said Allen.

Each player in the LCS has a minimum salary of $25,000 per year, offering a level of security that the vast majority of pro gamers in other games lack. Stars make far more with money from Twitch streaming and outside sponsorship money, but players who aren't as popular have a more secure career. Western teams have training houses near Riot's two studios in Los Angeles and Berlin, and the teams typically provide housing and food to players. By 2016, it was standard for teams to have more support staff like nutritionists and psychologists for players.

The LCS is a money loser for Riot, which has invested more than any other game developer. It not only pays the teams, but also rents out stadiums for events. It is in many ways a marketing expense. Ticket sales are a negligible source of revenue, and sponsorships, Twitch, and YouTube ads generate some money. But it isn't nearly enough to pay for expenses and the roughly one hundred Riot employees who work on eSports around the world. The eventual goal is that eSports will become its own sustainable revenue generator by attracting more sponsors and viewers, said Allen. But for now, it's a way to create excitement and bring in more new players.

By many metrics the LCS has been a spectacular success. It has the highest viewership of all games on Twitch and is rivaling traditional sporting events in spectacle and scale. The game has sold out the Seoul World Cup Stadium and Los Angeles's Staples Center for its world finals.

Wouter Sleijffers, CEO of Fnatic, one of the best teams in Europe and the champion of the first season, praises the LCS for its regularity and professionalism. "What I like about the LCS series is I know that Thursday and Friday, at a set time, our team will be playing and I'll be tuning in for that. But to be honest with you, I don't always know when our CS:GO team is playing," he said, referring to Counter-Strike's sequel, Global Offensive.

The LCS has also attracted unprecedented mainstream sponsorship. In August 2013, financial giant American Express sponsored League of Legends and created credit cards splashed with character images. Fans who used the cards would gain Riot Points in game that could be used to buy characters and items. Buying real goods could help them buy virtual goods. Two months later, Coca-Cola sponsored the Challenger Series and put the game's characters on its cans in South Korea.

League of Legends has also grown to become the most popular computer game in the world, with sixty-seven million players a month in 2014, and estimated annual revenue of over $1 billion. The game is complex to the point where someone who has played a few hundred hours is still considered a novice. With over a hundred Champions, there are over five quadrillion team compositions and matchups to experience.

This variety has made League of Legends almost infinitely compelling. Each match is different, and no one starts with a particular advantage beyond his or her developed skills and experience. There are thousands of decisions that are made differently in each match.

"You just have endless amounts of gameplay from that one map. The content you create is horizontal," said Stephanie

"Anuxinamoon" Everett, a video game art designer. "Those are the types of games that are the future."

Complexity can be a barrier for both players and spectators. Intricate plays based on intimate knowledge of advanced mechanics and split-second execution make hardcore fans scream in awe. For neophytes, fights read as unintelligible flashing lights and visual noise. Commentators and fans distill layers upon layers of game knowledge into insider terminology.

But the popularity of the game suggests that even in the age of mobile gratification, with casual puzzle and card games, there is a thirst for exceedingly complex, time-consuming, and competitive gameplay, thanks to the power of a vast community.

Riot has brought stability and structure to the often chaotic eSports scene, standardizing contracts between players and pushing for a set of rules that is consistent for all teams. It also hasn't hesitated to take disciplinary action to preserve what it sees as the game's purity.

Allen became known as an enforcer, handing out fines for poaching and other offenses like improperly registered rosters and players being verbally abusive in LCS games.

One of the harshest punishments would hit Chris Badawi, a patent lawyer who entered the eSports scene after nearly dying in a car accident and realizing that he wanted to work in gaming. At the beginning of 2015, Badawi tried but failed to acquire the team Curse Academy. So he decided to build his own team, called Renegades.

Badawi contacted a number of players signed to top teams and, after the talks were discovered by other owners, he was accused of tampering. In response, Riot banned Badawi from owning a team for a year.

The punishment was severe, but Allen notes that Badawi remains involved in Renegades even after the ban. He just isn't recognized as the official owner who is the point of contact for the league. Badawi argues that he was just speaking to players to give them more clarity about their own value. Because salaries aren't public, players have limited leverage for securing better financial deals. But League of Legends isn't a free marketplace. Riot controls the league and the game's copyright.

The dispute highlights the tension over Riot's decision to control all aspects of the league. Players have the ability to make a decent and potentially affluent living, but they also have virtually no bargaining power. (Riot declined to cooperate for this book.)

David Graham, a lawyer who focuses on eSports and a commentator for fighting video games, has advised clients not to sign Riot's contracts. But he realizes that there's little choice if they want to play the game professionally. "All the developers have too much power, even those that don't exercise it that much," said Graham. "They still can shut down any tournament they want. That really limits how tournaments and games can be played and how the scene can grow."

Players who aren't superstars are also in a precarious position because there are always players eager to agree to worse terms because eSports jobs are so scarce. Players are all independent contactors, so they don't have benefits like health insurance or retirement funding.

Players and team managers may have little recourse to appeal any regulatory decisions. Riot can also use a player's image and voice to promote League of Legends in any way. And players can't stop the uses even if they object to how they're portrayed.

A counterbalance in the relationship between teams and the league organizer would be a players' union and collective bargaining similar to traditional sports. But those unions took decades to develop. Identifying a source of funding for a union, like player dues, is also tricky when many players struggle to survive financially.

"I think there's a need for a union. But the problem is, there's not enough money for someone to undertake the labor of building out contracts and signing up all the players and battling with the owners," said Edward Chang, who has previously worked for compLexity, the IPL, and the eSports site Vulcun. "The owners are going to fight it tooth and nail. I don't blame them. At the end of the day, it's a business."

Another fear is that a players' union could be controlled by top players who are already financially successful, and its stances could favor the stars, rather than up-and-coming players.

A crucial ingredient of League of Legends' massive growth is its conquest of Asia, which was bolstered by its parent company Tencent's grasp on China. In 2014, Riot said 80 percent of its playerbase was in Asia. The game was a hit in South Korea's PC bangs, soon surpassing StarCraft II. Since it was free to play, piracy was not an issue.

And players who paid roughly a dollar an hour to play in PC bangs gained two huge benefits that players from home didn't get: through an agreement with Riot to lure players, a 10 to 20 percent bonus in Influence Points earnings to boost their acquisition of new digital goods, and they would have access to the game's entire roster of over one hundred Champions for free, instead of paying individually for each one.

"I think that reward system is so enticing. That's an instant gratification for playing that game," said William Cho, who previously worked with OnGameNet's League of Legends division, and now works at tournament organizer at ESL. And by removing the daunting multitasking of StarCraft to focus control on one Champion, League was a much bigger hit for casual players.

In 2013, South Korea and League of Legends found its next superstar: Lee "Faker" Sang-hyeok, a slim, quiet teenage prodigy who was signed to SK Telcom T1, the legendary team that had signed BoxeR in StarCraft.

In April 2013, Faker made his competitive debut against rival team CJ Entus's Blaze division. He faced off against Kang "Ambition" Chan-yong, a two-year veteran. Early in the game, Kang stopped for a millisecond to upgrade one of his abilities after leveling up. Faker used his Champion Nidalee's ability to transform into a cougar and pounced, slaying his opponent. Seconds later, he killed two more opponents in the bottom lane, stunning the crowd.

Later that year, Faker would battle Ryu "Ryu" Sang-wook of KT Bullets. The game was an unusual mode, so they were both playing the Champion Zed, a ninja assassin.

Ryu engaged on Faker, dropping his health to a sliver under a flurry of attacks. Faker used his ultimate ability, creating a shadow mirror that confused his opponent, feinting to the left, then the right. He used about six abilities in two seconds, killing his opponent and darting away. Faker's reflexes were jaw dropping, and his versatility was exceptional. Unlike most midlane players who play a handful of Champions well, Faker was dominant with dozens of heroes, including unconventional characters rarely seen in competitive games. An ESPN profile noted that his nickname was simply "God." In 2013, SKT won the championship in Los Angeles's Staples Center, and then became the first team to ever win two championships in 2015.

South Korea was dominating League of Legends like it had dominated StarCraft, but Riot's decision to have separate leagues in each region would insulate the game from some of the problems that plagued Blizzard.

After a few years as the top game in eSports, StarCraft was in trouble.

In 2012, Blizzard sought to have a formal, yearlong tournament similar to LCS that would determine the best player in the world. It partnered with existing organizers like GOMTV to create the World Championship Series, or WCS. But David Ting, who worked in Blizzard's eSports division after it bought the IPL's assets, said the tournament should have done more to keep up with rivals like League of Legends.

In October 2012, Steven "Destiny" Bonnell, a player with a popular stream on Twitch, wrote on Reddit that StarCraft would die unless Blizzard made some drastic changes. Tournament organizers weren't increasing their prize pools or making much money, he noted. Blizzard needed to make the game more social and more compelling for casual players, which could mean adding more superficial rewards like achievements and cosmetics, or the game's popularity wouldn't last.

In 2013, StarCraft's global finals had an average viewership of 92,404, a far cry from the millions watching League of Legends. It slipped to a distant sixth on the list of most-viewed games on Twitch.

"It is painful to see StarCraft being dethroned as the top eSport," said Ting, who has since left Blizzard to work for the Chinese game developer NetEase.

Part of StarCraft's disadvantage was its business model. The game required a one-time purchase of $60 when it was first released, a conventional model that has been used by the game industry for decades. But that structure has disadvantages compared to League of Legends' free-to-play model. It is a financial barrier to entry that requires players to commit to spending money on a game that they may have never played.

And because StarCraft didn't have any digital add-ons after the game was purchased, there were no recurring profits after the $60 players spent on the game. StarCraft attempted to introduce an "arcade" where fans could create their own maps and eventually sell them, but that plan was scrapped, so it was never going to be as financially robust as League of Legend's constant in-game sales.

StarCraft's decision to prioritize competitive and difficult gameplay also blocked players from enjoying it. Difficult multitasking was an essential part of making the game competitive, and there was always tension between maintaining a high skill barrier and being attractive to new players, a balance that League of Legends had reached with its design choices meant to appeal to casual gamers.

StarCraft is also an individual game. Grinding the ladder alone could be isolating and discouraging, and even pro gamers experienced burnout. The number of viable strategies was limited, and certain units became seen as overpowered, which made matches repetitive.

The dominance of South Korean players became a large problem in StarCraft, creating a repetitive narrative where, with a few rare exceptions, Western players didn't have a chance of winning. The WCS also wasn't initially "region locked," meaning that Korean players could qualify for the main championship by playing in the Americas and Europe, where they were superior to local players. South Koreans flooded into other regions, where competition wasn't as fierce as in Seoul.

In 2014, seven of sixteen players in the WCS's European division were South Korean. In the Americas, only one player was American; the others were thirteen Koreans and two Chinese players.

In four years of competition, only two non–South Korean players have qualified for the sixteen spots at the championships at the end of the year: Sweden's Johan "NaNiwa" Lucchesi in 2013 and David "Lilbow" Moschetto of France in 2015. South Korean players eliminated both players in the first round of the two events.

StarCraft II had a homogenous cast of competitors and deadened interest from some Americans and Europeans, who didn't have a local player to root for. Many Koreans also couldn't give interviews in English and spoke with respect toward opponents, which made for weak drama. There were a few exceptions, like the flamboyant Jang "MC" Min Chul, who would dance on stage and trash talk, but most of the Korean players had meek personas.

"Nobody wants to watch eight Korean players in the top eight. Nobody cares about it," said Alexander Kokhanovskyy, CEO of Natus Vincere, a Ukranian team that previously had Starcraft II players but no longer invests in the game.

"The most important thing about every game, and every challenge, is hype," said Kokhanovskyy. "If you have hype, the value is there. If you're decreasing the hype, you're losing everything. StarCraft is the perfect example."

Kokhanovskyy also blames teams for paying players six figures and says that salaries are now a fraction of what they were at their peak. The biggest culprit, he said, was Alexander Garfield's Evil Geniuses. "The salaries were completely insane," he said.

For the 2015 season, Blizzard implemented region locking, requiring players to establish permanent residency in the region they were competing in. Koreans could still battle in Europe and America, but they needed visas to stay.

But critics say it was too little, too late for StarCraft. "Stream-wise, events-wise, everything-wise, it's useless," said Kokhanovskyy.

Although South Korea has also won the last three world championships in League of Legends between 2013 and 2015, Riot has established local ecosystems for all major regions. The weekly games between local teams keep North American and European fans engaged, even if their teams are routinely beaten by Asia on the global stage.

South Korean players have also migrated to North American and European teams, but at least three of the starting players on a team must be long-term residents. The limitation isn't based on nationalism, but rather an effort to create compelling, long-term storylines with players who have connections with their regions, said Nick Allen, who was involved in making the rules at Riot.

Riot has also made an effort to foster competition in regions that have lagged behind due to less eSports investment and weaker Internet, such as South America and Australia. In those areas, a passionate local community pushed for the creation of a local league, said Allen, who left Riot to work for Twitch in 2015.

As StarCraft faded, GOMTV, the game's first competitive home in South Korea, also suffered. As viewership and revenue declined, the company couldn't afford to run its own English website. The site had relied on paid subscriptions for videos, since its mostly Korean sponsors weren't interested in advertising to a Western audience. But Twitch has made viewers used to free, high-quality streams. In February 2014, GOM shut down its website and began using Twitch and YouTube's free video archiving instead. John Park from GOMTV's business staff said he couldn't disclose revenue figures but said the company was profitable only from 2011 to 2012.

GOM became one of the rare channels that require subscribers to pay $10 a month for the highest quality stream on Twitch. Virtually every other major tournament allows viewers to view the highest quality for free.

"I honestly say that it makes more sense for GOM to pull out of eSports altogether and it was seriously considered at one point," said Park. "I am aware that there are many fans out there who feel GOM is greedy with a paywall for such low quality, but in our current situation, it's either that or we go bankrupt.

"Also, unlike LAN events overseas, we have no volunteers whatsoever, and every little thing costs money. ESports is legitimate business here, and like all business it needs investment and profit to sustain," said Park. "What keeps us going? Passion. It's absolutely essential. However, passion alone can't sustain an industry."

GOM's eSports staff shrank from over one hundred people to thirty, said Park. In August 2015, AfreecaTV, an online streaming site, acquired GOM's studio and took over the company in October, and Park soon left. The GSL would live on, but GOMTV's involvement was over.

Blizzard's format changes also made casting a stressful experience for StarCraft's two biggest casters, Tasteless and Artosis. "WCS fucked shit up pretty badly," said Tasteless. "I was actually personally quite depressed when that got implemented, because I felt like I really gave up a lot and really worked hard to try to build the show."

Blizzard began holding more events in the United States and Europe, and Tasteless felt the need to cast games in other regions, and at one point appeared at seventeen events in a year. "There were periods where I was in four different countries in a fucking month," said Tasteless. "I was jetlagged. I had gained weight. I was smoking way too much." He eventually cut down on traveling to focus on GOMTV.

Tasteless is still optimistic about StarCraft's future, and his love for the game hasn't dulled. Although the game is far from the largest title now, he was never interested in it because of its popularity.

"I'm still paid well. I still have a TV show that's viewed. The TV show is still the biggest thing in the genre," said Tasteless. "I'm fine wherever it is as long as I can keep doing what I want to do."

Blizzard declined to participate for this book. The company's focus has broadened to three new games, where it is investing millions in new tournament circuits: Heroes of the Storm, a five-versus-five strategy game based on DOTA; Hearthstone, a digital collectible card game, inspired heavily by Magic: The Gathering, the first trading card game; and Overwatch, a shooter game in the same genre as Counter-Strike, but with colorful characters. StarCraft II sometimes seems like an afterthought, but no matter how dim its future, the game was a turning point for eSports.

Chapter 6

UNBALANCED

WOMEN, RACE, AND GAMING

When Anna Prosser Robinson moved in to manage Evil Genius' team house in Arizona, she had to deal with the perception that she was the tag-along girlfriend of team captain Geoff "iNcontroL" Robinson, who is now her husband, rather than someone who was interested in eSports herself.

This impression wasn't coming from the largely male fan base, she said, but from the team's own male management. Despite growing up building computers and playing at LANs, she was female and had to battle the suspicion of faking enthusiasm for gaming.

Robinson, a former Miss Oregon, had sharp on-camera skills and began volunteering and interviewing players on camera starting in 2009. She was a polished, professional figure in a sea of amateurs. "Players generally don't receive much media training," she said. "They get a trial by fire."

She became a prominent host, but was troubled when other women tried to follow the same career path. She became tired of watching young women seek to work in gaming and eSports only to have their enthusiasm fade in the face of criticism and sexist remarks.

131

"Online negativity and bullying is pervasive, but the side that's directed to women—it can be scarring," said Prosser Robinson. She had to tune it out and seclude herself from it, but she wanted to do more. So she cofounded a group called Misscliks, which provides a supportive environment for female gaming content creators and players. In 2015, they were invited by the White House to give a presentation on eSports and women in gaming.

Gaming's portrayal of female characters and its marketing largely targeted at boys has led to accusations of sexism, and the Internet has only intensified the friction. The gamer stereotype consists of teenage boys screaming homophobic slurs and shooting virtual bullets, growing up into nerdy, isolated men.

In contrast, women are largely represented in games as digital eye candy. Lara Croft, the early buxom protagonist of the Tomb Raider series, was a digital novelty as graphics were sophisticated enough to give her crude, pixelated breasts. Around half of US gamers are women, and Lara Croft's more recent design is starting to reflect reality. Croft has become remade into a gritty adventurer, with realistic anatomy.

The 2014 controversy known as Gamergate epitomized the video game community's struggles over gender, and the vicious mysogyny of some gamers. Eron Gjoni, a vengeful ex-boyfriend of the independent game developer Zoe Quinn, posted an enormous blog post that detailed their relationship and accused Quinn of sleeping with gaming journalists to get positive coverage of her game, Depression Quest. The post ignited thousands of hateful comments and death threats directed at Quinn. Private details like her home address and telephone number were leaked, and she went into hiding. The movement eventually spread to other women developers like Brianna Wu and the critic Anita

Sarkeesian, who created a series of videos that detailed examples of misogyny in gaming.

Supporters of Gamergate allege that their movement is about "ethics in games journalism" and that gamers are being depicted unfairly by media. But any calls for change in the way that gamers are portrayed have been overshadowed by threats of violence.

Although the Gamergate controversy was a separate issue from the eSports industry, women in eSports have dealt with similar harassment. Part of the reaction might be seen as a backlash by a hardcore eSports fan base dealing with the popularization of the industry and exposure to more groups. There's often contempt for newcomers in gaming, an environment where expertise and experience are lauded. And being different in any way can make a person an object of scorn. Tournament organizers seem eager to hire attractive women to serve as hosts or interviewers, but they rarely compete at the highest level.

Detractors point to the unimpressive history of women in professional gaming as a sign that women are just worse players. They scoff that only two female pro players have made more than $100,000 in prize money, according to the website eSportsearnings.com. Over three hundred men and boys have surpassed that mark.

As of 2015, Katherine "Mystik" Gunn has won the most prize money of any female pro gamer, with $122,000. The money came largely from $100,000 in winnings from the second season of *WCG Ultimate Gamer*, a reality TV show on the cable network SyFy in 2010 that combined various games, including Halo: Reach. She won the remaining money at the now ancient CGS of 2007 and 2008, where she played Dead or Alive 4. In total, she has only three recorded events and hasn't competed since 2010.

The second highest earner has had a far more influential career. Her name is Sasha "Scarlett" Hostyn, and she is one of the most successful StarCraft II players, particularly among non-Koreans. She has career winnings of over $116,000 and is one of the few Western players who has been consistently able to beat South Koreans.

Scarlett grew up in Kingston, Canada, a city of 120,000 that juts into the Saint Lawrence River, which divides Northeast America from Canada. According to an extensive profile in the *New Yorker,* she had a steady diet of card and board games as a child, and won them all. She was similarly dominant in StarCraft, and she soon began training in Seoul and winning tournaments around the world. Her parents were hands-off, allowing her to pursue a gaming career with little interference, but they had concerns as she became the focus of online crowds.

Parental worry was heightened because Scarlett is a transgender woman, which has added another layer of prejudice from viewers. But she also became a fan favorite, not only for her differences but for her skill. Her wins were one of the few bright spots of a fading Western competitive scene. But at the beginning of 2015, she took a break from the game, and her future career is uncertain.

After Scarlett, there is a significant drop-off in overall prize winnings for women. Like Gunn, the next few top earners date back from the women's division of Dead or Alive 4 at the 2007 CGS. There have been only a handful of other prominent female StarCraft players. Another Canadian, Coryn "MsSpyte" Briere, reached the Grandmasters League and briefly joined the American team ROOT Gaming, but she retired after a few months, citing burnout. Olivia "Livibee" Seeto of Australia has also reached the Grandmasters level, but her focus has been streaming on Twitch rather than competing in tournaments, which have dwindled as organizers look to other titles.

She says that many male viewers who see her stream on Twitch say that she is "exploiting her gender," by trying to make money and gain attention based on appearance, rather than her passion for the game. She's hopeful that attitude will change and gamers will become more inclusive.

Female player representation is not much better in South Korea. Seo "ToSsGirL" Ji Soo was the only prominent female StarCraft I pro gamer, but she retired before the sequel came out. The StarCraft II player Kim "Eve" Shee-Yoon was signed "for her skills and looks," according to the female manager of her team. She later fled the scene after sexual harassment from men.

Even when they're successful, women can have second thoughts about continuing to compete. All of the struggles and sacrifices that male pro gamers deal with are compounded by being different. In August 2015, Maria "Remilia" Creveling became the first female pro player to qualify for League of Legends' LCS when her team, Renegades, triumphed in the Challenger promotion tournament. But she was torn about staying on the team both for financial reasons and because she had been the target of continual harassment and hate, including hate speech because she is a transgender woman. She asked Riot to avoid showing her on camera on LCS. After fans urged her to continue, she initially decided to play in the 2016 season. But the online harassment, particularly on Twitch chat, continued. In February 2016 she resigned from the team after a few weeks of play, citing issues with anxiety and self-esteem.

Some teams have deliberately sought to have all-female squads, such as Team Siren, a short-lived League of Legends team that disbanded, and Frag Dolls, sponsored by Ubisoft. But such teams can be seen as a gimmick and a cynical marketing effort to attract sponsorship funding while also attracting thirsty eyeballs from a male audience.

Women make up about half of all gamers, but the stereotype is that they gravitate toward more casual games like Bejeweled or Candy Crush.

There is a large gap between playing a free game on your phone and spending hundreds of dollars for a high-end gaming PC or video game console, never mind investing hundreds of hours to play a competitive game.

Southeast Asia is home to some prominent female gaming clans, such as PMS Asterisk. But there are still many barriers to being taken seriously. For example, the AsianCyberGames held a DOTA 2 female tournament entitled "Call for the Beauties."

"It really takes a lot of determination and resilience for any female gamer to make it in the pro circle," said Tiffani "Oling" Lim, the former manager of the DOTA 2 team Titan and leader of a competitive female team in Malaysia.

In traditional sports, men and women are segregated on basic biological differences: testosterone makes it easier to build muscle and strength and power. In gaming, in theory, there are no such physical barriers, but there are plenty of cultural obstacles that often make the industry an unsafe space. Female players often face more harassment, attention, and pressure from fans, and they are judged more harshly. There's an argument that there's no biological reason that women should struggle to compete in eSports compared to men. But that ignores the cultural and economic blocks, according to advocates.

"You have to realize the women you know who are interacting in this space are walking through a minefield," said Rachel "Seltzer" Quirico, a host and interviewer, at a panel on diversity at the Game Developers Conference in 2014. "And you guys are skipping through a daisy patch."

One of the first eSports has the longest history of women competitors: Counter-Strike.

Heather "sapphiRe" Garozzo grew up playing Counter-Strike in the early 2000s, along with her brother. She drove from her hometown in Milwaukee to her first CPL tournament in Dallas with a group of friends—three men and two women—to compete. They didn't have a sponsor, and didn't advance very far, but she was hooked. She's been playing over half her life.

"I've been telling myself for years, I have to stop," she said. "Thirty-one is coming up in a couple months, but I'm not done yet. I have so much more to do and win and so much more to learn. I can't give up yet."

Athletes of traditional sports, particularly punishing ones like football, also grapple with mortality. It's said that eSports is a young person's game, and older players in their late twenties will lose their reflexes. "I don't buy that at all," said sapphiRe. Many games are won with knowledge and communication. Pure reaction times are critical in some games, but Counter-Strike has the space for an older player to compete.

In high school, she gave up varsity softball to focus on gaming, when she realized while practicing on the field that what she really wanted was to go home and play the game. "I really like competing against other people, figuring out how I can outsmart them, out-aim them, and there's always something to improve on," she said.

She was initially reluctant to tell her teammates about her passion, but now, fifteen years later, her old high school friends will cheer her on when she posts about her events on Facebook. "It's a lot of the same people that I was so ashamed to tell them what I was doing on a Friday night," she said.

Like Anna Prosser Robinson, sapphiRe was treated differently because of her gender. She began dating Sal "Volcano" Garozzo of Team 3D, who is now her husband, and she was banned from watching the team compete at events because of a "no girlfriend" rule. "I wasn't going to the LANs to hang out with him. I wanted to watch Counter-Strike," she said.

Eventually, 3D's owner Craig Levine loosened up and realized that she was just as passionate about eSports as he was. She eventually worked for Levine's E-Sports Entertainment Association as a writer and helped with sponsorships.

In 2004 she began her studies at the University of Wisconsin, a "party school," where she studied communications. She also joined a pro team, breaking from her more casual teammates. "I enjoyed playing with my friends, but some of them didn't have the same drive that I did, and I didn't really want to be held back," she said.

She managed to earn decent grades, but there were other sacrifices. She lived with female roommates who would throw parties throughout the weekend in their dorm. "A lot of times, I had to sit upstairs in my room, practicing," said sapphiRe. "My friends didn't understand at the time. Now they're far more accepting of it."

She got to travel to events and meet people from around the world, many of whom remain friends. It was a social experience of a different sort, and she learned that life was about trade-offs. Her parents didn't tell her to stop. Her dad, who races cars as a hobby, shared her passion. "He loves competition. He understands what we do," she said.

At the 2012 ESWC world championship, sapphiRe's team, UBINITED, faced off against the German squad Team ALTERNATE. "We got smashed in the first map," she remembers. In the second round, they were losing with three points to twelve, but came back and won in double overtime. In game three, they came back from an unheard of thirteen-point deficit.

Years later, commentators will reference that comeback whenever a team is behind. Her performance became part of Counter-Strike history, and not because of her gender.

She eventually realized that all pro gamers are subject to some level of criticism. Male pros would be empathetic. "It made me feel better. 'Oh, it doesn't just happen to you. There are these people out there that are just attacking every player,'" said sapphiRe.

And she's proven that she can be competitive against the top male teams. She relished when they threw their mouse on their desk or slammed their headphones after losing rounds against her. "I'm making some of the best players in the world really upset, because I'm killing them. That felt really satisfying," she said.

She would later juggle a full-time job at a public relations company in New York while still competing, and then she worked at the insurance company Assurant Health, which let her freelance in eSports on the side. Her husband was doing programming at a hedge fund in New York, but he always wanted to work in gaming. In 2015, he was hired by Riot as a game designer.

SapphiRe wants to make eSports her career, but she's never managed to do it full time. "I really want to make my career in something that I love, and it's not just something like I want to rush home at the end of the work day to get to," she said. But it's hard to devote herself when she isn't a top player.

She's thought about quitting after hard losses, especially after putting sixty hours a week in practice and losing to someone who's been only playing for a couple years. And there was always the constant harassment, despite her calm personality and lack of trash talk.

"Now I've learned to just block it out. Those people don't matter and I shouldn't let them stop me from pursuing my dreams," she said. Often, pro players are supportive and it's the "fans" that will flame.

Men who harass female gamers are usually of lower skill, according to a study by the University of New South Wales and Miami University. They found that over 163 games of Halo 3, another first-person shooter, lower-performing male players would harass female players. Better male players were nicer. Men tended to treat each other the same. Insecurity fueled harassment.

"Low-status males that have the most to lose due to a hierarchical reconfiguration are responding to the threat female competitors pose," the study found. "High-status males with the least to fear were more positive, suggesting they were switching to a supportive, and potentially, mate attraction role."

Through her career, sapphiRe has won over $30,000 in cash and other prizes, which have mostly been computer parts. It's not nearly enough to make a living, but the experiences have been priceless, she said. A handful of her female teammates are now able to game full time thanks to streaming on Twitch, including donations and ad and subscription revenue.

"I want to have all these experiences while I can. Once I have kids some day and I'm older, it's just going to be harder to do these things. I want to grasp every possible experience that I can," said sapphiRe. Gaming brought her around the world. She saves photos and videos to share for her future kids and grandkids.

She has no problem with women who get dressed up to stream, revealing their cleavage and legs to tantalize the male gaze. But she has a problem when viewers cite the behavior of one streamer as an indictment of all female gamers.

When she streams, sapphiRe will wear pajamas, a hoodie, and no makeup, clutching a coffee mug. On another channel, a female streamer may wear a low-cut top and short shorts. "We don't all want to put on makeup and a dress to play Counter-Strike. I'm very, very uncomfortable if I'm dressed up and playing," she said. "I need to be in really comfortable clothes." Her team wears sports jerseys when competing.

SapphiRe's squad has struggled to qualify for Counter-Strike's largest tournaments against male teams, which are now predominately held for its sequel, Global Offensive.

Her team's main competitive appearances are at female-only tournaments, including the ESWC, Copenhagen Games, and ESL events. "It's a more comfortable environment. We'll hug. In Europe they'll kiss you on the cheek," she said.

They also have much lower prize pools, with only a few thousand dollars compared to the hundreds of thousands that top male teams can make. Female-only tournaments are a way to encourage more females to compete, which should support more gender diversity, but shouldn't be the only way, said sapphiRe. Her current squad, Team Karma, competes with men and was a few rounds from qualifying for a major tournament. "You're really limiting your skills if you only play against females," she said. "Male teams can teach you to get better." She doesn't want to see female-only tournaments as the only outlet for female gamers, but rather a supplement to the standard tournament circuit.

"We don't draw the biggest crowd. We aren't not the best players," said sapphiRe. "We're really not at the point where I think we're deserving of $250,000 tournaments. We have a lot to work up towards."

And sapphiRe believes that there are women who can compete on the same level as top male players, like her former teammate

Stephanie "missharvey" Harvey. She and Harvey played together on UBINITED, sponsored by Ubisoft and Intel.

Harvey's team won the biggest 2015 women's tournament, the Electronic Sports World Cup in Montreal. The prize pool for the women's tournament was $15,000 compared to $75,000 for the men. Harvey said that having a lower prize pool isn't offensive because the men's teams are better. But the presence of a tournament is important to encourage more female players. "It's hard for a female to find a role model. These tournaments are super important," she said.

Prior to the tournament, the team also became Counter Logic Gaming Red, a division of the popular League of Legends team. By joining CLG, Harvey found a partner whose goals she feels are aligned with promoting more female gamers. "They wanted to support diversity. That's exactly why we exist," said Harvey. "Not because they wanted to do a marketing thing."

That point is debatable. Having a female team can be beneficial for a team's marketing and ability to attract sponsors.

Harvey has also competed on mixed-gender teams before, but she feels that her gender is an excuse for them to kick her first. "I was the easy target because I'm the girl," she said. "It's a different atmosphere playing with girls. There's absolutely no fear for my spot. It's just my skill."

When she was younger, she could cut sleep to play, but as she enters her thirties, she's also considering quitting her job as a game designer at Ubisoft to compete in Counter-Strike full time. "I feel like I've been running for over twelve years, nonstop," she said. "I can't do it on the side. If I want to succeed, I have to do it 100 percent."

Gender disparity has become a larger part of the gaming conversation, as well as in the business and technology fields, which is encouraging to her. "Society as a whole needs to change," said Harvey. She looks to women's suffrage and the push for salary equality as historic precedents. Representation in eSports isn't as important as those fights, but it's still a critical issue if the industry wants to go mainstream, she said.

Harvey has also had her share of hate and intrusion. Her old home address was leaked to the public in 2015. "I'm used to being attacked and used to being targeted," she said. "I think it's an issue with the Internet as a whole."

Hollyanne "Set" Setola, a former professional gamer based in San Diego, disagrees that female tournaments are effective. She believes that they highlight the inequality between men and women, and the large disparity between prize pools reinforces the impression, especially to newcomers, that women are inferior gamers. "It's literally like women in the workforce that make less," she said.

Setola has also experienced seeing her personal information leaked, with users from the website 4chan harassing her. She's hopeful that the next generation, who grow up with no memory of a world before the Internet, will learn to be humane while online, with guidance from their parents and teachers. "We teach kids about bullying," she said, and now the next generation needs to learn that online socializing also requires courtesy.

The role of women in gaming can be complicated by Twitch streamers like Miki, a nineteen-year-old from New Zealand, who uses the name The Fluffiest Bunny. During one stream, she wore a red top, shiny black pants, and heels. She rolled a die and bent over to pick it up. Her pants were see-through.

On Reddit, a poster highlighted her as an example of "hot gamer girls" who use their appearance to gain hundreds of viewers, even if their gameplay is mediocre. "Please stop watching these channels. You are starting a trend and cheapening the community."

On July 27, 2015, she posted an apology video on YouTube. She wasn't apologizing for showing her cleavage or having fun. But she did make a commitment to highlight her gameplay instead of her looks. She regretted making a "mockery" of gaming and their competitive intensity. She had been working with a marketing consultant who had pushed her to play up her sexuality, escalating to pictures of her wearing only a towel. He gradually pushed her to show more and more, with the goal of getting her into amateur porn. She refused and ended the partnership.

There are thousands of women and men who perform live sex shows on explicit "cam" sites, and it is generally accepted as a part of the Internet. But using appearance as a marketing tool seems to many Twitch viewers to be disingenuous, a violation of the site's mission of highlighting gaming.

But going back to Justin Kan's 2007 stream, the site was also about personality and viewer interaction. To clarify its stance, Twitch updated its code of conduct to ban "sexually suggestive clothing" in 2014.

ESports' challenges with diversity extend beyond gender. When players are randomly matched with teammates who don't speak English, frustration can fuel xenophobia. On social media, DOTA players express a particular hatred of people who don't speak English in games, particularly Russians and Peruvians. These groups are accused of ruining games by not communicating properly. Players are already inclined to blame their teammates during losses, and an inability to communicate inflames that desire.

The nationalism of a competitive game can also lead to slurs based on region or race. The insults, particularly on Twitch chat, are wide in their urge to offend: Pinoys are shit at DOTA;

Peruvians are third-world failures; Americans are overweight, guzzling soda and hamburgers, and failing at gun control and health care. Some people are undoubtedly trolling to provoke a reaction and don't intend to be taken seriously.

But gaming forums appear to be one of the few corners of the Internet, outside of hate groups, where the word "faggot" is still commonly used as an insult. (No prominent pro player has ever come out as gay.)

Success in eSports has also concentrated in two racial groups: whites and Asians. China, South Korea, the United States, and Sweden have won the bulk of prize money in eSports' twenty-year history.

It's rare to see professional gamers who are Hispanic or black, except in one scene: fighting games, a genre with some of the most popular video game franchises, such as the gory rush of Mortal Kombat and the flagship Nintendo battler Super Smash Bros. Fighting games are largely two-dimensional, with clear health bars and combat between two foes. They may be the most accessible to newcomers, with clear action and swift rounds.

But the fighting game community has sought to separate itself from eSports, seeing it as too formalized, too corporate. The differences are apparent in the biggest fight game tournament, the Evolution Championship Series, or Evo, which began in 1996.

Typically, eSports tournaments have direct invites for top teams and qualifiers for lesser names to break into the tournament. This ensures, in theory, that the top competitors will be represented and the highest level of play will be broadcast. Evo is different. It is completely open to anyone who wants to register to play, and while professional players generally rise to the top of the standings, the tournament format is deliberately more accessible. The in-person culture of fighting games has meant that top players and newbies alike can face each other, in contrast to the online matchmaking that separates computer players by skill. There is no hidden information like in StarCraft, so competing side by side is fine. Likewise, while computer game tournaments have a stage, often soundproof booths, and barriers to prevent fans from coming too close outside of organized autograph sessions, the fighting game community still resembles the community-organized tournaments of the early 2000s.

In July 2015, Evo had over ten thousand players registered to compete in nine different fighting games in Las Vegas, becoming one of the largest communities in competitive gaming.

But the fighting game community has been wary of corporate sponsorship and breaking into the mainstream with the gusto of other games.

Part of this attitude has been a lack of support from developers. Between 2001 and 2008, there were no major competitive fighting game titles released. "There were many years where there were no new games coming out," said David Graham, the eSports lawyer who also commentates fighting games. "We got very used to being very underground and ignored."

That changed with the 2008 release of Street Fighter 4, which filled a void in a scene that was looking for a big title. "It has the big nostalgia factor," said Graham. The game is simple, slower, and has fewer mechanics compared to other games.

Game developer support has also lagged, which Graham attributes partially to Capcom's Japanese heritage, which historically didn't see eSports as a valuable part of business. Nintendo has also been wary. In 2013, they made a move to shut down a Super Smash Bros. competition at Evo based on a copyright claim. Rather than seeing competition as free marketing and a positive community gathering, Nintendo saw it as a threat.

Evo's more casual nature can provide compelling moments. At the 2015 competition, a player celebrated after a win and took his eyes off the screen as the third and decisive game was beginning. His opponent pounced and locked him into a lethal combination while he helplessly scrambled back to his seat, but it was too late and he was eliminated. The segment was later aired on ESPN.

Latency in online gaming has also prevented the growth of competitive fighting games in the same manner as first-person shooters and strategy games. The scene's shoulder-to-shoulder, in-person competition gives it an intimacy and community feel. But the lack of online play has also prevented the explosive growth that top computer games have experienced.

Fighting games were born in arcade competition, and Graham believes that the contrast between arcade gaming and online PC gaming has led to vast cultural and even demographic differences. Arcade games were played for a quarter per session, in contrast to the hundreds of dollars required for a personal computer. It is equivalent to the price difference between playing basketball and paying for equipment in hockey, which leads to player demographics separated by wealth. Arcades were usually in urban environments where there was enough dense population to support in-person play. Scenes were centered in areas like Los Angeles, San Francisco, and New York.

The cheap cost to enter arcades was a contrast to the hundreds, if not thousands, of dollars required for a gaming computer, good Internet, and top accessories like keyboards, mice, headsets, and chairs. This accessibility led to more racial diversity, particularly with more black and Hispanic players, said Graham. But it also made the scene less attractive for computer parts companies, which fund a huge portion of eSports teams.

Older technology is sometimes deliberately favored. Serious fighting game players use ancient, bulky cathode ray tube televisions because they have the lowest input lag compared to sleeker high-definition screens. Successful beat downs can be dependent on pushing the right button during a single frame, or a 16.67-millisecond window.

A culture of in-person competition rather than online anonymity can make the scene appear to be less inclusive in other ways, particularly toward females, said Graham. Respect had to be earned in the arcades, but he believes there was also more of a meritocracy, with skill mattering more than appearance.

The fighting game community has struggled with sexism, too. In February 2012, fighting game coach Aris Bakhtanians was commentating a tournament with female competitors, when he was asked about removing sexism in the fighting game community.

He responded: "You can't. You can't because they're one and the same thing. This is a community that's, you know, fifteen or twenty years old, and the sexual harassment is part of a culture, and if you remove that from the fighting game community, it's not the fighting game community—it's StarCraft. There's nothing wrong with StarCraft if you enjoy it, and there's nothing wrong with anything about eSports, but why would you want just one flavor of ice cream, you know? There's eSports for people who like eSports, and there's fighting games for people who like spicy food and like to have fun. There's no reason to turn them into the same thing, you know?"

Bakhtanians later said that he was speaking in the heat of the moment and apologized. He said that "mild hostility" had always been part of the scene, with arcades as a proving grounds and the face-to-face battling.

For all its aversion to going corporate, fighting games keep growing. Evo's prize pool is crowdfunded from each player's $10 registration fee, and the total prize money in 2015 was $303,500 across its nine games. That was almost triple the previous year's prize pool $111,959. In 2015, Capcom, Sony, and Twitch funded the Capcom Pro Tour, with a $500,000 prize pool.

Fighting game fans may not want to be labeled eSports. But like it or not, they're becoming part of the rapidly changing industry.

Chapter 7

BORN TO WIN

DOTA 2 RAISES THE STAKES

As League of Legends boomed, the longtime developer of DOTA had found himself a new job. IceFrog, the reclusive steward of the game, had long sought a partner for a true sequel to the venerable title, and he found it in Valve, the company behind Counter-Strike. The Bellevue, Washington–based company had also become a critical marketplace for computer games with its Steam platform, an online store for thousands of other publishers' computer games that functioned as an iTunes for the industry.

Valve was ready to launch another big title and announced that DOTA 2 would be unveiled at the video game festival GamesCom in Cologne, Germany, in August 2011. Instead of having a developer give a speech and showing some video footage, Valve would host a tournament called the International, and it would invite top DOTA teams from North America, Europe, China, and Southeast Asia.

The prize pool would be $1.6 million, a jaw-dropping number for the eSports community and exponentially more than any previous competition. The second-highest payout up to that point had been the $500,000 CPL World Tour Finals that Fatal1ty won back in 2005. The International also dwarfed the six-figure payouts of StarCraft II.

It was the first time a major game would be played competitively when it was still in the early stages of development, known as the beta. Although the game was essentially the same as the original DOTA, with the same map and mechanics, the graphics and interface were updated, and teams only had a few days to practice before competing. Perhaps most crucially, only forty-seven of the game's heroes were available, or about half of the full roster, which limited strategies.

The Chinese were the favorites to win the tournament. Just as South Korea was known for its StarCraft players, the Chinese were dominant in DOTA. In the late 1990s and early 2000s, thousands of Chinese youth grew up playing in Internet cafes known as *wangba* (net bars), blowing off stress and blowing up friends while competing in the country's rigorous school system. In 2000, the Chinese government banned video game consoles to shield the youth from gaming, but that only boosted PC gaming.

DOTA became a sensation, a five-versus-five game that you could play with your teammates sitting next to you.

"Most of the current crop of Chinese pros grew up in these environments and their habits at LAN events—not wearing headsets being the big one—still hearken back to those days," said Josh "Autumnwindz" Lee, who has worked as a Chinese translator for DOTA 2 tournaments.

In 2003, the Chinese government declared eSports, or *dianzi jingji*, as the country's ninety-ninth professional competitive sport. In 2008, the Warcraft III player Sky would carry the Olympic Torch in Hainan. ESports were seen as a separate entity compared to more casual games, or *wangluo*. They were serious competition rather than a leisurely diversion.

But in 2004, China's State Administration of Radio, Film, and Television banned the broadcast of online games on television, which prevented the rise of gaming channels, in contrast to South Korea. But eSports still attracted big money. The owner of Invictus Gaming, one of China's most successful teams, is Wang Sicong. He is the son of Wang Jianlin, chairman of Dalian Wanda Group Corporation Limited, and one of the richest men in China.

"Chinese teams and organizations in some cases have been around for nearly a decade and have very well-established relationships with their communities, partners, sponsors, even governments in some cases. There's a whole framework and structure to it all and people know what to expect as a general thing," said Josh Lee.

At the first International, EHOME was the giant of China, a legendary squad that had won ten consecutive DOTA championships in 2010. The team's manager, Tang "71" Wenyi, said the team would throw out trophies if they didn't win first place. Their roster had just been weakened with the departure of two players to Team DK, another Chinese squad, but EHOME easily reached the finals of the first International, battling for a historic prize pool of $1 million. EHOME's opponent was the Ukranian squad Natus Vincere, known as Na'Vi, Latin for "born to win."

Na'Vi's star was Danil "Dendi" Ishutin, who grew up in Lviv, Ukraine. He performed in musical theater and dance in school, which made him comfortable in front of large crowds. An avid gamer, he was entranced by World of Warcraft, Blizzard's massive online roleplaying game. But with a subscription fee of $15 per month, it was too expensive, and he stuck to the older Warcraft III. Then he discovered DOTA. He would play during the early morning, when the Internet was available in his house, and began attending local competitions.

DOTA's almost endless character combinations and nuances have kept Dendi enthralled. "It's insanely deep. It never repeats," he said. "I've been playing for ten years, and I find something new almost every day for myself. It's never-ending."

He became a star in the middle lane, which typically is a one-versus-one matchup. He would use his superior mechanics to dominate his opponent, and then overpower the other lanes with his advantage. "I like midlane because I'm not dependent on anyone. I'm more selfish," said Dendi. "I feel like I can create more for a team from this position." Dendi makes space for his teammates by occupying the attention of multiple enemies, giving the rest of his team time to get resources in the rest of the map.

Na'Vi's roots dated back to 2009, where it benefited from the funding of Murat "Arbalet" Zhumashevich Tulemaganbetov, one of the biggest eSports benefactors from Eastern Europe. Arbalet also organized over three hundred eSports events throughout the world, but he revealed few personal details. One report described him as a family man and a seller of tobacco, liquor, and tea.

Alexander Kokhanovskyy, a former pro player, became the manager of Na'Vi's Counter-Strike team in 2009. The following year, they won all the major tournaments in the world. Na'Vi's Counter-Strike team had skill, power of will, and hunger for victory, and a connection with fans, said Kokhanovskyy.

But in late 2010, Arbalet said he had run out of money for eSports after investing over $1 million. Na'Vi was now on its own, and it would have to attract sponsors, a challenge given its location in Eastern Europe, a less desirable place for marketers with its poorer demographics. But Na'Vi's champion pedigree drew investments from the eSports mainstays SteelSeries and the computer memory company HyperX.

The team decided to expand into DOTA and gathered the top Ukrainian players, including Dendi. He was initially paid $200 a month, which was a livable wage in Lviv, especially since he was still living with his parents. Even in 2016, it's about half of the median salary of his city.

At the International, facing EHOME, Na'Vi was wild, yelling and flipping off their opponents. "Our morale was super high," said Dendi. "It was really silly at that time, and maybe stupid sometimes, but it worked."

Dendi played the hero Enigma for the first time in a competitive game, with a game-changing spell called Black Hole, a huge area stun that crippled EHOME for four crucial seconds as his teammates beat them down. "Other people were using two, three strategies. We were using from seven to ten," said Kokhanovskyy. The hallmarks of Na'Vi were creativity and aggression, and a swagger that eased the pressure of battling for such high stakes.

Dendi's seemingly carefree personality is in sharp contrast to the sometimes tortured moods of his competitors when they lose. Dendi made winning look effortless, and even when Na'Vi has struggled, he projects a carefree personality, seemingly at odds with his lightning reflexes and his intensity on the digital battle-field. "He is natural. He is always smiling," said Kokhanovskyy.

"I don't have any plans for the future. I just live and enjoy," said Dendi. He dreams of a second championship, but he's content with his previous success. "I would like to, but if it doesn't happen, I won't be too sad."

Na'Vi's performance made them stars, and the buzz around the tournament made Valve commit to running the International every year, even though DOTA 2 would remain in its beta testing stage until 2013.

"Watching professionals play the product is the greatest demo you can get," Erik Johnson, a top Valve manager, later said. "As soon as we were one hour into the tournament, we already knew we wanted to do it next year partly because it was so fun and partly because our list of mistakes was awfully long."

In 2012, the second International was held at Benoroyal Hall, a concert venue in Seattle a few miles from Valve's headquarters in Bellevue. The prize pool was again $1.6 million, and this year, the Chinese teams were even more dominant.

EHOME was back, and new powerhouses like Team DK, LGD, and Tongfu emerged. Na'Vi were serenaded with chants of "USA! USA!" when they played. Despite being Ukranian, they were the West's best hope against China.

Na'Vi's playoff game against China's Invictus Gaming would immortalize them.

Invictus Gaming's carry, or their most powerful hero in the late game, Chen "Zhou" Yao, was playing Naga Siren, an imperious mermaid that was one of the top heroes of the tournament. Her ultimate ability, Song of the Siren, was a mythological reference that freezes the enemy team, making them temporarily invulnerable while sleeping, but setting up devastating combos with attacks that blanket an area.

Invictus Gaming paired Naga Siren with another nautical hero, Tidehunter, whose Ravage ability unleashes a burst of tentacles that knocks the opposing team out for a few seconds. They also had Dark Seer, whose Vacuum ability sucks opponents together. The three heroes were a fearsome combo, but unthinkably, Na'Vi allowed

Invictus Gaming to pick them all in the draft before the game, when the two teams each select and ban five heroes. Instead, Na'Vi picked Enigma again, along with Juggernaut, a Samurai-like attacker who could use his Bladefury ability to resist enemies' disabling attacks.

During a crucial engagement, Na'Vi appeared to be out of position, ready to be massacred. Commentator David "LD" Gorman would narrate the now infamous sequence: "They storm up the river, patience from Zhou, waiting in the wing, Na'Vi's about to be caught. Oh there's the Sleep, the Surge. He catches everyone! Oh this could be a total disaster!"

Na'Vi was seduced by Naga Siren, frozen in place for IG's devastating combination. "Vacuum in, Ravage on everyone!" shouted Gorman. But suddenly Na'Vi sprang into action, using a split-second window to activate their abilities that made them temporarily resistant to stuns. Dendi's Rubick, a masked magician that can steal opponents' spells, used his own Ravage, and suddenly Invictus Gaming was helpless.

What had seemed like an ambush became one of the most spectacular turnarounds, as Na'Vi killed all of their opponents and took the game. The fight would become simply known as "The Play" in DOTA lore.

Invictus Gaming would come back and beat Na'Vi 3–1 in the International's finals. The Ukrainians had fallen short, but their brave stand made them even more lovable.

Dendi's skills got him to the highest level, but his charisma is what made him a star and transformed him into an eSports icon. His shaggy, Beatles-esque moptop haircut, his huge smile, and his playful persona contrasted with the stern demeanor of many of his European and American peers. He has over three hundred thousand Twitter followers—more than Na'Vi's team page and more than the Ukranian national soccer team.

One of Dendi's signature heroes is Pudge the Butcher, a bloated, bleeding humanoid brute with a giant cleaver and meat hook, his menace somewhat tempered with a jolly English accent. Pudge is a flashy playmaker that exemplifies Dendi's strengths. His signature ability throws his grisly meat hook in a line, and if it connects with a unit—friend or foe—it drags them to Pudge. Other teams almost never use the hero competitively, yet Dendi had a supernatural ability to land hooks, anticipating where his opponents would walk. The hero encapsulates Dendi's appeal: humor, skill, and a willingness to be different.

Although Na'Vi has struggled with team instability and weaker results in later years, it remains a popular brand that's able to attract sponsorships based on its history. "Right now, the results are not essential, to be honest," said Kokhanovskyy. "Back in the day, it was crucial. Right now, no."

Disappointment never seemed to affect Dendi. He would break out in spontaneous dance or flash a goofy smile. "I don't play for money. I don't have pressure that I'm going to lose," he said. "I just want to show my best game. I don't have any troubles or struggles.

"I'm happy that I have really good friends. I'm happy that I have really good family, and I really love them. They love me. So I try to do my best for them. And they try to do their best for me," he said. "I'm a really lucky guy."

Dendi said that people have been criticizing him since he began competing. But he has maintained a cheerful outlook: "If I make someone smile, I am happy."

As Valve prepared for DOTA 2's official launch in 2013, it settled on a free-to-play business model. Like League of Legends, the foundation of DOTA 2's economy was cosmetic items that changed the appearance of characters but didn't affect gameplay. But unlike League of Legends, which locks items to the account they're purchased on, DOTA 2 items can be traded and sold directly on Valve's Steam platform. This online economy meant that some rare items, particularly those sold for a limited period of time, could eventually become far more valuable, like a courier, used to transport items to players in game, with a discontinued graphical effect that sold for $38,000 in 2013.

In contrast to League of Legends, Valve made all of its heroes free, so cosmetic items became the core of the revenue system.

Valve's Steam program was already well established, so the company had a lot of expertise in ecommerce and marketing. But Valve was a relatively small, private studio with only a few hundred staff. Their artists were already stretched thin, and to come up with enough variety in items to support an economy, they would need fresh ideas.

DOTA had originally been fan made, and Valve saw the community as a continued resource. The developer opened up design submissions to digital artists on the Steam Workshop. Community members could voice their support ("Super mega epic!") or displeasure ("Ewww") for items. Valve would ultimately decide which items to add to the in-game store.

To attract some top artists for new content, Valve held a contest for character designs at the art website Polycount in 2012. One of the contest entrants was Stephanie "Anuxinamoon" Everett, an Australian who had worked for a decade in graphic design for video game studios. She didn't even play DOTA 2, but the character design appealed to her, so she entered. She ended up being one of the ten finalists, and she won.

Everett focused on female characters, creating the character sets such as the "Winter Snowdrop" for Crystal Maiden, an ice mage who resembles Elsa from Frozen, and the "Blessing of the Wildkin" set for Enchantress, a forest dryad.

She was freelancing for other studios at the time, but was attracted by DOTA 2's flexibility. Artists who create items for the workshop have creative freedom and independence. "I dictate what I want to do, when I want to do it, and when I want to upload it," she said.

It takes her around two weeks to fully complete a set. Valve gets 75 percent of the revenue from item sales and creators get the remaining 25 percent, she said. Everett knows around twenty people who make items as a full-time job.

The model was so lucrative that in August 2013, Valve added cosmetic skins to Counter-Strike: Global Offensive, which helped launch the title from obscurity into one of eSports's top games, carrying the competitive torch of the original Counter-Strike. In 2013, Valve paid $10.2 million to 661 in-game item creators. Between 2011 and the end of 2014, the Workshop has paid out $57 million to over 1,500 artists for the games Team Fortress 2, DOTA 2, and Counter-Strike: Global Offensive.

DOTA 2 teams have also commissioned artists to make custom sets in partnership with players, who get a portion of the artists' royalties from sales. But the revenue that went to teams was initially delayed as Valve sent only a single check and didn't clarify what players were entitled to what royalties. Valve later provided more detailed data.

DOTA 2's virtual storefront also became a way to crowdfund the eSports scene. Tournament organizers can sell virtual tickets that allowed spectators to watch directly in the game, with full control of the camera, although the business model competes with the free streams on Twitch. Some organizers also offered exclusive cosmetic items, which were the main driver of sales.

Aside from the International each year, Valve has stayed hands-off in its approach to eSports, recognizing that its expertise is in design, not events. It is a small company with a few hundred employees, dwarfed by the thousands of workers at massive video game corporations like Blizzard, which is now merged with Call of Duty developer Activision. Valve has shown no desire to create its own yearlong league like Riot and Blizzard have done. If Riot is the rigid industrial farmer, reviewing every ounce of eSports grain and corn that is produced and distributed to a mass audience, Valve is the distant, sometimes absent gardener. Outside of running the International, Valve allows a thousand tournaments to bloom, but that approach has its own discontents.

Valve's hands-off business model has given independence to DOTA 2 commentators, in contrast to League of Legends commentators, who are mostly Riot employees and bound to the regimented schedule of the LCS.

In DOTA 2 independent studios have formed, starting with passion and transitioning to become businesses. One of the most successful ventures is Beyond the Summit, a commentary studio founded by Philadelphia native David "LD" Gorman, one of the announcers in the second International; and David "GoDz" Parker, an Australian former pro player. They initially focused on casting Asian events, which usually lacked English-language coverage.

But in 2013, they raised just under $40,000 on the crowdfunding site Indiegogo to build a full-time studio, and they both relocated to southern California to create the company. Beyond the Summit now provides coverage for all major DOTA 2 tournaments unless a rival studio, such as joinDOTA, has the rights. It sometimes streams for days without pausing when multiple tournaments are active.

As with players, the top eSports commentators can earn a solid living, but for those trying to start a career, money is scarce. Valve also controls the invitations to cast the International, and being selected or passed over can make or break a career. LD had the benefit of being a known personality after commenting the second International, but some of Beyond the Summit's newer commentators haven't secured in-person work at Valve's tournaments and have faded into obscurity.

When it comes to monetization, Beyond the Summit has lean margins, as it grapples with viewers of its Twitch stream using Adblock and other channels on YouTube stealing and uploading its content. When the studio began organizing its own tournaments, the largest of which was branded The Summit, it relied heavily on outside sponsors, just like eSports teams. Fans reacted negatively after the studio ran what was seen as excessive ads during the tournament, and some computers broke down, leading to outrage.

"When you're a tournament organizer, the community sees you as a business," said LD. In contrast, individual streamers on Twitch can get away with aggressively seeking donations. But Beyond the Summit has employees and a production crew to support, so that means getting outside financial support. The studio was founded because of passion for the game, rather than a desire to make money, but now the bottom line matters, and that can lead to backlash.

"This is something that I started out of love," said LD. "To hear people talk like that about something that we had worked eighty to one hundred hours a week on—it was heartbreaking."

While DOTA 2 and the International have set a new financial height in eSports with its massive prize pool, the enormity of the event has made it a make-or-break moment for both commentators' and teams' survival. Winning is everything, and players will drop out of rosters and try another set of teammates at early signs of failure or friction. It's typical for a pro player to try to play on numerous teams, disband, and try again in the course of a year in a futile effort to win it all.

"The International as it is definitely damages the scene," said Greg "WhatIsHip" Laird, a commentator and former DOTA 2 team manager. "The money is great but it completely fucks the scene up for four months."

But it still beckons as a shot at eSports immortality for the hopeful.

On December 11, 2011, twenty-year-old Jacky "EternaLEnVy" Mao posted a message on the Team Liquid eSports forum. He was ready to quit school and pursue his dream.

He was studying engineering science as a second-year student at the University of Toronto, a major that he described as an "extremely fucking retarded course that destroys your soul." He had a B-minus average.

He had been playing the original DOTA since he was fourteen. He was a diligent competitor, making friends with rivals and turning them into sparring partners. He would play dozens of games using one hero until playing it was second nature. EternaLEnVy began playing in an online group known as an in-house league, a semiorganized network that pitted top players against each other for practice. He became one of the best players.

Games were a way to escape. Having a dominant virtual self was empowering, no matter how anxious he was in real life. "It was my way of running away from life, the one thing I was proud of when I was pretty shit at everything else," he later wrote on Reddit. He reentered the competitive scene in his senior year of high school with Heroes of Newerth, a game heavily inspired by

DOTA. He played for hours and still maintained strong grades in high school.

Then he started watching old StarCraft competitions, which inspired him to become a pro gamer. His grades dropped as he discovered the burgeoning pro DOTA 2 scene and watched tournaments on weekends.

Now, he was contemplating tossing away his traditional career path to stream on Twitch's predecessor, Justin.tv, and coach weaker players to make money. Eventually, he wanted to gather a group of like-minded teammates to compete in tournaments. He figured that he could always go back to school in a few years. But he had concerns. Ad revenue on Justin.tv was paltry, at about $2 per thousand viewers, and Internet was slow in Canada.

Although he was posting on a forum founded to celebrate and discuss eSports, many respondents were not enthusiastic about his decision. He would be throwing away a stable career for a shot at success in an unstable industry. He would be playing against players who already had years of competitive experience.

But EternaLEnVy was undeterred: "THE PURPOSE OF THIS THREAD IS NOT TO CONVINCE ME OF STAYING IN SCHOOL. . . . It's only a year or two of my life. My financial issues aren't so bad that these two years would cost my life."

"Making a lot of money is not what concerns me," he added. His parents, Chinese immigrants, were skeptical, but he had saved up enough money for a year. He convinced them not to kick him out of the house.

EternaLEnVy's personality and obsessive desire to win manifest on his personal Twitch stream. Instead of the aloof, selfish focus that most pros have in public games, he tries to lead and direct his teammates, who are randomly matched with him. He is demanding from the start, begging his teammates to pick heroes that he thinks are the most powerful. He tries to lead like a general, but he can come off as obsessive, with an agitated stream of chatter. But it's all for one pure goal. "That intensity is because of his will to win," said Conrad Janzen, who would later be EternaL-EnVy's team manager. "I wish I had half the passion that Jacky has for any game. He is one of the most dedicated players."

People, particularly nongamers, look at the millions of dollars in prize pool money and joke that they should start playing. Or they sneer at kids with the dream job of gaming all day. They scoff that eSports is a sign that society is collapsing, or at least that people are valuing the wrong things.

In reality, professional gaming is one of the hardest industries to succeed in. Not only is competition structured to reward the few winners over the masses of losers, eSports still isn't fully established as a professional endeavor. The flow of money is slower than entrenched entertainment sources like television or film. And becoming a pro gamer is like striving to become a supermodel or Hollywood star. You need to network with the right people and convince someone with actual money to invest in you. Instead of amazing cheekbones, you need lightning-fast reflexes and deep knowledge of a game.

There are the millions of gamers, but only a few hundred have achieved anything in the professional scene. And even fewer have made a sustainable career out of it.

Like more traditional sports, becoming a pro requires single-minded focus, a thirst to win that consumes everything. It favors youth, those without financial obligations, and those who can put the game over all people. Becoming a professional requires the smarts to study the complexities of a game, the reflexes to perform, and a mind and heart that doesn't crumble under pressure and criticism. Talent is just the beginning.

Particularly in team games, communication and social interactions are crucial.

The top competitive games require hundreds if not thousands of hours of practice before a player can even begin to show mastery. A young person who has financial support from his or her parents can put the bulk of their energy into playing, without worrying about life's necessities. But becoming a pro also requires a certain social withdrawal, the minimization or elimination of human relationships. The game becomes your job, your craft, and your most significant relationship.

"People drive you away from the game," said Geoff "iNcontroL" Robinson of Evil Geniuses. Parents have to grapple with their kids dreaming of an industry that doesn't fully exist, with few templates of success. Friends are pushed aside for more practice. Reaching the top means sacrificing education, relationships, and other sources of income.

"Even if it made sense financially—let's say I win the lottery and I can compete professionally, I don't know if I would do it just because you have to give everything up for it," said David "GoDz" Parker from Beyond the Summit. "You have to devote everything, and you don't really know if that's going to succeed."

"I think EternaLEnVy's a good example of a success story, when he dropped out of college and gave up his life and everything to compete," said Parker. "But what people don't see is the countless people who do that and don't make a penny or make a hundred dollars winning some small, little tournament."

It was almost a year until EternaLEnVy played in a significant tournament. His team was called No Tidehunter, a reference to the game's hero. In October 2012 the roster was finalized with four Swedish players, including Jonathan "Loda" Berg and

Joakim "Akke" Akterhall, who had been playing together for a decade, since they were in high school.

Berg's girlfriend, Kelly "kellyMILKIES" Ong, the former maligned GSL StarCraft caster, became the manager of the team.

The other members were Henrik "AdmiralBulldog" Ahnberg, a Swedish newcomer who gained the friendship of Na'Vi's Dendi and showed off his skills as a substitute player for the Ukrainians, and Gustav "s4" Magnusson, another unknown.

At DreamHack Winter 2012, No Tidehunter played its first major LAN tournament and faced Alexander Garfield's Evil Geniuses in the finals. After losing the first game and facing elimination, they went for something crazy.

AdmiralBulldog was playing one of his signature heroes, Nature's Prophet, a druid that could teleport anywhere on the map and animate trees to fight. As the game was starting, he teleported to Roshan, a powerful neutral monster who can only be killed early by a specialized lineup. When he dies, Roshan drops the Aegis of the Immortal, an item that one hero can pick up for a one-time reincarnation. But killing Roshan was not the plan.

AdmiralBulldog was killed by the granite giant, to the amusement of the commentators, alerting Evil Geniuses to investigate. They moved to the low-ground by the pit, while the rest of No Tidehunter flanked from behind and ambushed them. Two Evil Geniuses players were killed, giving No Tidehunter an early advantage.

"No one has ever done that in the history of DOTA!" exclaimed Toby "TobiWan" Dawson, the game's commentator.

No Tidehunter rode the momentum to win the next two games, getting their first big championship and $15,000. EternaLEnVy had achieved his dream of becoming a professional player.

But after some mediocre results over the next three months, No Tidehunter sought change. His teammates wanted a fifth Swedish player so they could communicate in their native tongue, and they picked up Jerry "EGM" Lundkvist, whose name stood for "Enter God Mode." EternaLEnVy was kicked off the team.

In March 2013, No Tidehunter announced it had found a sponsor, computer accessory maker Razer, and changed its name to Alliance. The team's real owner would be revealed later: Alexander Garfield of Evil Geniuses. The prior year, Garfield had picked the team's veteran player Loda as someone to invest in and build a second brand around. And he had personally designed the team's silvery shield-like logo. It had been awkward when Alliance and Evil Geniuses faced off in the tournament finals, because Garfield had contracts with both teams.

With its new lineup, Alliance dominated. The next month they attended the G-1 Champions League Season 5 tournament in China, a country where no Western DOTA team had ever won a LAN. Alliance went undefeated, showing off new strategies that befuddled their Chinese rivals. With its victory, Alliance received a direct invite to the third International. Meanwhile, Evil Geniuses failed to qualify.

The tournament used a new tool to augment its prize pool: crowdfunding. Players had already demonstrated their desire for cosmetic items, so Valve offered the International Compendium, a program that listed all the teams that would compete at the event and came bundled with exclusive in-game items. Players could buy the Compendium for $10, and $2.50 of the purchase would go to the prize pool. Around 480,000 fans bought the program and boosted the tournament's prize pool from

$1.6 million to $2.8 million, setting another new prize record for eSports.

But the huge stakes didn't faze Alliance. Before the tournament, Loda showed supreme confidence in his team. When Garfield interviewed him for a video before the tournament, he was struck by how comfortable his chosen Swede was. "It's generally fear that makes people make mistakes," said Loda. "Even if I throw the game, my team will just respect me just as much."

Alliance's run in the International 3 was nearly perfect. They lost only one game on their path to the finals, where they faced Dendi and Na'Vi, battling to a final and decisive game five. It started with an unfair fight.

On the bottom lane, Loda's hero Chaos Knight, a towering horseman of the apocalypse, charged at an Ogre ridden by a diminutive alchemist, played by Na'Vi's Alexandr "Xboct" Dashkevich. Loda's allies, a sentient ball of energy known as Io and Crystal Maiden, an ice mage, backed him up. Alchemist threw a pool of acid on the ground and began mixing up an explosive chemical cocktail, which he hurled at the knight. Then he ran to his defensive tower.

Chaos Knight was stunned and blasted by the tower's powerful shots. He died, and Alchemist, hurt badly, stumbled to hide in the trees. First blood to Na'Vi. But the Alliance continued their assault. AdmiralBulldog, once again playing his signature Nature's Prophet, teleported in from the opposite side of the map, hunting his weak enemy. Alchemist juked through the trees, charged another stun, and flung it at Bulldog, leading to an unthinkable double kill for Na'Vi in a one-versus-four scenario.

The game was off to a dreadful start for Alliance, and it got worse.

In the midlane, Dendi's Templar Assassin, a psiblade-throwing femme fatale, dominated s4's Puck, an elusive faerie dragon who couldn't match Dendi's damage output. As the teams clashed, Dendi eviscerated Alliance's fragile supports with his psionic blades.

But in a decisive fight near the Roshan pit, Dendi was isolated and picked off. Alliance was still in it. Na'Vi kept fighting, charging through the middle lane and looking to smash Alliance's base.

There was no hope for Alliance to defeat Na'Vi in a direct confrontation. So Alliance dodged its opponent and put pressure on the two other lanes, known as split-pushing or pejoratively as "ratting," as if Alliance was infesting the map, sneaking around rather than fighting honorably. AdmiralBulldog's Nature's Prophet—the hero that earned him his first LAN win—had more mobility than any hero in the game with his global teleport, and he constantly pressured the side lanes. Alliance's Io could transport teammates anywhere with the ultimate ability Relocate, and as Na'Vi tore into Alliance's base down the middle lane, Alliance charged down the top and bottom paths.

Dendi had no room in his hero's inventory for a teleport scroll, which would allow him to return to his own base in the face of Alliance's counterattack. He told his team, but they said to keep pushing, victory was in sight.

"That's what makes teams really strong—it's trust," said Dendi. "You need to be friendly. You need to accept your teammates in all ways. You need to like them. You need to give them your trust. Then you're number one."

So Dendi trusted his teammates and kept attacking. But what if he trusted the wrong call?

Alliance's attack had reached Na'Vi's base, and the Ukrainians were losing their base more quickly than it could destroy their opponent's. The team retreated and began teleporting back to defend, but s4's Puck used his spells to stun them at the last second. They had to run back, helpless as Loda and AdmiralBulldog did massive damage. Despite their huge lead, the Ukrainian squad was crumbling. They couldn't pull off their trademark aggression when they were stuck defending, and Alliance demolished Na'Vi's entire base. The disaster of an early game was a distant memory.

In their booth, the Alliance embraced and jumped up and down. They had won $1.4 million, the biggest prize ever awarded in eSports. Confetti rained from the ceiling.

Alexander Garfield was watching from the stands near a Swedish flag. As Alliance hugged in victory, he collapsed. He was out for a few seconds. He called the moment a "fundamental rewiring of my brain." His Counter-Strike team had always been one win shy of that great triumph. His StarCraft players won more frequently, but they were always a step behind the South Koreans. His violin teacher had taught him that a craft was a path of pain, and to seek satisfaction rather than triumph.

But now, Garfield's victory was undeniable. He had chosen Loda. He had designed the team's logo. Though Evil Geniuses hadn't even qualified for the event, he had an Aegis of Champions, the trophy awarded to the winning team, to take home. He could be optimistic.

Garfield also added to his own coffers. AdmiralBulldog would later say on his stream that the Alliance organization took 20 percent of the prize pool, or around $280,000, and the Swedish government taxed 50 percent, leaving the five players with around $110,000 each. But winning the biggest DOTA 2 tournament was far more meaningful than the money.

EternaLEnVy didn't even get to compete against his former team in Seattle. He had launched a new team called Kaipi in March 2013, but Valve didn't consider it worthy of even an invitation to the qualifiers for the event. So he had his eyes on the next International and the next generation of champions.

For Kaipi, EternaLEnVy recruited a friend and practice partner: Artour "Arteezy" Babaev. Like EnVy, Arteezy's parents had immigrated to Canada. The seventeen-year-old was born in Tashkent, Uzbekistan, but grew up in Vancouver.

Arteezy had a fondness for rappers like Drake and Kanye West, even choosing his gaming ID in the same structure as Kanye's nickname, Yeezy. He matched EnVy's obsessive devotion to improving mechanics, and he was inspired to play seriously after watching Dendi. Arteezy would stream on Twitch for as much as twelve hours, playing the same hero over and over to discover its nuances. He soon became a top-ranked player in North America's in-house league, the proving ground for new talent.

"I can safely predict that Arteezy will become one of the best players that the West has ever seen. He is like a budding rose in a field full of dead weeds," said Sam "BuLba" Sosale, another pro gamer and practice partner.

As in League of Legends and StarCraft, North America was seen as one of the weakest regions in DOTA, with poor finishes in the first three Internationals. The scene was characterized by a constant churn of players forming teams and then disbanding after poor results.

But Arteezy's career seemed to end prematurely, before he could show off his skills. As his senior year approached in August, he left the team in order to focus on his studies again. Pro gaming was still risky, and he couldn't do it all.

Instead, EternaLEnVy recruited Kurtis "Aui_2000" Ling, who had also dropped out of studying at the University of British Columbia to play professionally, and WehSing "SingSing" Yuen, a popular streamer on Twitch. The team soon picked up a sponsor and was renamed Speed Gaming.

In one of the first big tournaments after the International, Speed and eight other top teams flew to Columbus, Ohio, to compete in Major League Gaming's first DOTA 2 event.

Another Speed Gaming player, Pittner "bOne7" Armand, lived in Romania and couldn't secure a visa, so the team had to bring in an emergency substitute. They turned again to Arteezy. The first day was a disaster. Flights were canceled, and Speed Gaming's players barely slept. The team lost its first three games on the first day as the new lineup struggled to adapt. Arteezy looked overwhelmed as he played unfamiliar heroes.

But on the second day, something clicked. Arteezy began exclusively playing in the midlane, the position he had practiced for thousands of hours, and began playing like a madman. He shined with the hero Outworld Devourer, a menacing Sphinx-like being that temporarily banishes opponents and steals their intellect to fuel his own damage. Speed Gaming won seven games in a row and secured a spot in the finals.

On the eve of their match, another crisis emerged. In a sudden move, Marco Fernandez, Speed Gaming's CEO, released the details of their contracts. It highlighted how financially precarious they were: they were signed for only three months and had a $1,000 a month salary, which would rise to $2,000 if they did well in the upcoming tournaments.

The players' relationship with Fernandez had been deteriorating for weeks. He was poorly organized, the players later said, and criticized them after losses and claimed the team wasn't trying hard enough to win.

But the team had to push that aside. They had to face Team DK, a new superstar squad from Asia with a trio of Chinese veterans and two of Southeast Asia's brightest stars.

The first game went for over an hour, with Speed Gaming trying to break DK's base. Arteezy's Outworld Devourer was stacked with items, but DK struck decisively and wiped them out with the hero Earthshaker's Echo Slam, a powerful earthquake that gets stronger when more enemies are clumped together. With a fierce counterattack, DK won game one.

Facing elimination, EternaLEnVy picked Clinkz, a flaming skeletal archer with powers of invisibility and brutal damage output. He made the unconventional choice of getting a Blink Dagger, an item that let him teleport short distances and increased his mobility. He dashed around the map, picking off DK's players. Speed won the second and third games with the same strategy and took home $68,445. "Thank you for believing in me again. It's been a long time since I've done anything in DOTA," EternaLEnVy said to the crowd. Their manager, Marco Fernandez, was fired from the team for incompetence.

Garfield watched Arteezy's performance with interest. Evil Geniuses had been crushed in the group stages of the MLG tournament, finishing second-to-last. Alliance—the world champion just a few months ago—had also looked shaky and didn't make it to the final four. Garfield was tired of mediocrity. He had recruited IdrA and HuK, and he had won a championship with Loda. It was time to make Evil Geniuses' DOTA team worthy of its name. Garfield had hesitated to recruit Arteezy, despite the hype surrounding him because other people said he was too immature. But after attending

MLG and watching Arteezy dominate in person, Garfield was ready to make a deal.

Arteezy had committed to staying in high school. But with the MLG win, he began to reconsider. Perhaps, he thought, he could finish his classes and still play full time.

Garfield experienced Arteezy's personality firsthand over Skype, as they negotiated a contract. Garfield later sent the chatlogs to the satirical humor website ESports Express, which published them on April Fool's Day. One partially censored part read:

[12:56:45 AM] Alexander Garfield: you're gonna have to chill a little bit on language while on stream
[12:56:52 AM] Arteezy: i am aware
[12:56:52 AM] Alexander Garfield: stuff like that is not as okay
[12:56:54 AM] Arteezy: i am just getting it out
[12:57:15 AM] Arteezy: how come i cant use _____ though
[12:57:23 AM] Alexander Garfield: it's an offensive word to a lot of people
[12:57:29 AM] Arteezy: it seems subjective
[12:57:34 AM] Alexander Garfield: can't say _____, either
[12:57:45 AM] Arteezy: >?
[12:57:47 AM] Arteezy: _____?
[12:57:49 AM] Arteezy: WHAT th ehlel
[12:57:54 AM] Alexander Garfield: hell is fine
[12:58:04 AM] Arteezy: isn't
[12:58:08 AM] Arteezy: _____ = female dog
[12:58:14 AM] Alexander Garfield: you're cute
[12:58:14 AM] Arteezy: how is _____ offensive
[12:58:18 AM] Arteezy: U FUCKIN MKOTHERUFK ER

It was partially an act, an immature silliness that formed a protective shell over Arteezy's emotional investment in the game. But Arteezy's personality would also be attractive for fans who appreciated his sometimes ridiculous antics.

Arteezy's skills and reputation would also give confidence to the rest of the team. "You need someone who will be a magnet to other good players," said Garfield. "When that many people idolize you, you start to become who they think you are." As he had with Loda, Garfield was going to build a team around Arteezy.

Garfield had originally championed Evil Geniuses' leader to be Clinton "Fear" Loomis, who had grown up in Medford, Oregon, and begun playing DOTA in 2003. He was born in 1988, nearly a decade before the game's younger prodigies. And with his beard and weary-looking eyes, Fear became known as the "Old Man." When he was two, his father left his family, and his mother raised Fear and his brother while she studied law and worked a part-time job. To occupy her kids, she bought them a Sega Genesis, which became the gateway for Fear's love of gaming.

Fear was also an avid athlete, skateboarding and playing soccer, but he failed to make the varsity basketball team, perhaps because he was too short. Gaming became the fuel for his ambitions. Even as he studied computer science at a local university, gaming was his focus, and he soon dropped out. The obsession became a source of tension with his mom.

After Fear joined a mostly European team and had to practice late at night to sync time zones, the family dog kept barking, denying his mother precious sleep. She made him move out, but Fear was still determined to play, and his team, Online Kingdom, finished seventh in the first International, netting $25,000. It was a far cry from Na'Vi's million-dollar triumph, but he got the attention of Garfield as one of the only standout

American players. He became the elder statesman of the Evil Geniuses' DOTA team, but they couldn't break through.

Garfield still believed in Fear, as well as the team's quiet playmaker, Saahil "UNiVeRsE" Arora. The three other Evil Geniuses players, Fogged, Jeyo, and MSS, were dismissed after just four months. "It's always been hard for me to cut people. That was my decision at the end of the day," said Garfield.

Now the team needed its final members: two supports, the heroes that are least reliant on getting their own items and that help their teammates by roaming around the map and setting up kills.

Two candidates stood out: Peter "ppd" Dager and Ludwig "zai" Wåhlberg, a Swedish player. They had only been playing DOTA 2 for about a year each, but as teenagers, they had played the DOTA-like game Heroes of Newerth and traveled the world to compete. They showed off their skills by playing in the same in-house league where Arteezy had risen to fame.

Critically, Evil Geniuses also needed a true leader, a shotcaller who didn't hesitate. It needed more than Arteezy's swagger. It needed a steely decisiveness.

At the beginning of his career, ppd wouldn't have been able to lead. But he had grown after trying to run his own independent DOTA 2 team. Without the support of an organization with sponsors or a manager, he had to function as a sort of "team mom," organizing practices and calling his teammates when they overslept. "If that player doesn't show up, I can't practice, so I can't get better," he said. "You have to swallow your pride and make sure it gets done."

Although he hadn't had much experience as a captain beyond his boyhood soccer team, it was a role that he became more comfortable with. "I knew that the best way to get something you want is to take charge and do it yourself," he said. "People kind of rallied around me."

He was also obsessive about learning the metagame, or which heroes were strongest during the current version of DOTA 2, which would shift as Valve released game updates, or patches. Sometimes he would dream about the game. Armed with that knowledge, ppd could choose the most effective lineup for his team.

With ppd's potential as captain, Evil Geniuses added him and zai to the new roster, although Garfield would wait and see how the team performed before making a final commitment.

The team was initially called SADBOYS, after a song by the rap group Yung Lean, which Arteezy liked. Their first game in January 2014 was against Team Liquid, a familiar foe from the StarCraft era. They were slaughtered. A Reddit post joked: "Impressive start."

But then the team played its first major tournament, the Electronic Sports Prime Shock Therapy Cup. They went undefeated, winning eight games and beating four other top teams. Soon after, the team officially became the new Evil Geniuses. Charlie Yang, an eSports veteran who had worked with EternaLEnVy's team, became Evil Geniuses' manager, overseeing team logistics.

Ppd and Arteezy were polar opposites in their in-game roles. Arteezy was the hard carry. His job was to gain as much gold as quickly as possible, stashing an arsenal of items until he became a killing machine in the late game. Although he idolized Dendi from Na'Vi's flashy plays, Arteezy's' play style wasn't so much reliant on split-second reactions as relentless, repetitive efficiency. He was often on his own, slaughtering computer-controlled monsters and looting them for more gold, as his team created distractions around the map.

The team's carry hero usually begins the game on one of the map's side lanes, where it would be protected by the team's supports. But with Arteezy's stellar mechanics, he was comfortable playing the hero in the midlane, where he could dominate in a one-versus-one matchup.

Meanwhile, ppd played the hard support role, buying items for the team at the expense of his own progression. He would almost always be the poorest character in the game, even when Evil Geniuses was winning. But he was the brains of the team, dictating their movements and engagements.

Arteezy would often get the glory, dominating with his efficiency and wealth, while ppd's dictatorship kept the team focused and proactive. "The best teams in DOTA know what they want to do and don't let anyone get in the way of that," said ppd, and with Arteezy's skills and his leadership, the team always had a plan.

Outside of the early victories, the team became a source of fascination for the community. Arteezy had a mixture of young cockiness and innocence, and a bizarre taste in music that was playfully mocked.

"I owe my life to Arteezy. I got in a horrible car crash and I was in a six-month coma. The nurse switched to the Twitch channel of Arteezy's stream. I awoke from my coma and muted it," said one meme that his fans frequently reposted in chat.

In contrast, ppd came off as cerebral and intolerant of dissent. He was portrayed as perpetually "salty," sometimes showing contempt for opponents. He was critical, demanding, and effective.

He reluctantly admits to being a bully in high school, and he freely admits that he can be an asshole. "Sometimes it takes an asshole to crack the whip and get your guys going," he said.

But he was also selfless, sometimes sacrificing himself to save a teammate.

It was a role he embraced. Instead of glorifying himself, he made the team better. He had studied communications and journalism in college at Indiana, and while he dropped out of school to play DOTA 2, his leadership would sometimes resemble an interview. "What do you need? How can I make your game go better?" he would ask his teammates.

As the spring of 2014 approached, the team prepared to play its first LAN tournament at the Monster Energy Invitational, with a modest $15,000 prize pool, but held on the prominent stage of SXSW, the tech and music gathering in Austin, Texas. And a win could transform the fate of the team that won. The winner of the tournament would likely receive a direct invitation to the fourth International to represent North America.

As he competed in his second LAN tournament, Arteezy felt a new emotion: uncertainty in himself. He was choking and dying too much. But his teammates bailed him out with their own stellar play, and Evil Geniuses beat EternaLEnVy's team in the finals. It was Evil Geniuses' first LAN victory in DOTA 2, after three years of failings, and EternaLEnVy was on the verge of tears from losing to his former upstart teammate.

Between April and June of 2014, the new Evil Geniuses become the most dominant team in North America's history, winning five more tournaments. Arteezy's greedy efficiency, ppd's leadership, Fear's stability, UNiVeRsE's playmaking, and zai's flexibility were almost unstoppable. And the roster was free from the drama that seemed to plague their constantly reshuffling peers. The team appeared unflappable, almost emotionless in the way it handled pressure. With its strong performance, Evil Geniuses got the elusive invite to compete in Seattle. This year, it wouldn't have to battle its way through the qualifiers.

But as the fourth International approached, Fear's arm began hurting. He saw medical specialists but nothing seemed to work. He couldn't practice for the eight or more hours needed to stay at the top of the game. So Evil Geniuses found a temporary stand-in, Mason "mason" Venne. He would say off-color things and was unpopular with some fans, but the team kept winning with him. Fear would be the team's coach, for now.

For the fourth International, Valve announced that the Compendium had returned, and the digital rewards were even more vast, with new items like new music and in-game emoticons that players could acquire after achieving various in-game goals. Or they could spend more money on top of the base $10 to unlock content faster, which led to a new surge. In a five days, the prize pool leaped to $5 million. It was now the biggest prize pool in eSports, bigger than the previous three Internationals combined. By August, the prize pool was $11 million, and the winner would get $5 million.

Evil Geniuses' most threatening opponent was Team DK, the Chinese superstars that Arteezy had beaten in his first tournament. The team was a darling, not just in the East, but also in the West. DK was creative, daring, and, perhaps most seductively, a group of five players that had never won an International. They always came one fight, one game, one play short of reaching the finals.

Evil Geniuses finished a powerful group stage with ten wins and four losses. There was one last game: Alliance. The Swedes, defending champions, had been battered by updates to the game that weakened their play style, and the previous year's championship had damaged their chemistry. With six wins and eight losses, Alliance could survive and make it to the playoffs only with a win against Evil Geniuses.

Evil Geniuses had clinched their upper-bracket spot and were guaranteed at least sixth place in the tournament, so they had far less pressure, although winning would still help their standings.

As the two teams prepared to play, Alexander Garfield got a surprise visitor. Erik Johnson, one of Valve's most senior managers, was worried about match-fixing. Garfield owned both teams, and Evil Geniuses could lose on purpose to let Alliance through. Garfield was taken aback. Of course both his teams would compete as hard as possible. And he planned to sit in the middle of the arena, away from all supporters of either team, and remain completely silent.

Evil Geniuses picked Omniknight, a Paladin healer usually shunned by top teams, which further fueled suspicions that they really were going to lose on purpose. But it turned out to be an effective pick. Alliance attempted a retro strategy, drafting the same Chaos Knight and Wisp that they had won with in the previous year's International. In a bitter forty-seven-minute slugfest that saw both teams' bases in tatters, Evil Geniuses triumphed. Alliance, the defending champions, were going home, and Evil Geniuses was ascendant.

In the playoffs, Evil Geniuses showed off some new strategies built around securing Roshan and toppled Team DK, who were seen as the tournament favorites, to advance.

But then Evil Geniuses faltered against the remaining Chinese teams, Vici and Newbee, and finished third. The finals were inexplicably held on Monday afternoon, already a bit of a hype killer, and the games were disappointing. The two teams had perfected the deathball strategy, focusing on winning team fights and then quickly crashing through the other team's towers and base. Newbee won three games, and Vici only managed one win, with no game lasting more than thirty minutes. Vici seemed paralyzed, picking the same heroes with the same poor results.

Newbee won over $5 million, and Vici won nearly $1.5 million. Evil Geniuses won over $1 million for third place. DOTA 2 lacked the stability of League of Legends' regulated tournament circuit, and its rival still had a much larger player base. But the aggressive crowdfunding model meant that DOTA 2's prize money was shattering precedents. And Evil Geniuses had made its mark, but it still wanted more.

Chapter 8

CAPITAL FLOOD

BIG MONEY COMES TO ESPORTS [AGAIN]

Hardcore video gamers, who are still largely male and in their twenties, present a dilemma for advertisers. The demographic represents enormous spending power, with billions of dollars, but they're hard to reach with the decline of traditional media, and they crave authenticity. Gaming is a bridge to consumer spending that marketers crave.

"You are not selling products to the eSports community. What you do sell is emotions. You create a bond between fans, players, organizations, and your brand that if cultivated properly is powerful enough to hold a lifetime," said Bjoern Franzen, an eSports consultant who has worked at SK Gaming, Razer, and AMD.

Despite millions in new investment money in recent years in teams, tournaments, and startups, the eSports industry remains a frontier, a digital Wild West that is being settled but still filled with danger. The spike in media coverage and focus on superstars suggest glamour and fortune, but for the vast majority of people, work is uncertain and job instability is common.

It isn't the first time capital has flooded the industry—DirecTV's CGS's prize pool is still one of the largest in the history of eSports, but that investment quickly fizzled, which devastated the American competitive scene.

The question now, amid the mid-2010s tech boom, is whether the growth in eSports investment is sustainable and a harbinger of an established industry with stable careers, or is it another bubble?

One sector of the eSports industry epitomizes the surge of money entering the space and has extracted millions of dollars for both investors and fans: betting websites.

Like sports betting, eSports betting allows fans to wager on the outcome of competitive matches. Typically, a host website will set odds and bettors will select which team they think will win. The house makes its profits by skimming a portion of bets for itself and paying out the rest to the winners.

Traditional sports betting sites have expanded to list competitions in League of Legends and StarCraft, such as the prominent betting website Pinnacle Sports, which registered its millionth eSports bet in December 2014. "It's eclipsing traditional sports like golf and rugby," said Philip Hudson, a former acquisitions manager at Pinnacle.

Pinnacle has sponsored its own tournaments and hired Jonathan "DarKFoRcE" Belke, a former StarCraft II pro gamer, as one of its eSports traders, who determine betting odds.

While betting is a source of fan engagement, it can also present a strong temptation for the professional players, who can match fix by betting against themselves and intentionally losing to make a profit. In the absence of stable salaries or prize winnings, it can often be more profitable to match fix and lose than to win. If discovered, the practice has ended careers and cast suspicion over the integrity of competition.

One of the first and largest scandals was in 2010, when Ma "sAviOr" Jae Yoon, one of the most renowned South Korean Star-Craft players, was implicated in an eleven-person match-fixing ring that stunned the country and led to a lifelong ban from competitive play. His championship titles were vacated. The Seoul Central Court sentenced him to 120 hours of community service and two years of probation.

In 2013, Russia's Alex "Solo" Berezin was a promising young player on the DOTA 2 squad Rox'Kis, when he was exposed as betting on the website Egamingbets against his team and losing on purpose in a game in the Starladder league. He was kicked off his team and received a one-year ban from Starladder, a punishment that some thought was too mild.

Solo reportedly won $322 from match-fixing, and "322" became a meme that viewers spam in Twitch chat when other teams make mistakes, suggesting that they're internationally throwing the match. Solo has since returned to play after his ban, but the nickname follows him.

The following year, Arrow Gaming, a young DOTA 2 team from Malaysia, was suspected of intentionally playing poorly during matches and betting accounts were linked to the players. Arrow player Kok Yi "ddz" Liong initially attempted to deflect blame and said their girlfriends had bet without their knowledge. A day later, he confessed to betting and said the team was "underpaid" and "were desperate for money."

"All that bottled-up anger led to the eventual match-fixing that, according to the players, was an act of revenge on the management as well as a way to earn some extra income to feed themselves," said Tiffani "Oling" Lim, the former manager of the DOTA 2 team Titan, who follows the Southeast Asia eSports scene closely. "That said, however, I don't think it should in any way justify their actions—match-fixing is wrong and should be punished severely no matter what made them do it."

Southeast Asian eSports suffers from lack of funding and tournaments with big prize pools. Some of the region's biggest stars have left to join Chinese teams, a much bigger market.

"China offers a lot more exposure for the players in terms of opportunities, as the scene there is much more advanced, with lots of money being pumped into the industry. However, with that comes a much higher level of pressure on the players to improve, and with the level of exposure, every move you make will be scrutinized," said Lim.

Male payers in Singapore face another challenge: a mandatory two-year national military service for all men at age eighteen. South Korea also has a similar policy, but is more flexible, requiring men to serve by age thirty-five.

"It highly limits the players' training schedule, and prevents the players from making any decisions to venture overseas or forming serious, full-time pro teams within those two years when they're eighteen and nineteen years old," said Lim.

In March 2014, a South Korean League of Legends player, Cheon "Promise" Min-Ki, said that financial pressures had driven him to attempt suicide by leaping from a twelve-story building. He said his coach had pressured him to match fix in order to cover the team's expenses. He only survived because his fall was broken by the roof of a recycling center, and while he was able to make a recovery, he dropped out from competing.

In January 2015, Valve banned seven players tied to match-fixing in Counter-Strike: Global Offensive from iBUYPOWER, a team sponsored by the computer maker of the same name, which lost suspiciously. The online news site Daily Dot published chat logs and screenshots that implicated the players. Valve banned them from Valve-sponsored events, which are the biggest tournaments in CS:GO, effectively ending their careers.

Despite the numerous examples and rumors of match-fixing, the betting scene powers on, with game developers who are unwilling or unable to stop the activity. Regulators have also been ineffective. The United States has banned Internet gambling since the Unlawful Internet Gambling Enforcement Act in 2006, and in October 2014, Singapore also passed legislation to block "remote" gambling through the Internet. But loopholes, such as using a virtual private network, allow the betting to continue in areas where it's banned.

The in-game economy of Valve's Steam platform has enabled a giant new gambling empire to emerge: DOTA 2 Lounge. The site began in July 2012 as an item marketplace. Players can bet on matches using in-game cosmetic items, with odds shifting depending on what team is more favored. Users win items and the Lounge takes a cut, although founder Rob Borewik has said that it doesn't turn a profit and the items are held as "reserves." It has also expanded into Counter-Strike: Global Offensive bets with CS:GO Lounge.

The site's legal status is hazy. Cosmetic items have value, from a few cents to thousands of dollars. But is betting cosmetic items the same as betting cash? It's an issue that the US government hasn't yet bothered to rule on.

Some are concerned that the ease of sites like DOTA 2 Lounge encourages young teenagers who play the games to become vulnerable to gambling addictions. The site itself doesn't require a credit card or any sort of verification to sign up—players just need to log in using the same free account information on Valve's Steam program that they use to play DOTA 2 and CS:GO. Valve has also made no move to block the site and allows its "bots," automated accounts that hold the items that have been bet, to use the service Steam. DOTA 2 Lounge says in its rules that users must confirm that they're following their local gambling laws, including being eighteen years or older. But many community members suspect that younger teenagers are using the site, since there are no enforced restrictions.

DOTA 2 Lounge and CS:GO Lounge are a big source of viewers, particularly to smaller tournaments. Bettors who use the site and have items at stake may care about obscure events that they would otherwise ignore. Betting also increases engagement and emotional excitement when something is on the line, a boon for tournament organizers. That power has led the sites to reportedly refuse to list games for smaller tournaments unless they provide free advertising to the sites by displaying their logos as part of the broadcast.

In September 2014, CS:GO Lounge reportedly demanded free advertising from DreamHack on the event's video stream or said it wouldn't list bets for the event. DreamHack refused and bets weren't listed for the early stages, but, perhaps in recognition that the event was too big to ignore, the site added later games.

The opportunity of expanding betting in eSports has attracted new players from the technology sector. Rahul Sood, the creator of startup incubator Microsoft Ventures, and his business partner Karl Flores launched an eSports betting site named Unikrn in April 2015, in partnership with Australia's Tabcorp. It raised $10 million in 2015, attracting celebrity investors like the actor Ashton Kutcher and billionaire Mark Cuban, owner of the NBA's Dallas Mavericks. "The rapid growth of eSports has created an entire new category of competition," Cuban said in a statement. Unikrn is careful about legality, only offering real-money betting outside the United States and noncash contests where gambling is illegal.

Daily fantasy sports have also entered the eSports sector, with an effort to differentiate itself from betting. As with the decades-old hobby of fantasy sports, participants draft players on their rosters and earnings points based on their performance. Coworkers and friends have played season-long fantasy leagues and usually earn little more than bragging rights, but daily fantasy has accelerated the payouts with contests that are held every day, with money changing hands.

One of the best-funded efforts to fuse eSports and daily fantasy is Vulcun, a website founded by Ali Moiz and Murtaza Hussain, who previously operated a League of Legends team with the same name. In April 2015, the website raised $12 million in Series A funding from investors, including top venture capital firm Sequoia Capital, Yahoo, Google Ventures, and Zynga. By June, it announced that a player named Yjingtong had won over $100,000 by playing on the site, more money than many of the pro gamers who actually competed in tournaments have earned.

Vulcun grew alongside FanDuel and DraftKings, the two biggest daily fantasy sites for traditional sports, each with valuations of over $1 billion. As the 2015 NFL season began, the sites blasted fans with constant television ads. They seemed to have support from within the league, as owners of the Dallas Cowboys and New England Patriots of the NFL bought stakes in DraftKings and Comcast and NBC invested in FanDuel.

The sites have portrayed themselves as a fun way for fans to be more passionate about the competition and show off their skills in picking players, and maybe win some money on the side. Proponents say fantasy sports, just like video gaming itself, aren't inherently harmful and shouldn't be outright banned like online betting has been. They seek to differentiate themselves from gambling by citing the ruling that fantasy sports is defined as a "game of skill," which is legal under US law.

For one thing, there are more decisions beyond betting's binary choice of who will win the match. Users of Vulcun and similar sites have to draft multiple players from a list of the teams competing, which supporters say takes skill.

And even if game publishers wanted to regulate betting and fantasy, they have limited tools. "Betting is not going anywhere. It's only going to get bigger. Fantasy's not going anywhere," said Edward Chang, who joined Vulcun as head of business development soon after it launched. "Publishers can't stop us from running fantasy. We might as well work together and see what we can do."

Riot, which operates its own fantasy league without cash prizes for fans lets Vulcun use images from League of Legends but won't allow the site to sponsor teams directly. Nick Allen, Riot's former director of North American league operations, said that the developer recognized that betting was legal outside of the United States and it was going to happen, so it didn't try to fight it and focused instead on being vigilant about match-fixing.

Valve, which also has some DOTA fantasy league support, in its typical hands-off fashion, doesn't care what Vulcun does.

Chang also claims that Vulcun and daily fantasy sites are more resistant to match-fixing, because scoring is based on stats like kills, deaths, and assists rather than just wins and losses. He says the site works to monitor suspicious behavior and communicates with publishers. But it also seeks to attract pro players to play on the sites themselves, and it sponsors tournaments directly. It's another example of eSports' limited ecosystem leading to potential conflicts of interest.

In September 2015, scandal rocked DraftKings and FanDuel. Ethan Haskell, a DraftKings employee, admitted to winning $350,000 on FanDuel by using information on the most popular players, a move described as insider trading.

A month later, Nevada, the epicenter of gambling, banned the sites and said they required gambling licenses to operate. Vulcun also ceased operations in the state as a precaution. The Department of Justice and the FBI investigated the sites to consider if they were gambling.

In November, Eric Schneiderman, New York's attorney general, banned daily fantasy sports in the state, pending an investigation. DraftKings and FanDuel are fighting the ban, which would destroy their business in one of the country's largest markets.

Vulcun responded by banning players from playing in New York and Nevada, but with more regulations potentially looming, it laid off a quarter of its staff in January and eliminated real-money prizes too. Chang was among the departures. Technology changes swiftly, particularly when billions of dollars are at stake.

The question of whether more money is good for eSports remains unsettled. It can mean more financial opportunity for all involved, but also a shift toward reliance on businesspeople and investors with no emotional ties to eSports. Their focus is revenue, users, and growth. That's all fine when the eSports industry is booming. But when the next downturn or crash happens, they're unlikely to have much loyalty to the people who built it and were invested purely on passion. "That's my biggest worry—it's just a lot of people trying to cash out," said Conrad Janzen, a former DOTA 2 team manager, who now works for Twitch.

Another favored target for direct eSports investment has been League of Legends' North American LCS. Riot has a rule that allows team owners to sell their spots at the end of seasons, which allows new owners to completely revamp player rosters and create new brands that are guaranteed one of the ten spots in the league in the next season. Riot allows team spots to be sold because it gives a way for owners to exit the obligations of running a team, said Nick Allen.

"We didn't want to trap owners into the LCS," he said. "We wanted teams to be able to make drastic changes if they weren't performing well."

As the LCS has grown, team spots have shot up in value. At the end of the 2015 season, three weaker teams' spots reportedly sold for between $800,000 and $1.2 million each, triple the price of the previous season.

The prominence of some of the new owners is also unprecedented: co-owners of the Sacramento Kings of the NBA bought a spot and formed a new LCS team called NRG eSports, which later attracted investment from sports megastars Shaquille O'Neal and Alex Rodriguez. The retired NBA champion Rick Fox also created a team called Echo Fox. The moves suggest that LCS owners aren't merely looking for wealth but also the cachet of team ownership.

The most successful new team through the first half of 2016 play is a team called Immortals, which drew a slew of investors from the video game outlet Machinima; Lionsgate Interactive Venture and Games; a co-owner of the Memphis Grizzlies; and Machine Shop Ventures, the investment arm of the superstar band Linkin Park.

Flush with cash, the new team signed up Seong "Huni" Hoon Heo and Kim "Reignover" Ui-jin, two of the South Korean–born stars of the European team Fnatic, which had finished in the semifinals of the 2015 world championships in the previous season. A team with such a strong result would usually avoid roster changes, but as Fnatic CEO Wouter Sleijffers acknowledged prior to the moves, the United States has a larger market for advertisers compared to Europe. Thus, European teams face challenges competing when it comes to getting big sponsorships and having the same resources in recruiting talent. The competitive disadvantage is compounded when the outside money dwarfs existing eSports teams.

Money is also changing the Challenger Series, the tournament that aspiring LCS teams must battle through to get promoted to the main tournament. It's potentially a cheaper way for new investors to get an LCS spot if they're able to field a strong enough roster that can qualify during the twice-a-year promotional playoffs. Team Ember, part of an eSports organization founded by former Riot employees, raised $2 million from Signia Venture Partners and, in an unprecedented move, published its player salaries, which started around $70,000 including bonuses. According to Ember's leadership, it was a move to increase transparency and show players what they were worth.

Some cheered the move, but one established team, Counter Logic Gaming, said that the numbers showed how venture capital was inflating and distorting the market. The team's CEO, Devin Nash, noted that the first investment round for some of the new teams dwarfs the entire value of teams that have been playing in the LCS for years, creating an "unhealthy" ecosystem.

"This ecosystem broadcasts one message: money wins," Nash wrote, adding that if the trend continued for a few years, "it's impossible to have an e-sports team unless you're a behemoth. You then lose classic brands who can't keep up, or cash out and don't choose to." And if revenue doesn't keep up with investment, the result is another collapse, with capital drawing back and salaries plummeting once more.

As one of the oldest League of Legends teams in North America, Counter Logic Gaming has seen firsthand the economic instability of eSports. Despite years of strong placements in the LCS, in early 2015, the team was days away from bankruptcy. The team recovered with a sponsorship from DraftKings, but a year later DraftKings dropped its eSports investments as it grappled with regulatory scrutiny. Another Counter Logic Gaming sponsor, the video game marketplace G2A, ran afoul of Riot after it sold League of Legends accounts and services to hire people to boost the rankings of accounts. Riot banned teams from displaying the site's logo on team jerseys during tournaments.

Investing in an LCS spot is also inherently more risky than buying an NBA or NFL team, because the league is structured so that any team can be eliminated if it performs poorly through the relegation system. The five-man roster also means a team's performance can vary wildly if it loses just one or two of its star players, compared to the larger rosters on sports teams.

In the spring of 2016, Ember advanced to the playoffs of the Challenger Series but failed to qualify for the LCS. Days later, the team released almost all of its players after its investors reportedly pulled out. It turned out that its high salaries were worthless if the team didn't win.

Consolidation and deal making remain in full swing in the eSports event space. In June 2015, Sweden's media conglomerate Modern Times Group (MTG), bought a majority stake in veteran eSports tournament organizer Turtle Entertainment, the parent company of ESL (Electronic Sports League), which is now the largest tournament organizer in the world. In November 2015, MTG also bought DreamHack for around $28 million, giving it dominance over the sector. A month later, Blizzard bought a faltering Major League Gaming for $46 million, less than the $67 million in equity funding that the company had raised.

Live events have become a crucial piece of legitimizing eSports as a cultural force and building a community. The challenge is in creating an experience that offers more than watching games online. In sporting events, there is an actual physicality to be seen on the field or rink. In eSports, the players are largely static, sitting in gaming chairs or soundproof booths.

ESL has sought to increase interaction between fans and players, with autograph sessions and sometimes games with fan participation. It also has hired side attractions like balloon makers and temporary-tattoo booths.

"It's about creating an experience," said Craig Levine, the former owner of Counter-Strike's Team 3D and now an executive at ESL, speaking at Kasico Research's 2015 eSport conference in San Francisco.

One of ESL's largest events is in Katowice, Poland. The city's economy was historically based on coal mining, but now it seeks to attract youth and tourism. It gives ESL economic incentives and marketing help, which has made it the location of one of the largest eSports events in the world despite its modest population of three hundred thousand.

Historically, eSports events haven't been held as often in primary cities like New York because of the numerous other entertainment options and the high cost of renting out venues, said Ulrich Schulze, managing director of pro gaming at ESL. But that's changed, and ESL has thrown two events at Madison Square Garden and the Commerzbank-Arena in Frankfurt. In New York, ESL worked with partners including ReedPOP, the event organizer behind Comic Con, and attracted big corporate sponsors including Pizza Hut and

T-Mobile US, Inc. to contribute to the event's roughly $1 million budget.

ESL now holds around fifteen big events and thirty to forty smaller online tournaments a year, about triple the amount that it held just a few years ago. "Most arenas are struggling a little bit," said Schulze. "So they're looking for new opportunities."

ESL also found itself unexpectedly taking a regulatory stand after Kory "Semphis" Friesen, a former player on Cloud9's Counter-Strike: Global Offense team claimed that the entire team had been using Adderall during a competition in 2015. Shortly afterwards, ESL said it would begin randomly drug testing, something that other tournament organizers have resisted doing because of regulatory uncertainty.

Riot, for example, declined to drug test because it may create an employer-employee relationship with its players, according to Nick Allen. That would subject it to having to pay benefits like health insurance, which the developer was unwilling to do.

The industry also continues to draw new large sponsors. One of eSports most deep-pocketed supporters is Red Bull, which makes the most popular energy drink in the world, with over $5.6 billion in revenue in 2014. The company's Santa Monica, California–based production arm, Red Bull Media House, produces event coverage of things like Felix Baumgartner's free fall from twenty-four miles above the Earth's surface, which drew fifty-two million live viewers on YouTube.

Red Bull popularized so-called extreme sports like snowboarding, skydiving, and biking, aiming its marketing toward younger viewers. And starting in 2011, it has been one of the biggest brands to invest heavily in eSports. It's sponsored individual players such as Call of Duty player Matt "NaDeSHoT" Haag, who has over two million subscribers on his YouTube channel. Red Bull was wary of investing in a violent game like Call of Duty, but Haag's charisma won them over, said a company official.

Red Bull has gone far beyond just throwing money at players. It's become an eSports event organizer itself, hosting over a dozen tournaments in StarCraft II since 2012 and branching into DOTA 2 in 2015. It combined gaming training with physical conditioning for pro gamers by flying them to the Red Bull North American headquarters in Santa Monica and mixing workouts with team-building exercises.

An ecosystem has also sprouted around community-based live events, growing out of community efforts to make eSports more social and personable. Glen Bower of Seattle started the first barcraft—a play on "bar" and "StarCraft"—in 2011, at Asian eatery Chao Bistro, which played StarCraft tournaments live on its televisions and featured a menu with dishes based on game characters. The owner couldn't keep up with demand. (The restaurant has since closed, but Barcraft became a staple of eSports.)

The *Wall Street Journal* covered another barcraft in San Francisco on its front-page A-hed section, reserved for offbeat stories. Some traditional sports fans were horrified by the weird games being broadcast through Twitch on televisions that normally had quarterbacks and point guards, not Marines and Siege Tanks.

AFK Lounge in San Jose is trying to take the barcraft model further. Founders Tyler Peckham and Kevin Isaac Wick met while studying business at San Jose State University around 2013. They wanted to create a gaming space that appealed to adults as well as younger gamers, which meant having a restaurant and bar.

The space opened in April 2015 in downtown San Jose, a city of around a million people, an hour south of San Francisco and a nexus in Silicon Valley. It is near the SAP Center, where the San Jose Sharks play, which has also hosted ESL tournaments.

The building's management was struck by AFK's different take on the restaurant model. Peckham recalls their reaction as "Hey, you guys are different from a normal bar. Our normal restaurants here can't bring anybody in when it's not a big Sharks game going."

AFK is also a team house, sponsoring teams for the games Heroes of the Storm and Smite. They live upstairs and play matches downstairs for work. AFK pays a one-time relocation fee and provides housing. The teams will play under the AFK name, but they are free to get other sponsors.

AFK Gamer Lounge is part of an effort to create a grassroots community and local loyalty to eSports teams. "Our goal is to create local economies for eSports," said Peckham. "We're using this to prove concept. If it works, there's no reason why you wouldn't have AFK teams everywhere."

As a newcomer, AFK Lounge ran into barriers from established eSports brands. "There's a very select few teams that are basically handling all of the marketing," said Peckham. "Sometimes when you don't want to work with them, they start to throw their weight around and it starts to close doors in other places. They potentially view us as a threat."

A challenge to growth is luring more mainstream companies, such as tech and other corporations. There are cultural biases: traditional television is still seen as more influential compared to online video, and many potential investors don't get gaming at all.

"They throw huge dollar values at TV commercials because Nielsen ratings say that ten million people are watching it," said

Peckham. "You get that same statistic proving ten million people are watching eSports. But because it's the Internet and because it's computer gamers, it's not validated in the same way.

"The people that are controlling budgets at top-tier companies are more likely of the generation that doesn't understand eSports yet. As those are replaced, it becomes easier and you notice it when a company has a young marketing team, a team that understands new demographics. They want to throw money at a place like this.

"Whereas other companies, you have to be like, 'This is a computer game, and people play them competitively for money,' and they're like, 'So like, Pac Man?'"

Chapter 9

THE ROAD TO
$18 MILLION

THE FIFTH INTERNATIONAL

At the end of 2014, Alexander Garfield wasn't satisfied. He had established Alliance and Evil Geniuses as top teams, but he moved to sign more DOTA squads as rosters shuffled after the fourth International. Garfield had grown beyond just Evil Geniuses, establishing GoodGame Agency, an eSports company that acted as a player agent, marketing firm, and content creator, so adding more players to connect with advertisers was a natural move.

Garfield was in talks with some of the most popular Western players to form a new top DOTA 2 team, beginning with buyouts of two players from Fnatic: Johan "N0tail" Sundstein, a cherubic Dane; and Tal "Fly" Aizik, a beefy guy from Israel whose father, Moni Aizik, created the martial art Commando Krav Maga. Fnatic had been fan favorites but had never achieved a big win.

They would join Na'Vi's two support players, Clement "Puppey" Ivanov and Kuro "KuroKy" Takhasomi, who were disappointed with the team's poor finish at the fourth International. Na'Vi's charismatic, reckless play had obscured a major weakness: they barely practiced. It wasn't a big deal when they could rely on their phenomenal skills, but as other teams began adding coaches, analysts, and training regimes, Na'Vi's results had slipped, and they were eliminated in the first round of the 2014 International's playoffs.

The fifth member of the team would be Gustav "s4" Magnusson, the Swedish superstar who was looking to leave Alliance, which had had an even worse tournament, having been eliminated by Evil Geniuses before the playoffs had started. The formation of the new team would shatter Garfield's first successful DOTA 2 squad.

Puppey and KuroKy were also tired of the lack of financial transparency on Na'Vi. After they won a string of tournaments, they had received only a modest raise, even though Na'Vi had become a worldwide darling They wanted more say in the direction of their team and better insight into the economics of a team, something Garfield was willing to do.

But then things changed. KuroKy had been leading negotiations, and it soon became apparent that the deal with GoodGame Agency was going to fall through. Discussions broke down and they became one of the only major DOTA 2 teams where the players controlled the company, despite Fly, N0tail, and s4 still being contracted to Garfield's GoodGame Agency. It would be called Team Secret. "Kuro just ended up being a very smooth character," said Garfield. "We never got paid for any of them."

There was little he could do. Team Secret was made up of some of the most popular players in all of DOTA 2. There was no way to fight a breach of contract without more damaging publicity, something that Garfield had dealt with in other games.

"I have a lot of respect for the guy. He was a very convincing person to the public and these players that he recruited," said

Garfield of KuroKy. "His biggest strength was having enough blind belief in himself."

Team Secret soon emerged as a new kind of team: players controlled the brand, and therefore didn't have to give up a cut of their prize winnings to a corporation. But winning was even more critical for Team Secret's survival, because it didn't have sponsors. Garfield wanted another team, but instead he got a new rival.

Garfield's moves had raised concerns even at the hands-off Valve, which barely regulated DOTA 2. Riot Games had also previously prevented Garfield from directly owning both an Alliance team and an Evil Geniuses team in the LCS, so he had licensed the brands to two separate owners.

A subsequent revision to the league rules required the teams to completely rebrand, so they became Winterfox and Elements. These moves perpetuated the idea that Garfield was always trying to expand his reach, and other owners were worried that he was breaking rules. Garfield denies this, and said owning more teams was never about his own personal glory.

If his company, GoodGame Agency, offered the best marketing and management and business relationships, why shouldn't more teams want to work with him?

Despite millions of dollars in annual revenue, Evil Geniuses and GoodGame Agency had never been profitable, he said, because he kept reinvesting the funds into new teams and new games. "That was self-inflicted in the sense that we didn't have to keep recruiting," he said. Garfield's own salary had maxed out at $60,000 a year, although he had perks like an apartment in pricey San Francisco.

Garfield didn't have a family to support like his old rival Jason Lake of compLexity, and that allowed him to make splashier deals with six-figure salaries. It also allowed him to invest in players of less lucrative competitive games like Street Fighter because he thought it was a cool thing to do.

Treating players better and giving them more money was something that he emphasized. "I'm very proud of that, even though in retrospect it was a pretty foolish, high-risk business decision," he said. "I had that leg up. I was young and hungry."

But he didn't like what he saw in the rest of the industry. Players usually didn't know how much money their teams, such as Na'Vi, were making off of their success, and compensation around the industry was usually a mystery. "I felt our business model was broken because we were paying players really well, but we couldn't win their trust because there was no transparency in the model," said Garfield. To help eSports move forward, Garfield felt, he needed a bigger platform. He had to give up some control.

Garfield knew that Twitch's leaders, Emmett Shear and Kevin Lin, were gamers themselves and shared his passion. And he wanted more resources and more certainty. On December 9, 2014, Twitch, which had just sold itself to Amazon a few months prior, announced that it had acquired GoodGame for an undisclosed sum. Garfield was now an employee of Amazon CEO Jeff Bezos. "I believed that selling at that time would allow me to be more of like a stabilizing influence," said Garfield.

It was a hard choice. As a big Dilbert fan, he wasn't into bosses, and for around a decade, he had operated Evil Geniuses as an independent empire. But now he was giving that up.

It was important for Garfield, who had shunned the spotlight, to get the right message out this time. He was worried about being seen as a sellout, and he crafted a letter to the community that highlighted his passion for eSports and desire to help more players, teams, and tournaments find success. The financial upside was relevant, but he wasn't going to cash out on his life's work.

The eighteen GoodGame Agency employees moved from their loft-like offices in San Francisco's South of Market into the Twitch office at 225 Bush Street, with its endless snacks. Before the sale, they were all independent contractors with no health insurance, and now they had benefits.

Garfield is adjusting to the new, more corporate culture. GoodGame's once-independent staff took a room in a corner of the Twitch office. Trophies gleam along the wall. Garfield's desk is in the corner, by the window.

But team owners' concerns have intensified that Garfield is seeking to control more of the industry now that he has the backing of Twitch. He is trying to balance seemingly conflicting goals. Does he want to have the best team in the world? Or does he want to make eSports the biggest entertainment industry in the world, even if he loses a competitive edge? He's still figuring that out.

On Garfield's left arm, he has a tattoo with words from Homer's Iliad: "The old horseman Peleus urging his son Achilles, 'Now always be the best, my boy, the bravest, and hold your head up high above the others.'" It's an aspirational message, not a flaunting of ego, a motto for his work and the child that he might have one day. "It's the kind of thing I would want to tell my son," he said.

But would he want his kids to work in eSports, knowing all the obstacles and potential pain?

"I would not push them into eSports any more than I would push them into any other activity," said Garfield. "One of the biggest gifts that my parents gave me was really the ability to choose what I did with my time as long as it was appropriately balanced in different areas.

"I would be very unhappy with my children only playing video games and neglecting their education and physical health. That would be unacceptable."

For the Evil Geniuses DOTA 2 squad, the priority was winning the next International. The fall of 2014 was centered on one roster spot: was Fear, who had been the team's coach, healthy enough to play? His arm was still pained, but he had recovered to the point where the team wanted him back. Despite the team's third-place finish at the International, Mason, who had joined the team originally as a substitute, was kicked out. Mason didn't have a good attitude about practicing and had insulted other players during practice games with racial slurs. Some of his teammates no longer wanted to play with him. He had won over $230,000 in prize money in four months.

As the top Western team of the year, Evil Geniuses could have signed almost any player, but ultimately it was Fear who regained his spot. Ppd initially had his doubts. For someone who had been playing DOTA 2 since the first International, Fear had few accomplishments. But he was a stabilizing force, rarely having a bad game. And he backed up ppd's leadership, telling ppd to make a choice with confidence in moments of doubt.

Evil Geniuses' players lived far apart—in California, Indiana, Canada, and Sweden—so practicing against the better European teams was challenging, since they would insist on playing on the Luxembourg server, which led to lag. Evil Geniuses dwarfed all the American teams, so finding good local practice partners was also difficult.

When the team played scrimmages against other teams, Arteezy and zai would lose focus and find it hard to play seriously. A front-page story on eSports in the *New York Times* quoted ppd criticizing a teammate during a scrim: "I can't play DOTA this way," he said. "What you're doing makes no sense. Just follow your teammates." That teammate was Arteezy.

The solution was playing online tournament matches against teams as practice, and the lack of scrims didn't appear to hurt the team's results. In the fall of 2014, they won Starladder in Ukraine and DreamHack in Sweden, taking home about $140,000 between the two tournaments. They won despite not understanding the metagame and learning things on the fly. "We still won everything, but we had no real practice," said Charlie Yang, the team's manager. "Lack of practice led to resentment."

The team had played four big tournaments in three continents over three months. They had been successful but were fatigued. It was a stressful time, and fissures developed.

A disagreement over the best strategy for the current version of the game emerged. The metagame had changed since the twenty-minute deathballs of the fourth International. Arteezy believed that a team needed to have a powerful late-game carry hero, with four players making space for one hero—his hero—to get all the glory. Ppd was unconvinced.

Simmering tensions erupted at the Summit 2, an intimate tournament held at the house of casting studio Beyond the Summit, in a suburb of Los Angeles. In the semifinals, Evil Geniuses faced Arteezy's old friend EternaLEnVy once again. EternaLEnVy's team was now signed as a division of the prominent team Cloud9, a League of Legends stalwart. But even with the new branding, Evil Geniuses had a seemingly insurmountable psychological advantage, having never lost to them in a LAN.

Evil Geniuses played in a dim, spare room at the Beyond the Summit house, with only their computers for illumination. A webcam recorded their reactions for a secondary Twitch stream. The team's mechanical keyboards were a constant clank, punctuated by terse communications. Evil Geniuses jumped to a six-kill lead, destroying Cloud9's trio of outer towers and kept the pressure up. But then a few fights turned against them.

"We fucking see them. We just let them jump on us. What is the reasoning for that?" said ppd.

"How do we stop them from jumping on us? What do we do?" asked Arteezy.

"Just walk away. You have to kite them through all of this," said ppd.

There was silence. Then Fear murmured, "There's no way I should have died there."

"We fucking see them walk on us and we just sit there and hit the tower. Panda got a four-man, like three-man Clap there. It doesn't even make sense," said ppd, referring to Cloud9's Brewmaster hero hitting three Evil Geniuses players with his Thunder Clap ability.

No one responded.

A few minutes later, Evil Geniuses lost another team fight. Their early lead was a mirage. "I'm dead. This game's lost," said ppd, as he typed out "Good Game." "All right, go new?"

He took two gulps of Monster Energy (a team sponsor), took off his headset, and left.

"There's no way we can win this game," said Arteezy.

"We want to do this push strategy but no one's calling to go down a lane and push a lane," said Fear.

"You can't even win with this team fight. That's why no one's calling, 'cause they're hesitant, 'cause they know they can't win a fight so they don't want to just send everyone—just go down a lane and suicide," said Arteezy.

"If we can't group up and push, this strat's fucking garbage," said Fear.

"It is garbage," said Arteezy.

"Well, it's hard to push into Panda," said UNiVeRsE, the teammate who rarely spoke, trying to calm the mood. The recording ended.

Evil Geniuses came back and won the next two games, setting up a decisive game five.

They battled for over an hour, but after a crucial fight, Cloud9 destroyed two-thirds of Evil Geniuses' base. They had never been challenged so fiercely.

Then, it looked like a comeback. At sixty-six minutes, Evil Geniuses wiped all five players on Cloud9 and marched toward their base. Arteezy advanced with Naga Siren, one of the most powerful late-game heroes, and Fear's insectoid hero Weaver laid siege with searing, armor-piercing attacks, demolishing one, then two sections of Cloud9's base. Suddenly, the teams were on even footing.

But Cloud9 turned it, killing Fear and coming back. EternaLEnVy played the hero Faceless Void, a violent brute whose signature ability, Chronosphere, encases and freezes heroes, ally or foe, as Void bashes them in. His final Chronosphere caught Arteezy and Fear in their base, and Cloud9 had triumphed for the first time.

Ppd and Arteezy had slight smiles as cameras followed them after the game, but they were seething. Arteezy believed that playing for a long game was the better strategy, but it turned out that his friend and one-time mentor EternaLEnVy could execute the strategy even better, at least this one time.

Evil Geniuses was eliminated from competing in the finals, but they had to play Team Secret, which had lost its quarterfinals, to decide the third-place team. Despite the prize difference of $18,000, playing more games was a burden. For the perennial champions, it was perhaps a humiliation. For Team Secret, it was another unsatisfying result for a roster made of top players. Evil Geniuses were stomped 3–0 by Secret, who were also disappointed by failing to reach yet another finals. Secret had been heralded as a dream team, but their results had been mediocre. And Cloud9's victory over Evil Geniuses was only a temporary triumph, as it fell to the elite Chinese team Vici Gaming in the Summit's grand finals.

"It got pretty cancerous," said Yang. "Artour and Peter had a big argument."

Arteezy rebooked his flight and immediately flew home.

Zai mingled with his competitors, and spoke with Team Secret. The superstar squad wasn't winning, and they needed changes too. They were planning to kick out Tal "Fly" Aizik. Did he want to join?

Zai had one stipulation: take Arteezy, too.

But Arteezy didn't want to leave Evil Geniuses after one loss. He thought his team just needed to communicate better. It was clearly still a top contender. He met with his teammates. They would keep fighting together.

In 2014, Evil Geniuses had earned over $1.5 million, second only to Vici Gaming and Newbee, the top two teams of the fourth International. Evil Geniuses was no longer known for giving up big leads and failing to qualify for tournaments. It was now one of the best teams in the world.

There was one last game before Christmas, a semifinals match in the small tournament DotaPit, against Virtus.pro Polar, a

Russian squad that was the organization's B-team. Again, it went to a game five, and again, the game surpassed sixty minutes. And again, Evil Geniuses lost.

"Everything we talked about was completely not there. It felt like there was a complete disconnection. Zai kept on feeding. I kept on getting mad because we were playing like retards," Arteezy later reflected on his Twitch stream.

"Artour took that loss and thought it meant more than it actually did," said Yang. "For him, it was a culmination of all the issues he had with Peter in the last two months."

Arteezy began to reconsider. If he joined Team Secret with zai, he would be playing with Puppey, a towering leader who had led Na'Vi to glory, and s4, the Alliance midlane champion. KuroKy, who had been playing carry, would even switch back to the support position to accommodate him.

He didn't sleep well for three nights as he finalized his decision. "You have to be selfish in what you do to be successful. If that means you have to break some friendships . . . to get what you want, it's worth it," he said on his Twitch stream. "I want to win so bad so that other things like temporary friendship and temporary praise to me doesn't matter. I just want to win so I can satisfy myself."

KuroKy had already convinced three players to ignore Alexander Garfield's contracts. Soon it would be five. Team Secret also kicked Johan "N0tail" Sundstein to make room for Arteezy. "They didn't care that Artour was still contracted," said Yang, Evil Geniuses' manager. "Secret is all about first place."

Garfield was willing to take other measures to make Arteezy stay. But he asked Yang if he thought the team would be stronger without Arteezy. Yang said yes.

Their partnership—and their friendship—had splintered, and Evil Geniuses couldn't go on. "I think it was an absolute necessity for EG to get a roster change, for EG to be reborn again, to be a good team again," said Arteezy.

Traditional sports has many tales of superstars switching allegiances, and money is often the deciding factor. Personal loyalty means little when millions are on the line. But it isn't just economic considerations that drive roster switches.

"If you have a player that you used to enjoy playing with, but then his attitude starts changing or he gets complacent because you have a sponsor, you don't want to play with that type of person ever again," said Ioannis "Fogged" Loucas, a former Evil Geniuses player who has struggled to compete on a stable team. "It just completely destroys your view on them. Even if they were great to play with at first, that stuff just tarnishes it completely."

Arteezy and zai's move set off a chain of shuffling. N0tail, now off Secret, reached out to Cloud9, and an unsuspecting Aui_2000 put him in touch with EternaLEnVy. Aui_2000 thought the team would work through their issues, too. After all, they had just beaten Evil Geniuses. It was time to enjoy the holidays. Then EnVy wrote six sentences to him in Skype, and he was out along with his teammate Johan "pieliedie" Åström. They were replaced by N0tail and Rasmus "MiSeRy" Filipsen, another European player.

"I think the idea that you form a team with your friends—it's almost like a pipe dream. It doesn't really happen," said Yang. "Alliance was a rare, rare case. The chemistry that existed within that team is something that you're not going to have again. It's better to have a business-like relationship with your teammates. You can be friendly with them, but I think founding a team on friendship and loyalty first is not healthy to yourself."

Evil Geniuses now had to replace two players. They asked everywhere for replacements, but it was a sharp contrast to just a few months before, when everyone wanted to be on the squad. Without Arteezy and zai, they were seen as weak, as the losers of the reshuffle. Ppd was unsure if the team would be good anymore.

Evil Geniuses had to gamble, and there was another teen prodigy who had displayed skill in the in-house league: Syed "SumaiL" Hassan, a sixteen-year-old who grew up in Karachi, Pakistan. In his native country, SumaiL didn't have his own computer and had to travel to the Internet cafe. He even had to sell his bicycle to fund his passion.

SumaiL had moved in the previous spring to a suburb of Chicago with his family, fitting two parents and six kids in a three-bedroom apartment. All he cared about was DOTA 2. He was a top player on the public ladder, but he had never before played at a live tournament. But his mechanical skills were so impressive that he was recommended for the team.

Yang flew to Chicago to talk to SumaiL's mother, Huma. He was reportedly offered a salary of around $4,000 a month. SumaiL would stay in school and attend classes in between playing at tournaments around the world, and Yang talked to his teachers to work out his schedule. Yang would later inadvertently admit on a Twitch stream to doing SumaiL's homework to ensure that he attended a tournament.

Then, Evil Geniuses got news that Aui_2000 was available. It was serendipitous. Aui_2000 had almost the same hero pool as the recently departed zai, and they both played as greedily as they could, letting the other support sacrifice themselves for the team.

Aui_2000 joined, and the new Evil Geniuses was complete. The new lineup would be tested almost immediately at the DOTA 2 Asia Championships, at the beginning of 2015. The Chinese tournament used a crowdfunding program similar to the International, and the prize pool ballooned to $3 million.

With the addition of Arteezy and zai, Team Secret dominated with an undefeated run in the group stage, winning fifteen straight games. But then they faltered in the semifinals against a resurgent Evil Geniuses, losing in two straight games. It was sweet revenge, as SumaiL demonstrated that he was a supremely talented player, winning matchups in the midlane with heroes where he should have had huge disadvantages. "It was just ridiculous the things that he did," said ppd. "It was unheard of the lanes he was winning."

In a one-versus-one matchup, SumaiL was dominant, but his skill had to be tempered with caution. DOTA is a team game, and the midlane is often the focus of aggressive rotations by supports. SumaiL would take risks to secure more last hits, leaving him exposed to unfair fights. "In his mind, winning the lane is more important than winning the game," said ppd.

In the finals against the Chinese team Vici Gaming, SumaiL controlled a hero named Storm Spirit, which relies on a strong early game. As he gathers more kills and items, Storm Spirit's mana pool grows, allowing him to zip across the battlefield with his Ball Lightning ability, becoming unstoppable. But in the early game, he is slow and vulnerable, and Vici's supports abused that fact. SumaiL was killed four times in the opening minutes.

"OK, I'm mad now," he said in the booth. This time, he didn't need ppd's direction, and he roared back and finished with seventeen kills. Evil Geniuses won another $1.2 million to start 2015. The new blood sustained them as a powerhouse.

"One less ego one more championship," ppd posted on Twitter after the victory.

In May and June, the new Team Secret finally found its stride, winning four major LANs on three continents and beating Evil Geniuses twice in finals. It was reminiscent of Alliance's dominance in 2013, and the upcoming International seemed like it could be a coronation.

KeyArena sits in an urban park called Seattle Center, just beyond the shadow of the city's iconic Space Needle. It is surrounded by lush trees and lawns and a fountain. In August 2015, it hosted the fifth International, the most lucrative eSports tournament ever. Fans, with their insatiable appetite for digital items, propelled the International 5's prize pool to $18 million, bigger than the first four Internationals combined. First place would win $6.6 million. The huge prize pool was a testament to the intensity of the players and the depths of their connection to the game. It was also a sign of Valve's marketing brilliance.

The challenge for Valve was making a physical space for a digital event compelling. They transformed the stadium, decorating it with DOTA characters draped in banners over the façade leading to the entrance. A viewing screen was set up in a grassy field.

Arsenio Navarro, a jolly guy with an easy laugh, is Valve's "shopkeeper," who heads up the company's merchandising and physical products. He works with item creators to produce a slew of T-shirts, figurines, mouse pads, and other trinkets, ranging from $20 for a plush doll to over $200 for a keyboard, which are all sold at the Secret Shop, a merchandise booth at the tournament whose name is a reference to an in-game location. Some of the items come with in-game digital chests. Independent artists, known as workshop creators, designed many of the items, and they got their own gallery in KeyArena.

Valve rented out private suites for all sixteen teams, their logos pulsing in groups of four around the arena. As teams were eliminated their logos dimmed into shadows.

Before the six-day main event, the teams played a grueling four-day group stage at the Westin Seattle. A total of 120 games were played and broadcast on three concurrent Twitch streams. Each team played about fourteen games.

As expected, Team Secret and Evil Geniuses dominated, along with the Chinese stalwart LGD Gaming, now led by xiao8, the former leader of the champion from the previous year, Newbee. But one upstart surprised everyone: CDEC Gaming, which performed nearly as well as Evil Geniuses and was placed into the upper bracket for the playoffs.

The team had started by gathering talent from an in-house league in China, the Chinese DOTA Elite Community, where amateurs practiced together. It was originally affiliated with LGD, but was spun off into its own organization. CDEC's players were relative unknowns. They had placed second at a few Chinese tournaments but had never won a LAN.

CDEC showed a mastery of the game's strategy, with their carry Sun "Agressif" Zheng living up to his name, fighting early. The team invaded their opponent's territory, frequently bullying their way to controlling more territory.

On August 3, the main event began at KeyArena. Gabe Newell, Valve's chief executive, made a brief appearance and told an anecdote about how he and his coworkers had traveled to the previous year's Super Bowl where their hometown team, the Seattle Seahawks, was playing. Instead of watching football, they just wanted to play DOTA. A live orchestra played the game's theme, and a video retrospective highlighted the tough road that the teams had taken to get to the tournament.

Kacey Atkinson, a local television news reporter, was hired to host the tournament for the third year and acted as a bridge to the wider world. She was not a gamer, but was amazed by the passion. Despite being a neophyte to gaming culture, she became a fixture at the event. The tournament is also notable for its lack of ads. The massive crowdfunded prize pool means that no sponsors are needed.

Na'Vi, a shell of its former self, had finished near the bottom of the group stages. On the first day of the main event, Na'Vi faced Vici Gaming, the second-place finisher from the previous year and was eliminated. "Na'Vi! Na'Vi!" the crowd chanted as the Ukranians lost.

Evil Geniuses picked compLexity in the first round in the winner's bracket. It had been almost seven years since Alexander Garfield poached Jason Lake's Counter-Strike team, but here was an unexpected chance for revenge at the biggest tournament in the history of eSports. CompLexity got off to a strong start in the first game, but then an Internet problem paused the game for nearly two hours. When the game resumed, Evil Geniuses came back and took the series.

In the other upper-bracket match, Team Secret unexpectedly lost to China's EHOME, falling to the bottom bracket in the double-elimination tournament. Arteezy said they had been too cocky, but he said in a post-game interview that he was glad that Secret had lost and would be forced to play more games. "Playing elimination changes the team. It forms more trust and more unity," he said. But in reality, tensions were boiling. KuroKy, the cerebral German player who had masterminded the formation of the team, was irking Arteezy.

In the winner's bracket, CDEC upset LGD with an aggressive strategy. They had secured a top-three finish, an unprecedented result for a team that hadn't received a direct invitation and had battled through qualifiers to even appear at the main event.

Evil Geniuses faced EHOME in the quarterfinals, the team that had knocked Secret to the lower bracket. The half-full crowd roared "USA! USA!" and did the wave. They were the last American hope in a sea of Chinese teams, which made up four of the top six teams.

They lost the first game but then shocked the Chinese by picking the hero Techies in the second game. Techies is unlike any other, relying on placing invisible mines around the map, completely changing the game. The character was seen as a joke. But ppd's brother, who played DOTA 2 casually, had played hundreds of games with the hero and taught Aui_2000 a plethora of unexpected places to hide mines. The chaotic playstyle of the hero caught EHOME completely off guard. For the rest of the tournament, the Chinese teams would ban Techies in the pregame draft, giving Evil Geniuses a strategic edge.

In the lower bracket, Team Secret faced off against Virtus.pro, the same team that Arteezy and zai had played their final match against as members of Evil Geniuses. In the third and decisive game of the series, Arteezy played the soul-stealing demon Shadow Fiend, standing tall as he tried to bring his team back against an early ten-kill deficit, sometimes fighting alone against multiple opponents. But the Russians were relentless, and Team Secret, despite its dominant streak, were eliminated. The players were visibly bickering in the booth. Arteezy said that KuroKy was a horrible teammate, and KuroKy later dismissed Arteezy as young and emotional. Evil Geniuses would never face Team Secret in the entire tournament.

"I could have tried harder to bring out the best in s4 and tried to ignore my hate for Kuro. I could have done more, but I blew the fuck up," Arteezy later said on Twitch.

217

After Secret's defeat, Alexander Garfield was outside the arena and saw Arteezy, who managed to muster a "hey."

"I'm sorry," said Garfiel as they walked passed each other.

A minute later, Garfield saw zai, who wanted a hug.

"I hope you guys win," he told Garfield.

"Yeah, I hope so too," Garfield remembers saying.

But before the tournament moved forward, it was time for an annual tradition: the All Star Game, where fans selected their favorite ten players to battle each other. This year, Dendi dressed up in a Pudge costume for the All Star Game. The Na'Vi star had been eliminated, but he was still making people smile.

In the next round, Evil Geniuses played the surprising upstarts CDEC and lost swiftly, dropping down to the lower bracket for the first time. Aui_2000 despaired, bringing the team down. It was shades of the defeatism of Cloud9—who had already been eliminated from the tournament—and an attitude that ppd wouldn't tolerate. The team had overcome so much, and they would have a chance to come back the next day.

August 8, 2015. Championship Saturday. American flags with the Evil Geniuses logo replacing the stars were distributed to hype up the crowd while CDEC fans countered with Chinese flags.

In the lower-bracket finals, Evil Geniuses overcame LGD, with the hometown support roaring its approval, setting up a rematch with CDEC.

The teams traded wins, and Evil Geniuses went up two games to one. CDEC was terrified of Aui_2000's Techies and banned it every single game.

In the twenty-eighth minute of the fourth game, Evil Geniuses was up fourteen kills to seven. SumaiL had died a few times but was greedily positioned in CDEC's jungle. They glimpsed his character and feigned a move up the midlane, before pouncing and chain-stunning SumaiL's signature Storm Spirit. With Evil Geniuses' most dangerous hero dead, CDEC took a gamble, rushing to the Roshan Pit and grouping up as five.

They didn't see ppd and UNiVeRsE approaching. Ppd's hero Ancient Apparition launched Ice Blast, a ball of frost that devastates a circular zone. UNiVeRsE's hero, Earthshaker, was attuned to punishing proximity with his Echo Slam ability, which does more damage when opponents are clustered in one area. CDEC was exposed, and four of the five players immediately died to the crash of ice and earth. Evil Geniuses rode the momentum and didn't look back.

In the end it wasn't SumaiL who had the play that defined the victory. It was the quiet UNiVeRsE and ppd, the less flashy players on the team.

Good game.

A flash of sparks engulfed the stage's perimeter. Golden confetti streamed from the ceiling. Evil Geniuses yelped in their booths and embraced as five. They walked out to a roar from their hometown crowd, shaking hands with CDEC before approaching the white pillar where the golden Aegis of Champions was embedded. After a moment, ppd lifted the Aegis. Aui was speechless, only sputtering and grinning when he was asked how he felt. The team seemed dazed. They were exhausted after playing six games.

From the player suites, Arteezy smiled. He was jealous, but he couldn't help but be happy, especially for Fear, who had been striving for the victory for five years.

"That was EZ," the always cocky SumaiL tweeted.

With the $6.6 million win, Evil Geniuses more than doubled its total prize winnings, shooting up to $11 million, the most of any team in eSports history. Every Counter-Strike struggle, every

StarCraft II win, the short-lived League of Legends teams—it was all eclipsed. And it was the biggest eSports win ever for North America.

After the victory, the team gathered on the second-floor suite. SumaiL drank a soda, wearing his neck pillow. Ppd held the Aegis. There was no post-game press conference, but the players filmed interviews with a camera crew on the side. ESPN would broadcast a documentary a few months later.

The team walked past a giant line of fans to board a black bus and prepared to head to the after-party. Alexander Garfield stood outside, wearing a backpack and smiling, but didn't get on. He had expected the victory. He was looking forward to throwing a celebration for the fans who weren't in Seattle, back at Evil Geniuses and Twitch's hometown of San Francisco.

Later that night, a *thump, thump* reverberated in the silvery EMP Museum for the International's after party, filling the silvery structure designed by architect Frank Gehry. Pulled pork, noodles, and mashed potatoes were spread through the venue. EternaL-EnVy and Arteezy sat together on a couch, rising to take photos with fans. Their tournaments had been a bust, but they were still adored. "Anyone got a lighter?" Arteezy asked around, and the two walked away into the night. They would talk about creating a team together and pairing their formidable carry skills in the next year.

On the Friday evening the week after the International, Aui_2000 uploaded a video on his YouTube channel detailing some of his practice regime. His mom had redecorated his room in Vancouver to read "Aui_1000000+" in reference to his prize winnings, and he posted a photo on Twitter to his ninety thousand followers. Garfield retweeted him. Meanwhile, Arteezy was streaming on Twitch.

The day shifted to early evening, and the sun faded from the West Coast. At 6:40 p.m., Aui_2000 posted a Tweet: "i have been kicked from eg after winning ti. i actually hate people."

Fans were flabbergasted. Had he been hacked? Two of his heroes, Techies and Naga Siren, had been considered too dangerous by the Chinese, who had used two of their hero bans to ensure he couldn't play them. Sixteen minutes later, Aui_2000 posted again, "can someone from eg just fucking confirm so idiots stop tweeting me its fake."

Three minutes later, SumaiL chimed in: "@Arteezy is joining EG."

Aui_2000 had been backstabbed, fans said. Ppd was an awful person. Evil Geniuses was a terrible organization that didn't care about its players, and perhaps they wanted Arteezy back because he was better for sponsorships.

But no team has ever won the International twice. Every winner has gone on to stagnate, leading to future roster shuffles and failures. Loyalty and friendship may be second to business. The team was doing what it felt was best, said ppd.

The backlash grew, and the following Tuesday, August 18, ppd wrote a blog post while he was on vacation at St. John in the Caribbean to defend himself. Despite their victories, playing with Aui_2000 had become unbearable. He "talked a lot but said very little," and questioned ppd's leadership. After the first loss to CDEC, he had brought the team down. There was no amount of winning that could be worth the amount of stress that he caused, said ppd, and the rest of the team agreed. Aui_2000 had been welcomed onto the team in part because of necessity, because the team had had to fill a spot. And while his work ethic and game knowledge were world class, he would panic and overwhelm the team's communications. Afterward, ppd regretted making the comments, but he had felt the need to defend himself in the face of thousands of hateful messages.

Plus, the team wanted Arteezy back. He had reconciled with ppd, with both apologizing in private messages. He was coming home, an older and more mature player.

When he got back from vacation, ppd moved from Indiana to San Francisco, where Garfield had relocated years before, and Justin Kan and his friends had built their dream company. Sure, he could save money by living in the Midwest, but now was the time to enjoy life in the big city.

A few days later, Aui_2000 announced his new team had formed, Digital Chaos. And Valve announced that the International would no longer be the only huge tournament of the year. In an effort to provide some structure, there would be three other big tournaments, known as Majors, each with a $3 million prize pool. The first one would be in just a few months in the fall, in Frankfurt.

There was always another tournament, another goal, and now, another rival to beat. Competition was eternal, win or lose. And as one former pro player put it, "Anyone who struggles for the top will be transformed."

EPILOGUE

Twitch boomed in 2016. Viewers watched 292 billion minutes of gaming streams, up from 50 billion in 2015.

The company signed an office lease for 185,000 square feet in an under-construction tower in San Francisco, one of the city's largest deals of the year. It hired hundreds of new employees. Memories of the cramped industrial quarters occupied by Justin Kan and his friends faded.

Competitive gaming was also smashing records. League of Legends sold out Madison Square Garden in New York. ESPN embraced eSports, dedicating a section of its website to the topic. It was a timely move, as owners of teams like the Philadelphia 76ers and Sacramento Kings started eSports squads.

It was the biggest eSports had ever been. But Evil Geniuses wasn't growing, despite now being a subsidiary of Twitch. Aside from the return of Artour "Arteezy" Babaev, the flashy player acquisitions that characterized Alexander Garfield's tenure were absent. It wasn't expanding into new games.

Evil Geniuses was now owned by Twitch, which was owned by Amazon. That led to a backlash, according to veteran Evil Geniuses player Geoff "iNcontroL" Robinson. He claimed that Evil Geniuses didn't sign a Counter-Strike: Global Offensive team, despite its roots in the franchise, because other teams threatened to boycott Twitch if that happened. Cloud9 owner Jack Etienne led the opposition, said iNcontroL. Etienne denied the accusations.

The new Evil Geniuses DOTA 2 squad was good but not great, taking third place in the first $3 million Major tournament in Frankfurt. They looked for redemption in the spring of 2016 at the second Major in Shanghai.

On the eve of the team's flight to China, captain Peter "ppd" Dager reflected on two years of victories. He had made over $2 million playing DOTA 2, the most of any eSports player aside from his teammate Saahil "UNiVeRsE" Arora.

"The players have all the power currently. Some players don't realize that yet, but I think a lot of the older players are starting to see how much value we actually have," he said.

"At the end of the day, we own our team," he said. "Maybe we don't have ownership in the team or a stake in its equity, but if we don't want to play in this tournament or we want to play in this tournament, we're gonna do it, nobody's going to stop us."

For instance, Evil Geniuses had declined an invitation to an ESL tournament in Manila, which was devastating to the organizers, said ppd.

"I've realized how much business is like a game. Everyone is just trying to get the biggest piece of whatever's happening right now," he said.

"We're in this giant period of transition that never ends. All these companies are trying to make exclusive tournaments and sell their media rights. It's a crazy time right now. There's guys throwing money at teams that aren't really worth that much," said ppd.

In traditional sports, a team's spot in the league is not in jeopardy. A mediocre team may not play games in the playoffs, but it won't get kicked out of the league if it sucks. In eSports, a team has a risk of collapsing every year. Even in League of Legends, a championship team can disband or lose its spot in the league by underperforming. In DOTA 2, teams could disband at any moment, and most of them did if they failed to qualify for big tournaments.

"Tomorrow, our team could disband. Artour could be like, 'I fucking hate you, Peter, I'm never going to play with you again,' and then our team is destroyed, right?" said ppd. "Then we're not going to go to big tournaments. We're not going to get top placements."

"I've very fortunate and I'm very lucky in the position I'm in. A majority of players don't have that," he said. "I could be kicked from my team tomorrow."

The next day, ppd was not kicked, and he flew with his team to Shanghai.

Evil Geniuses was strong, advancing to the second round of the upper bracket, where it faced its nemesis, Team Secret.

Secret's lineup was nothing like the year before. Only Clement "Puppey" Ivanov remained. Four new players, including Jacky "EternaLEnVy" Mao, were on the team.

The match went to a third, deciding game. Arteezy was playing the hero Sven, a burly armored warrior with a massive sword and some of the highest damage output in the game. But he's a melee character, weak to ranged attackers and disables.

In the fifty-fifth minute, with its base almost destroyed, Evil Geniuses marched down the middle lane. Arteezy moved confidently forward. With two Divine Rapier items, he dealt over 1,200 damage per strike.

Then Team Secret's Nature's Prophet summoned a ring of trees, temporarily encasing Arteezy. He was impotent, dying beneath an onslaught of ranged damage.

Evil Geniuses dropped to the lower bracket, facing elimination. They would play Team Liquid, and again, Arteezy played Sven and was countered by Nature's Prophet. Third place again.

Team Secret stomped Team Liquid in the finals, three games to one. They won $1.1 million.

Three weeks later, March 22, 2017. A whirlwind of social media announcements: Despite winning the year's biggest tournament so far, Team Secret was kicking two of its members. Arteezy and UNiVeRsE were leaving Evil Geniuses and joining Secret.

Ppd was right. A team's future was fragile, even if it placed third. Even if it won the entire tournament.

Facing a crisis, Evil Geniuses re-signed two old faces: Sam "BuLba" Sosale and, improbably, the player it had kicked months before: Kurtis "Aui_2000" Ling. The next big Major tournament in Manila was a disaster, as Evil Geniuses were eliminated in the first round. But shockingly, so was Team Secret. It turned out that Arteezy and EternaLEnVy's greedy play styles were not complementary. UNiVeRsE, the supreme playmaker on Evil Geniuses, looked lost and was ineffective.

The shuffle began again, weeks before the sixth International was to take place in August. UNiVeRsE returned to Evil Geniuses, and Ludwig "zai" Wåhlberg rejoined the team, having just finished his high school studies. BuLba, kicked again, joined Team Secret.

Crowdfunding surged, and the sixth International's prize pool grew to $20.7 million, with $9 million to the champion.

The new Team Secret managed to qualify for the tournament, but faded quickly, losing to the Chinese team LGD in the first round of playoffs. Evil Geniuses looked like they'd had a return to glory, marching toward the semi-finals.

"It can be hard to appreciate things these days. This @Evil-Geniuses team is a special group at a special moment - let's all try to enjoy it," Evil Geniuses' chief Alexander Garfield said on Twitter. He declined to comment further.

They faced Digital Chaos, a team with two of the players that Team Secret had previously kicked. It went to a third game, and again, Evil Geniuses lost. Third place. It was a far better performance than ppd had anticipated, but not the miracle of the previous year's championship.

Nine days after the Chinese team Wings won the International, on August 22, 2017, Garfield announced he was leaving GoodGame. Sources said it wasn't amicable.

Weeks later, Evil Geniuses announced it was severing its relationship with Twitch. The team would be independent again, and Peter "ppd" Dager was the new CEO.

As eSports looked to new heights, one of its oldest names was free to grow once more.

THE PLAYERS

THE TEAMS

compLexity

Jason Lake, CEO

Counter-Strike, 2006
   Matt "Warden" Dickens
   Justin "Sunman" Summy
   Danny "fRoD" Montaner
   Tyler "Storm" Wood
   Cory "tr1p" Dodd

Team 3D

Craig "Torbull" Levine, CEO

Counter-Strike, 2006
   Josh "Dominator" Sievers
   Kyle "Ksharp" Miller
   Mikey "method" So

Ronald "Rambo" Kim
Griffin "shaGuar" Benger
Sal "Volcano" Garozzo

Evil Geniuses

Alexander Garfield, CEO

Counter-Strike, WCG 2005
Jimmy "Lin" Lin
Matt "bl00dshot" Stevenson
Griffin "shaGuar" Benger
Pasha "LaRi" Lari
Robert "blackpanther" Tyndale

StarCraft II
Chris "HuK" Loranger
Geoff "iNcontroL" Robinson

Former Players
Greg "IdrA" Fields
Lee "PuMa" Ho Joon

DOTA 2, The International 2015 Champions
Clinton "Fear" Loomis
Syed Sumail "SumaiL" Hassan
Saahil "UNiVeRsE" Arora
Kurtis "Aui_2000" Ling
Peter "ppd" Dager
Charlie Yang, manager
Philip Aram, assistant manager
Sam "BuLba" Sosale, coach

Alliance

DOTA 2, The International 2013 Champions
Jonathan "Loda" Berg
Gustav "s4" Magnusson
Henrik "AdmiralBulldog" Ahnberg
Jerry "EGM" Lundkvist
Joakim "Akke" Akterhall
Kelly "kellyMILKIES" Ong, manager

Natus Vincere

Alex Kokhanovskyy, CEO

DOTA 2, The International 2011 Champions
Oleksandr "XBOCT" Dashkevych
Danil "Dendi" Ishutan
Dmitriy "LighTofHeaveN" Kupriyanov
Clement "Puppey" Ivanov
Ivan "Artstyle" Antonov

Fnatic

Wouter Sleijffers, CEO
Sam Cook, founder
Patrik "cArn" Sättermon, chief gaming officer

Team Secret

DOTA 2, The International 2016 Eighth Place
Artour "Arteezy" Babaev

Gustav "s4" Magnusson
Ludwig "zai" Wåhlberg
Kuro "KuroKy" Takhasomi
Clement "Puppey" Ivanov
Matthew "Cyborgmatt" Bailey, manager

SK Telecom T1

Lim "BoxeR" Yo-Hwan, StarCraft I champion

League of Legends World Champions, Season 3, 2013
Jung "Impact" Eon-yeong
Bae "bengi" Seong-ung
Lee "Faker" Sang-hyeok
Chae "Piglet" Gwang-jin
Lee "PoohManDu" Jeong-hyeon

THE DEVELOPERS

Riot Games

Brandon Beck, CEO, cofounder
Marc Merrill, president, cofounder
Ryan "Morello" Scott, the lead designer of League of Legends
Nick Allen, former director of North American league
    operations

Valve Corporation

Gabe Newell, Mike Harrington, founders
IceFrog, lead DOTA 2 designer

Jess Cliffe, cocreator of Counter-Strike

Minh "Gooseman" Le, cocreator of Counter-Strike, former employee

Blizzard Entertainment

Michael Morhaime and Frank Pearce, cofounders

Dustin Browder, game director of StarCraft II

David "dayvie" Kim, StarCraft II balance lead

Chris Metzen, senior vice president, story and franchise development, lead design of StarCraft

Kim Phan, director of eSports

Former employees

David Ting, former head of online publishing

Rob Pardo, former chief creative officer, lead designer of StarCraft: Brood War

James Phinney, lead designer for StarCraft

THE INFRASTRUCTURE

Justin.tv Founders

Emmett Shear

Justin Kan

Michael Seibel

Kyle Vogt

Twitch

Kevin Lin, COO

Marcus "djWHEAT" Graham, director of programming
Jeff Bezos, CEO of Amazon.com

Beyond the Summit

David "GoDz" Parker
David "LD" Gorman

joinDOTA

Toby "TobiWan" Dawson

GSL

John Park, former contents manager
Nick "Tasteless" Plott
Dan "Artosis" Stemkoski

ESL

Ralf Reichert, founder and CEO
Craig "Torbull" Levine, CEO of Turtle Entertainment
    America Inc. (ESL parent company)
Ulrich Schulze, managing director of pro gaming
William Cho, host and creative producer

ACKNOWLEDGMENTS

Before each game, it's customary to write "gl hf"—or "Good Luck Have Fun"—to your opponent. Those two things have also been crucial ingredients to the success of eSports: the luck of good timing and having the technology to support a rapidly growing industry, and the fun that has created passion and pleasure for gamers around the world.

The roots of this book are partially from my own childhood spent gazing at computer screens, battling pixelated monsters controlled by strangers on the Internet. But the idea of eSports didn't quite come into focus until the spring of 2010, when I was a senior about to graduate college. I came across some YouTube videos of StarCraft II beta matches, commentated by Alex "HDStarCraft" Do and Mike "HuskyStarcraft" Lamond. They aren't active anymore, but their work helped kick off the latest and biggest wave in what's become a life-changing industry, and one that I've spent thousands of hours following.

I'm hugely grateful to my editor Maxim Brown, publicist Ashley Vanicek, and Skyhorse Publishing for the amazing opportunity to document one of the most quickly changing and fast-growing phenomena of my lifetime.

Most of the material of the book comes from my five years of following eSports as a personal passion, lots of reading, and over fifty interviews conducted during 2015.

Special thanks to Alexander Garfield, who was very generous with his time, and his past and current colleagues: Anna Prosser Robinson, Geoff Robinson, Robert Tyndale, Charlie Yang, Peter Dager, Greg Fields, Ioannis Loucas, and Conrad Janzen.

Over at Twitch, thanks to Kevin Lin, Marcus Graham, and Chase. It was also a treat to hear Justin Kan and Michael Seibel talk about the early days of what was once Justin.tv.

Thanks to Jason Lake and Craig Levine, two of the original makers of the North American eSports scene. And to Dan Stemkoski and Nick Plott for telling the story of their incredible journey to South Korea, and John Park for an unfiltered look at the business triumphs and struggles of GOMTV.

Thanks to Minh Le, the only game designer I was able to talk to directly, for memories of Counter-Strike.

Thanks to Heather Garozzo, Stephanie Harvey, Hollyanne Setola, and Olivia Seeto for thoughtful interviews on women in gaming.

Thanks to David Graham for legal and fighting game insights, and to Andy Reif for a candid look at the CGS. Thanks to Nick Allen, Travis Gafford, William Cho, and Brad Bao for a League of Legends education. Thanks to David Ting for making IPL.

Thanks to Dimitri Valente and Josh Lee for a look at Chinese DOTA 2. Thanks also to Greg Laird and Stephanie Everett, and Beyond the Summit's two Davids, David Gorman and David

Parker. Thanks to Alexander Kokhanovskyy and the singular Danil Ishutin, known better as Dendi.

Thanks to Ulrich Schulze at ESL, Tyler Peckman at AFK Lounge. For a European perspective, thanks to Bjoern Franzen and Wouter Sleijffers.

Thanks to Blizzard, Riot, and Valve for making all of the games that we love. Attending the fifth International was something I'll never forget.

This book wouldn't have been possible without the mountains of data and news at sites like TeamLiquid.net and the incredibly helpful Liquipedia tournament database, E-sports earnings, Reddit, Kotaku, GosuGamers, archival footage from YouTube, Twitch, and the Game Developers Conference, and mainstream media sources.

I also hope this builds on two previous works: T.L. Taylor's *Raising the Stakes* and Michael Kane's *Game Boys*.

Thanks to my parents for letting me play—but not too much. Thanks to Johan Harjono and Heather Holland for feedback on drafts.

I can't wait to see what happens next. As we say at the end, win or lose: good game, well played.

Roland Li
Oakland
March 2016

NOTES

Pre-Game

1 "Reliably, at any nighttime moment": Stewart Brand, "Spacewar Fanatic Life and Symbolic Death Among the Computer Bums," *Rolling Stone*, December 7, 1972. www.wheels.org/spacewar/stone/rolling_stone.html.

2 Atari created the Space Invaders Championship: "'Space Invaders' revel at New York superbowl," UPI. www.retroist.com/2013/05/20/it-is-1980-and-the-national-space-invaders-tournament-finals-is-approaching.

2 *Starcade*: See www.starcade.tv/starcade/tv/starcadetv-shows.asp.

2 Nintendo World Championships: Frank Cifaldi, "The Story of the First Nintendo World Championships," *IGN*, May 13, 2015. www.ign.com/articles/2015/05/13/the-story-of-the-first-nintendo-world-championships.

2 cash prizes that reach seven figures: An extensive database of tournament winnings can be found at www.esportsearnings.com.

4 revenue will exceed $100 billion: See newzoo.com/insights/articles/global-games-market-will-reach-102–9-billion-2017–2.

4 Deloitte projecting eSports revenue: See www2.deloitte.com/eg/en/pages/technology-media-and-telecommunications/articles/tmt-pred16-media-esports-bigger-smaller-than-you-think.html.

4 Roger Ebert claimed: Roger Ebert, "Video Games Can Never Be Art," Roger Ebert's Journal, April 16, 2010. www.rogerebert.com/rogers-journal/video-games-can-never-be-art.

5 **"What does it take to get really good?"**: Frank Lantz, interview with the author.

5 **Is eSports actually a sport?**: For more on this topic see T.L. Taylor, *Raising the Stakes: E-Sports and the Professionalization of Computer Gaming* (The MIT Press, 2012).

6 **dedicated eSports section on its website**: See www.espn.com/esports.

6 **if competitive gaming is characterized as a sport**: Nick Wingfield, "In E-Sports, Video Gamers Draw Real Crowds and Big Money," *New York Times*, August 30, 2014. www.nytimes.com/2014/08/31/technology/esports-explosion-brings-opportunity-riches-for-video-gamers.html; see comments by James Lampkin.

7 **estimated $278 million**: See newzoo.com/insights/articles/esports-q3-report-revenues-to-reach-765m-in-2018-as-enthusiasts-grow-to-165m.

7 **$10 billion for the NFL and $21 billion by European soccer leagues**: Prashob Menon, Liam Boluk, "Why the next sports empire will be built on eSports," *Redef*, April 12, 2015. redef.com/original/good-game-why-esports-is-the-next-major-league-sport.

7 **hit 32 million in 2013**: Dustin "RedBeard" Beck, "One World Championship, 32 million viewers," Riot Games, 2013. na.leagueoflegends .com/en/news/esports/esports-editorial/one-world-championship-32-million-viewers.

7 **A peak of 120 million**: Frank Pallotta, "Super Bowl XLIX posts the largest audience in TV history," CNN, February 2, 2015. money.cnn.com/2015/02/02/media/super-bowl-ratings.

7 **Global brands like Coca-Cola, American Express, and Intel**: See www.coca-colacompany.com/tags/coke-esports,about.americanexpress.com/news/pr/2013/amex-prepaid-partner-league-of-legends.aspx, and www.intelextrememasters.com.

Chapter 1

9 **"Terrorists Win"**: This is a general description of gameplay and isn't specific to a particular match.

10 **truly broke through in the 1990s with Doom**: David Kushner, *Masters of Doom: How Two Guys Created an Empire and Transformed Pop Culture* (Random House, 2003).

10 **a magnet for controversy**: Kevin Simpson and Jason Blevins, "Did Harris preview massacre on 'Doom'?" *Denver Post*, May 4, 1999. extras.denverpost.com/news/shot0504f.htm.

11 **"It really wasn't about eSports"**: All Minh Le quotes from interview with the author.

12 **"I thought it was insanely frustrating"**: All Alexander Garfield quotes from interview with the author.

13 **"I grew up working . . . Too often people are afraid of failure"**: Istvan Hargittai, "Deeds and Dreams of Eugene Garfield," *Chemical Intelligencer*, October 1999. www.garfield.library.upenn.edu/papers/chemicalintelligencerp26y1999.pdf.

15 **The first major US video game tournament**: John Gaudiosi, "CPL Founder Angel Munoz Explains Why He Left ESports And Launched Mass Luminosity," *Forbes*, April 9, 2013.www.forbes.com/sites/johngaudiosi/2013/04/09/cpl-founder-angel-munoz-explains-why-he-left-esports-and-launched-mass-luminosity/#634bfc2454d9.

16 **The early days were lean**: For the most in-depth account of CPL and the compLexity and Team 3D rivalry, see Michael Kane, *Game Boys: Triumph, Heartbreak, and the Quest for Cash in the Battleground of Competitive Videogaming* (Viking, 2008).

18 **"There are very few areas that so beautifully marry"**: Ehtisham Rabbani, interview with the author.

19 **"You have to have a real insider's perspective"**: All Robert Tyndale quotes from interview with the author.

21 **Levine began working at an East Village Internet café**: Craig Levine, interview with the author.

22 **"I never went into it with the idea"**: Sal Garozzo, interview with the author.

22 **"I really thought this was the sport of the future"**: All Jason Lake quotes from interview with the author.

23 **Stockholm was home to the gaming festival DreamHack**: See www.dreamhack.se/DHS11/event-information/what-is-dreamhack.

23 **Angel Munoz realized that he preferred being an entrepreneur**: Gaudiosi.

23 **Munoz stopped paying prize money**: Dominic Koller, "G7 Teams not to attend CPL," SK Gaming, November 7, 2007. www.sk-gaming.com/content/12657.

23 **after he was profiled in the *Washington Post***: Jose Antonio Vargas, "Big Games Hunter," *Washington Post*, October 25, 2005. www.washingtonpost.com/wp-dyn/content/article/2005/10/24/AR2005102401859.html

24 **MTV had run a documentary in 2005**: See footage here: www.youtube.com/watch?v=PXGkNHsXm2w.

24 **The Australian native would pretend to work**: Kane.

25 **"Dead or Alive was picked for being cinematic…"**: All Andy Reif quotes and most CGS material from an interview with the author.

26 **he spent the last $500**: Stuwart Lowman, "Turning fun into profit," January 3, 2006, *Brainstorm*. www.brainstormmag.co.za/index.php?option=com_content&view=article&id=1028:turning-fun-into-profit.

30 **a reported fifty million viewers**: Corin Cole, "The Fall of CGS," *Esports Heaven*, December 2, 2008. www.esportsheaven.com/articles/view/128/the-fall-of-cgs.

31 **The World Series of Video Games closed**: Andy Chalk, "Cyberathlete Professional League Shuts Down," *Escapist*, March 2008. www.escapistmagazine.com/news/view/82350-Cyberathlete-Professional-League-Shuts-Down.

32 **"We hope that the team's rich history"**: See druidz.se/nyheter/3/129.

33 **"A traitor is a traitor"**: Corin Cole, "coL.CSS Move to EG, Lose Rambo," *Esports Heaven*, December 14, 2008. www.esportsheaven.com/news/view/47810/col-css-move-to-eg-lose-rambo.

Chapter 2

35 **fastest Internet on the planet**: Mark McDonald, "Home Internet May Get Even Faster in South Korea," *New York Times*, February 21, 2011. www.nytimes.com/2011/02/22/technology/22iht-broadband22.html.

35 **the government invested $11 billion**: Dal Yong Jin, *Korea's Online Gaming Empire* (The MIT Press, 2010).

36 **Players view the map from an aerial perspective**: Gameplay descriptions from many games of StarCraft played by the author.

39 **"Rush strategies are important"**: Soren Johnson, "Designer Notes: Rob Pardo," October 30, 2014. www.idlethumbs.net/designernotes/episodes/rob-pardo-part-1.

39 **"My high school years were like a dark tunnel"**: A BoxeR fan with the TeamLiquid user name Marencielo translated the book. A commercial copy of the book doesn't appear to be available. A cached version of the translation can be found at web.archive.org/web/20110725083823/http://boxerbiography.blogspot.com/.

41 **reportedly died of starvation:** Mark Tran, "Girl starved to death while parents raised virtual child in online game," *Guardian*, March 5, 2010. www.theguardian.com/world/2010/mar/05/korean-girl-starved-online-game.

41 **A Taiwanese gamer went into cardiac arrest**: Katie Hunt, Naomi Ng, "Man dies in Taiwan after 3-day online gaming binge," CNN, January 19, 2015. www.cnn.com/2015/01/19/world/taiwan-gamer-death.

41 **curfews for Internet cafés**: Geoffrey Cain, "South Korea Cracks Down on Gaming Addiction," *Time*, April 20, 2010. content.time.com/time/world/article/0,8599,1983234,00.html.

41 **is reviewing research**: Stephanie Sarkis, "Internet Gaming Disorder in DSM-5," *Psychology Today*, July 18, 2014. www.psychologytoday.com/blog/here-there-and-everywhere/201407/internet-gaming-disorder-in-dsm-5.

41 **Sinabro approached Lim**: From his memoir.

42 **BoxeR, wearing a silvery jacket**: See www.youtube.com/watch?v=rv3dqjgLeCg.

43 **swelled to over a half million members**: Patrick Howell O'Neill, "The Emperor strikes back: the rise of Boxer," *SK Gaming*, January 15, 2011. www.sk-gaming.com/content/31853-The_Emperor_strikes_back_the_rise_of_Boxer.

43 **Air Force ACE**: See wiki.teamliquid.net/starcraft/Air_Force_ACE.

43 **"Korea is a society driven by competition"**: John Park, interview with the author.

44 **Dal Yong Jin, a communications professor**: Jin.

45 **forming the Korean e-Sports Association**: Ben McGrath, "Good Game," *New Yorker*, November 24, 2014. www.newyorker.com/magazine/2014/11/24/good-game.

45 **In New Hampshire, Dan "Artosis" Stemkoski**: All Dan Stemkoski quotes from interview with the author.

47 **Tasteless wore a pink T-shirt**: See www.youtube.com/watch?v=v0fV5KADifY.

47 **"He was better than me at the time"**: All Nick Plott quotes and narrative from interview with the author.

Chapter 3

52 **brute of a man**: See www.youtube.com/watch?v=aUXoekeDIW8.

52 **"Really? That weird thing in Korea?"**: See Dustin Browder's talk at www.gdcvault.com/play/1014488/The-Game-Design-of-STARCRAFT.

55 **"We joke about how StarCraft is bad for you"**: All Nick Plott quotes from interview with the author.

55 **Artosis had his friend**: All Dan Stemkoski quotes from interview with the author.

56 **selling over 1.5 million copies**: Matt Peckham, "StarCraft II Sales Top 1.5 Million Copies in 48 Hours," *PCWorld*. www.pcworld.com/article/202460/starcraft_ii_sales_top_1_5_million.html.

56 **Blizzard wanted royalties**: Kim Tong-hyung, "Blizzard vows to take MBC to court," *Korea Times*, December 2, 2010. www.koreatimes.co.kr/www/news/tech/2010/12/133_77381.html.

56 **required StarCraft II to be played online**: Jason Schreier, "Why StarCraft II Still Doesn't Support Local Multiplayer," Kotaku, June 20, 2012. kotaku. com/5919892/why-starcraft-ii-still-doesnt-support-local-multiplayer.

57 **"It was extraordinary to see"**: All John Park quotes from interview with the author.

57 **Kim "Fruitdealer" Won Ki**: See www.youtube.com/watch?v=WrfzEO2yTe0.

58 **Alex "HD" Do and Mike "Husky" Lamond**: See www.youtube.com/ watch?v=SvDBBXqthrY. (This was the tournament that got the author interested in eSports and can be considered the genesis of this book.)

59 **Day[9] Daily**: See www.youtube.com/watch?v=NJztfsXKcPQ.

61 **Ong stopped casting**: See www.complexitygaming.com/news/2536.

61 **He was color-blind**: Jake Sklarew, interview with the author.

61 **thread on Reddit**: See www.reddit.com/r/starcraft/comments/qlpfk/orb_ gets_really_mad_when_he_loses_lol.

62 **Garfield didn't think he was actually racist**: All Alexander Garfield quotes from interviews with the author.

62 **Garfield fired Sklarew**: See www.teamliquid.net/forum/starcraft-2/319018- orb-dismissed-from-evil-geniuses-broadcasts.

63 **"Nobody thought $200 was going to get them"**: Geoff Robinson, interview with the author.

63 **Major League Gaming**: Alan Feuer, "Seeking to Be Both NFL and ESPN of Video Gaming," *New York Times*. www.nytimes.com/2013/08/11/nyregion/seeking-to-be-both-nfl-and-espn-of-video-gaming.html

63 **stint in juvenile prison**: Jeff Fraser, "Canadian pro-gaming prodigy earning a Starcraft salary abroad," *Global and Mail*, July 17, 2012. www. theglobeandmail.com/technology/gaming/canadian-pro-gaming-prodigy-earning-a-starcraft-salary-abroad/article4423093.

64 **11.7 million viewers**: See www.majorleaguegaming.com/news/mlg-2012-season-generates-334-growth-in-live-online-viewers.

64 **"I hated losing"**: All quotes from an interview with Greg Fields.

67 **"I thought Nick"**: All Alexander Garfield quotes from interviews with the author.

68 **"It's not like not caring about the game"**: See www.youtube.com/watch?v= jRheYNwLWk4.

69 **HuK conjured a fleet**: See www.youtube.com/watch?v=4Occy9kljvI.

71 **"It's not just TSL"**: Radoslave Kolev, "NASL champion Puma joins Team EG," *GosuGamers*, July 21, 2011. www.gosugamers.net/ news/16279-nasl-champion-puma-joins-team-eg?comment=364761.

73 **"potentially life changing"**: See www.teamliquid.net/forum/news-archive/ 255528-farewell-liquidhuk.

Notes

73 **His face was expressionless**: See www.youtube.com/watch?v=z49n0LaxagE.

75 **"i genuinely hope something bad"**: See i.imgur.com/LPgTR0W.jpg.

76 **"Winning is at best tangentially related"**: See www.teamliquid.net/forum/starcraft-2/411483-the-giant-evil-geniuses?page=4#67.

76 **"As most of you are already aware"**: See www.teamliquid.net/forum/starcraft-2/411840-evil-geniuses-releases-greg-idra-fields.

77 **"On some level"**: Geoff Robinson, in an interview with the author.

78 **"If I wanted to continue"**: See www.teamliquid.net/forum/starcraft-2/442589-leaving-starcraft-idra.

Chapter 4

80 **In April 2005**: The majority of this narrative is from interviews with Justin Kan, Michael Seibel, and Kevin Lin.

81 **Graham was initially reluctant**: See old.ycombinator.com/start.html.

82 **Livingston, a former**: See paulgraham.com/jessica.html.

82 **"Emmett only learned to program"**: See areallybadidea.com/34320844.

83 **Kan had the idea of selling**: See areallybadidea.com/selling-kiko.

84 **"I'll fund that just to see you make a fool"**: Joyce Guo, "Sitting down with Justin Kan," *Yale Herald*, November 20, 2014. yaleherald.com/voices/sitting-down-with-justin-kan.

85 **nick named the "Yscraper"**: Jessica Guynn, "Justin.tv to get boot from S.F. landlord," *San Francisco Chronicle*, April 28, 2007. www.sfgate.com/business/article/Justin-tv-to-get-boot-from-S-F-landlord-2599257.php.

85 **"This is a once-in-a-lifetime opportunity"**: All Michael Seibel quotes from interview with the author.

85 **"I wanted to do things"**: All Justin Kan quotes from interview with the author.

86 **published a front-page story**: Jessica Guynn, "It's Justin, Live! All day, all night!" *San Francisco Chronicle*, March 30, 2007. www.sfgate.com/news/article/IT-S-JUSTIN-LIVE-ALL-DAY-ALL-NIGHT-S-F-2606536.php.

86 **"Is it about being understood?"**: See www.youtube.com/watch?v=6E2-osqW6Vs.

86 **later told the *Yale Daily News***: Rachel Dempsey, "Alum stars in own 'Truman Show' online," *Yale Daily News*, April 5, 2007, yaledailynews.com/blog/2007/04/05/alum-stars-in-own-truman-show-online.

87 **The band's managers called**: See justinkan.com/three-stories.

89 **"There were thousands of people"**: All Kevin Lin quotes from interview with the author.

90 **raised a Series A funding round**: See www.crunchbase.com/organization/justintv.

245

90 **The UFC sued**: Michael David Smith, "UFC Sues Justin.tv, Says 50,000 People Viewed UFC 121 Illegally," *MMA Fighting*, January 21, 2011. www.mmafighting.com/2011/01/21/ufc-sues-justin-tv-says-50-000-people-viewed-ufc-121-illegally.

92 **grown to about $10 million**: Justin Kan, interview with the author.

92 **sold it to the software company Autodesk**: Ryan Lawler, "Mobile Video Sharing App Socialcam Acquired By Autodesk For $60 Million," *Techcrunch*, July 17, 2012. www.techcrunch.com/2012/07/17/socialcam-autodesk-60-million.

93 **streamer reportedly gets $2:** Jay Egger, "How exactly do Twitch streamers make a living? Destiny breaks it down," Daily Dot, April 21, 2015. www.dailydot.com/esports/twitch-streaming-money-careers-destiny.

94 **"Twitch represented the ideas"**: Marcus Graham, interview with the author.

96 **growing to twenty-eight million unique visitors**: See blog.twitch.tv/2013/03/twitch-announces-record-breaking-growth.

96 **Twitch was fourth**: Drew Fitzgerald, Daisuke Wakabayashi, "Apple Quietly Builds New Networks," *Wall Street Journal*, February 3, 2014. www.wsj.com/news/articles/SB100014240527023048511045793612016553653302.

97 **featured in the *Wall Street Journal***: Ian Sherr, "Videogames Become a Spectator Sport," *Wall Street Journal*, November 24, 2013. www.wsj.com/articles/SB10001424052702304607104579210140721840928.

97 **Felix "PewDiePie" Kjellberg**: See www.youtube.com/user/PewDiePie.

97 **he admitted using drugs**: Philip Kollar, "Popular Twitch streamer comes clean about drug use on stream," *Polygon*, December 8, 2015. www.polygon.com/2015/12/8/9871816/twitch-stream-manvsgame-man-vs-game-drug-use.

98 **id of eSports**: Ben McGrath, "Good Game," *New Yorker*, November 24, 2014. www.newyorker.com/magazine/2014/11/24/good-game.

98 **Kappa**: See twitchemotes.com.

99 **Abraham Biggs, a Florida college student**: Brian Stelter, "Web Suicide Viewed Live and Reaction Spur a Debate," *New York Times*, November 24, 2008. www.nytimes.com/2008/11/25/us/25suicides.html.

101 **Amazon.com emerged**: Eric Newcomer, Amir Efrati, "Amazon to acquire Twitch for $970 million," *The Information*, August 25, 2014. www.theinformation.com/Amazon-Nears-Deal-to-Acquire-Twitch.

102 **"There's an awful lot of influence"**: Jason Lake, interview with the author.

102 **later expressed regret**: See www.youtube.com/watch?v=Sh3iE1G79wk.

102 **"basically zero headway in China"**: Josh Lee, interview with the author.

103 **ESPN2 enraged many sports fans**: Nick Schwartz, "ESPN people are freaking out because ESPN televised eSports," *USA Today*, April 26, 2015. ftw.usatoday.com/2015/04/espn-esports-heroes-of-the-dorm-reaction.

103 **"Mostly, I'm interested in doing real sports"**: Dawn Chmielewski, "Sorry, Twitch: ESPN's Skipper Says eSports 'Not a Sport,'" Re/code, September 4, 2014.   recode.net/2014/09/04/sorry-twitch-espns-skipper-says-esports-not-a-sport.

104 **"Those were young"**: Joe Brown, Peter Kafka, "ESPN's John Skipper Calls the Plays on Digital Content, eSports and Diversity," Re/code, February 26, 2016. recode.net/2016/02/26/espns-john-skipper-calls-the-plays-on-digital-content-esports-and-diversity/?curator=MediaREDEF.

104 **Turner Broadcasting plans**: See www.e-league.com.

104 **Twitch's first ever convention, TwitchCon**: Author attended.

Chapter 5

106 **making nearly $500,000**: Ran Liu, "FOX officially unveils record signing Moon," *SK Gaming*, March 12, 2009. www.sk-gaming.com/content/22880-FOX_officially_unveils_record_signing_Moon.

107 **A creator known only as Eul**: See web.archive.org/web/20090417003613/www.gamesetwatch.com/2008/05/column_the_game_anthropologist_defense_of.php.

109 **Beck and Merrill met**: See www.marshall.usc.edu/about/voices/2011/we-started-riot.

110 **Mescon shut down the website:** See www.playdota.com/forums/showthread.php?t=274600.

111 **"I was a twenty-six-year-old CEO"**: See www.youtube.com/watch?v=gxif15cxvzU.

111 **considered two: Riot and Zynga**: Brad Bao, interview with the author.

112 **leaking ceiling**: See www.riotgames.com/articles/20131107/983/riots-making-move.

113 **took around $18 million**: David Segal, "Behind League of Legends, E-Sports's Main Attraction," *New York Times*, October 10, 2014. www.nytimes.com/2014/10/12/technology/riot-games-league-of-legends-main-attraction-esports.html.

113 **"Our game and most games"**: All Marc Merrill quotes from www.gdcvault.com/play/1013805/LEAGUE-OF-LEGENDS-Postmortem-One.

114 **1.6 million people watched:** John Funk, "League of Legends Championship Draws 1.69 Million Viewers," *Escapist*, June 23, 2011. www.

escapistmagazine.com/news/view/111254-League-of-Legends-Championship-Draws-1–69-Million-Viewers.

114 **He and his wife bonded**: David Ting, interview with the author.

115 **The opening interested Nick Allen**: All Nick Allen quotes from interview with the author.

116 **8.2 million viewers**: Tracey Lien, "League of Legends final attracts 8.2 million viewers, Season 2 Championships most-watched eSports event of all time," *Polygon*, October 23, 2012. www.polygon.com/2012/10/23/3542424/league-of-legends-final-attracts-8-2-million-viewers-season-2.

117 **"Riot's always had a hard time"**: Travis Gafford, interview with the author.

117 **News Corp sold IGN**: Sarah Lacey, Michael Carney, "Sources: Ziff Davis is close to buying IGN," *PandoDaily*, February 1, 2013. pando.com/2013/02/01/sources-ziff-davis-is-close-to-buying-ign/.

118 **Riot set the standards**: Nick Allen, interview with the author.

119 **$25,000 per year**: See the contract at riot-web-static.s3.amazonaws.com/lolesports/Rule%20Sets/2015_LCS_Rule_Set_2.01.pdf.

119 **The LCS is a money loser for Riot**: Segal.

120 **"What I like about the LCS series"**: Wouter Sleijffers, interview with the author.

120 **American Express sponsored**: See about.americanexpress.com/news/pr/2013/amex-prepaid-partner-league-of-legends.aspx.

120 **Coke sponsored**: See www.coca-colacompany.com/tags/coke-esports.

120 **sixty-seven million players . . . $1 billion**: Segal.

120 **"You just have endless amounts of gameplay"**: Stephanie Everett, interview with the author.

121 **Chris Badawi**: Samuel Lingle, "Chris Badawi and the LCS team owners: Investigating one of League of Legends' biggest controversies," Daily Dot, August 12, 2015. www.dailydot.com/esports/chris-badawi-poaching-allegations-league-of-legends/.

122 **"All the developers have too much power"**: David Philip Graham, interview with the author.

123 **"I think that reward system"**: William Cho, interview with the author.

124 **found its next superstar**: Mina Kimes, "The Unkillable Demon King," ESPN, June 11, 2015. www.espn.go.com/espn/feature/story/_/id/13035450/league-legends-prodigy-faker-carries-country-shoulders.

125 **should have done more**: David Ting, interview with the author.

125 **StarCraft would die**: See www.reddit.com/r/starcraft/comments/11m21k/starcraft_2_will_be_dead_before_legacy_of_the.

127 **In four years of competition**: See wiki.teamliquid.net/starcraft2/2015_StarCraft_II_World_Championship_Series.

127 **"Nobody wants to watch eight Korean players"**: Alexander Kokhanovskyy, interview with the author.

129 **"I honestly say that it makes more sense"**: John Park, interview with the author.

129 **"WCS fucked shit up pretty badly"**: Nick Plott, interview with the author.

Chapter 6

131 **she had to deal with the perception**: Anna Prosser Robinson, interview with the author.

132 **Around half of US gamers are women**: See www.theesa.com/wp-content/uploads/2015/04/ESA-Essential-Facts-2015.pdf.

132 **controversy known as Gamergate**: Eric Johnson, "What Is Gamergate, and Why Is Intel So Afraid of It?" Re/code, October 9, 2014. recode.net/2014/10/09/what-is-gamergate-and-why-is-intel-so-afraid-of-it/.

133 **more than $100,000 in prize money**: See www.esportsearnings.com/players/female_players.

134 **Scarlett grew up in Kingston, Canada**: Ben McGrath, "Good Game," *New Yorker*, November 24, 2014. www.newyorker.com/magazine/2014/11/24/good-game.

134 **she retired after a few months**: See www.reddit.com/r/starcraft/comments/2du3so/why_msspyte_retires_starcraft_watch_first_minutes.

135 **"exploiting her gender"**: Olivia Seeto, interview with the author.

135 **"for her skills and looks"**: Becky Chambers, "All About Eve: The Story of StarCraft 2's First Female Pro," *The Mary Sue*, August 17, 2011. www.themarysue.com/all-about-eve-the-story-of-starcraft-2s-first-female-pro.

135 **She resigned from the team**: Callum Leslie, "The first female LCS player has stepped down," Daily Dot, February 5, 2016. www.dailydot.com/esports/remi-leaves-renegades.

136 **"It really takes a lot of determination"**: Tiffany Lim, interview with the author.

136 **"You have to realize the women"**: See www.gdcvault.com/play/1022030/Growing-the-Participation-of-Women.

137 **"I've been telling myself for years"**: Heather Garozzo, interview with the author.

140 **"Low-status males that have the most to lose"**: Michael Kasumovic, Jeffrey Kuznekoff, "Insights into Sexism: Male Status and Performance Moderates Female-Directed Hostile and Amicable Behaviour," *PLoS*

ONE, July 15, 2015. journals.plos.org/plosone/article?id=10.1371/journal.pone.0131613.

142 **"It's hard for a female to find a role model"**: Stephanie Harvey, interview with the author.

143 **"It's literally like women in the workforce"**: Hollyanne Setola, interview with the author.

144 **she posted an apology video**: See www.youtube.com/watch?v=DFDWdtWq8GA.

144 **Twitch updated its code of conduct**: Casey Johnson, "Twitch to streamers: no shirt, no service," *Ars Technica*, October 2014. arstechnica.com/gaming/2014/10/twitch-bans-sexually-suggestive-streamers.

146 **Evo had over ten thousand players**: See shoryuken.com/2015/07/01/evo-2015s-final-registration-numbers-released-see-where-your-favorite-game-stands.

146 **"There were many years where"**: David Graham, interview with the author.

148 **"You can't. You can't because"**: Patrick Klepek, "Aris 'Aris' Bakhtanians Releases Statement on Recent Comments," *Giant Bomb*, Februry 29, 2012. www.giantbomb.com/articles/aris-aris-bakhtanians-releases-statement-on-recent/1100–4007.

Chapter 7

150 **functioned as an iTunes**: Nick Wingfield, "Game Maker Without a Rule Book," *New York Times*, September 8, 2012. www.nytimes.com/2012/09/09/technology/valve-a-video-game-maker-with-few-rules.html.

150 **DOTA 2 would be unveiled**: See Valve's documentary on the event: www.youtube.com/watch?v=UjZYMI1zB9s.

151 **"Most of the current crop"**: Josh Lee, interview with the author.

151 **the country's ninety-ninth professional competitive sport**: Chris Luo, "Chinese gamers win US$5m top prize in international video game tournament," *South China Morning Post*, July 22, 2014. www.scmp.com/news/china-insider/article/1557200/chinese-gamers-win-us5m-top-prize-international-video-game.

152 **banned the broadcast of online games**: Marcella Szablewicz, "From Addicts to Athletes: participation in the discursive construction of digital games in urban China," *AoIR*, October 10, 2011. spir.aoir.org/index.php/spir/article/view/35.

152 **The owner of Invictus Gaming**: Phill Cameron, "iG celebrate their Dota 2 International win with a massive party thrown by their billionaire owner," *PCGamesN*, August 15, 2012. www.pcgamesn.com/dota/

ig-celebrate-their-dota-2-international-win-massive-party-thrown-their-billionaire-owner.

152 He performed in musical theater: Danil Ishutin, interview with the author.

153 One report described him: Danila Otavin, "Who is Arbalet?" *Esports Heaven*, May 26, 2010. www.esportsheaven.com/articles/view/579/who-is-arbalet.

153 had skill, power of will: Alexander Kokhanovskyy, interview with the author.

155 "Watching professionals play": See www.youtube.com/watch?v=lCIGtLpzgFw.

156 "The Play": See www.youtube.com/watch?v=Ldq1afiKQb8.

158 sold for $38,000: Jeremy Peel, "Dota 2 courier fetches $38,000, partly because it's pink," *PCGamesN*. www.pcgamesn.com/dota/dota-2-courier-fetches-38000-partly-because-its-pink.

158 Valve held a contest: Stephanie Everett, interview with the author.

159 Valve paid $10.2 million: Emily Gera, "Valve paid $10.2M to Dota 2 and Team Fortress 2 item creators," *Polygon*, January 17, 2014. www.polygon.com/2014/1/17/5318402/valve-paid-10–2m-to-dota-2-and-team-fortress-2-item-creators.

160 raised just under $40,000: See www.indiegogo.com/projects/beyond-the-summit-esports-studio.

161 "When you're a tournament organizer": David Gorman, interview with the author.

162 "The International as it is": Greg Laird, interview with the author.

162 Mao posted a message: See www.liquiddota.com/forum/dota-2-general/454226-going-on-leave-from-university-to-play-dota-2.

162 "It was my way of running away from life": See www.reddit.com/r/DotA2/comments/325ek3/my_younger_brother_wants_to_quit_education_and/cq8l9v9.

164 "That intensity is because of his will to win": Conrad Janzen, interview with the author.

165 "People drive you away": Geoff Robinson, interview with the author.

165 "Even if it made sense financially": David Parker.

166 "No one has ever done that": See www.youtube.com/watch?v=MAWK5kNDDlM.

167 No Tidehunter announced: Tezzeret, "nTh becomes the Alliance," *joinDOTA*, April 12, 2013. www.joindota.com/en/news/8399-nth-becomes-the-alliance.

167 Garfield had picked: Alexander Garfield, interview with the author.

168 "It's generally fear": See www.youtube.com/watch?v=gN7H8fK4Ueg.

168 **It started with an unfair fight**: See www.youtube.com/watch?v= -8HBr1EGX1I.

170 **"fundamental rewiring of my brain"**: All Alexander Garfield quotes from interviews with the author.

170 **AdmiralBulldog would later say**: See www.youtube.com/watch?v= vfuRkFcsDiI.

171 **"I can safely predict that Arteezy"**: Johan Järvinen, "Kaipi adds CWM and Arteezy," joinDOTA, April 29, 2013. www.joindota.com/en/ news/8857-kaipi-adds-cwm-and-arteezy.

172 **The first day was a disaster**: See www.youtube.com/watch?v=qrP4oey2_ys.

172 **released the details of their contracts**: Johan Järvinen, "SpeedGaming manager reveals contracts without players' permission," *GosuGamers*, November 19, 2013. www.gosugamers.net/dota2/news/26010-speedgaming-manager-reveals-contracts-without-asking-players.

172 **He was poorly organized**: Aaron Stern, "EternaLEnVy and Aui_2000 on the Thyton drama," *OnGamers*, November 27, 2013. web.archive.org/ web/20150813024842/www.ongamers.com/articles/eternalenvy-and-aui-2000-on-the-thyton-drama/1100–209/.

174 **[12:56:45 AM] Alexander Garfield**: See esportsexpress.com/2014/04/ arteezy-skype-logs-with-eg-owner-leaked.

175 **Clinton "Fear" Loomis**: Will Partin, "Nothing to Fear but Fear Himself," *Evil Geniuses*, February 10, 2014. evilgeniuses.gg/read/ 251,nothing-to-fear-but-fear-himself-part-i/.

176 **"If that player doesn't show up"**: Peter Dager, interview with the author.

177 **"Impressive start"**: See www.reddit.com/r/DotA2/comments/1w7z7u/ impressive_start_for_s_a_d_b_o_y_s_against_team.

179 **"What do you need?"**: See www.youtube.com/watch?v=KGgyfa9UZAU.

179 **Arteezy felt a new emotion**: See web.archive.org/web/20150115060449/ www.reddit.com/r/DotA2/comments/2shbcx/live_transcript_ arteezys_thoughts_on_the_drama.

181 **Garfield got an unwelcome visitor**: Alexander Garfield, interview with the author.

Chapter 8

183 **"You are not selling products"**: Bjoern Franzen, interview with the author.

184 **"It's eclipsing traditional sports"**: Philip Hudson, interview with the author.

185 **Ma "sAviOr" Jae Yoon**: Lukasz Gzelak, "sAviOr admits to match-fixing," *GosuGamers*, June 25, 2010. www.gosugamers.net/news/12308-savior-admits-to-match-fixing.

185 **Alex "Solo" Berezin**: Johan Järvinen, "Solo out of RoX.KiS," joinDOTA, June 26, 2013 www.joindota.com/en/news/10165-solo-out-of-rox-kis.

185 **"underpaid . . . were desperate for money"**: Lawrence Phillips, "Arrow: We are DDZ, and we DID 322," joinDOTA, October 20, 2014. www.joindota.com/en/news/22381-arrow-we-are-ddz-and-we-did-322-update

185 **"All that bottled-up anger"**: Tiffani Lim, interview with the author.

186 **Cheon "Promise" Min-Ki**: Ferguson Mitchell, "'League of Legends' pro attempts suicide after match-fixing scandal," Daily Dot. www.dailydot.com/esports/league-of-legends-promise-suicide-match-fixing.

186 **Valve banned seven players**: Richard Lewis, "New evidence points to match-fixing at highest level of American Counter-Strike," Daily Dot, January 16, 2015. www.dailydot.com/esports/match-fixing-counter-strike-ibuypower-netcode-guides.

187 **DOTA 2 Lounge**: See story by the author: www.polygon.com/features/2014/10/1/6080299/dota-2-hustlers.

188 **Unikrn in April 2015**: Dean Takahashi, "Ashton Kutcher invests in esports startup Unikrn as it launches a global platform," *Venturebeat*, September 1, 2015. www.venturebeat.com/2015/09/01/ashton-kutcher-invests-in-esports-startup-unikrn-as-it-launches-global-platform.

189 **Vulcun, a website**: Dean Takahashi, "Vulcun raises $12M for fantasy e-sports tournament startup," *Venturebeat*, April 9, 2015. www.venturebeat.com/2015/04/09/vulcun-raises-12m-for-fantasy-e-sports-tournament-startup.

190 **"Betting is not going anywhere"**: Edward Chang, interview with the author.

190 **developer recognized that betting was legal**: Nick Allen, interview with the author.

191 **it laid off a quarter of its staff**: Casey Newton, "The DraftKings of e-sports just laid off a quarter of its staff," *Verge*, January 11, 2016. www.theverge.com/2016/1/11/10750510/vulcun-layoffs-fantasy-e-sports.

191 **"That's my biggest worry"**: Conrad Janzen, interview with the author.

192 **reportedly sold for between $800,000 and $1.2 million each**: Joshua Brustein, "What Happens When Real Sports Money Moves Into Video Game Sports? "*Bloomberg*, January 15, 2016. www.bloomberg.com/news/articles/2016-01-15/what-happens-when-real-sports-money-moves-into-video-game-sports-.

193 **United States has a larger market for advertisers**: Wouter Sleijffers, interview with the author.

193 **"This ecosystem broadcasts one message"**: See www.twitlonger.com/ show/n_1so3r17.

194 **days away from bankruptcy**: Darren Heitner, "From Near Bankruptcy To Making Millions In eSports," *Forbes*, September 30, 2015. www. forbes.com/sites/darrenheitner/2015/09/30/from-near-bankruptcy-to-making-millions-in-esports/#16dff2023e2d.

194 **dropped its eSports investments**: Jacob Wolf, "DraftKings drops sponsorships from major esports organizations," Daily Dot, February 25, 2016. www.dailydot.com/esports/draftkings-drops-esports-sponsorships.

194 **Riot banned teams**: Jacob Wolf, "Riot asks teams to remove G2A logos as it mulls sponsorship ban," Daily Dot, October 6, 2015. www.dailydot. com/esports/riot-g2a-sponsorship-ban.

194 **its investors reportedly pulled out:** Jacob Wolf, "Ember's investors back out, team will release all players except Contractz," Daily Dot, March 21, 2016. www.dailydot.com/esports/ember-release-players-contractz.

194 **bought a majority stake**: Callum Leslie, "Swedish media giant MTG now effectively owns both DreamHack and ESL," Daily Dot, November 12, 2015. www.dailydot.com/esports/mtg-buys-dreamhack/.

194 **A month later, Blizzard bought**: Thiemo Brautigam, "MLG sells 'substantially all' assets to Activision Blizzard for $46 million, DiGiovanni replaced," *Esports Observer*, December 31, 2015. www.esportsobserver.com/mlg-sells-substantially-all-assets-to-activision-blizzard-for-46-million.

195 **"It's about creating an experience"**: See www.twitch.tv/kisacoresearch/ profile.

196 **"Most arenas are struggling"**: Urich Schulze, interview with the author.

196 **randomly drug testing**: Nick Wingfield, Conor Doughterty, "Drug Testing Is Coming to E-Sports," *New York Times*, July 23, 2015. www. nytimes.com/2015/07/24/technology/drug-testing-is-coming-to-e-gaming.html.

196 **$5.6 billion in revenue**: "Red Bull profit without wings," *Sky News*, September 19, 2015. www.skynews.com.au/business/business/shares/2015/09/19/ red-bull-profit-without-wings.html.

197 **Haag's charisma won them over**: Conversation at Red Bull Battlegrounds in San Francisco.

197 **covered another barcraft**: Amir Efrati, "Geeks Beat Jocks as Bar Fight Breaks Out Over Control of the TV," *Wall Street Journal*, August 23, 2011. www.wsj.com/articles/SB10001424053111904070604576516462736084234.

198 **"Hey, you guys are different"**: Tyler Peckham, interview with the author.

Chapter 9

200 Alexander Garfield wasn't satisfied: Alexander Garfield, interview with the author.

202 teams to completely rebrand: Samuel Lingle, "By their powers combined, Alliance is now Elements," Daily Dot, January 8, 2016. www.daily-dot.com/esports/alliance-rebrands-elements.

203 announced that it had acquired GoodGame: See www.goodgame.gg/twitch.

205 Some of his teammates: Peter Dager, interview with the author.

206 A front-page story: Nick Wingfield, "In E-Sports, Video Gamers Draw Real Crowds and Big Money," *New York Times*, August 30, 2014. www.nytimes.com/2014/08/31/technology/esports-explosion-brings-opportunity-riches-for-video-gamers.html.

206 "We still won everything": Charlie Yang, interview with the author.

207 Evil Geniuses played in a dim, spare room: See www.youtube.com/watch?v=fk6PuRsLBN8.

208 They battled for over an hour: See www.youtube.com/watch?v=c9b-H5-zgxo.

210 "Everything we talked about": See web.archive.org/web/20150115060449/www.reddit.com/r/DotA2/comments/2shbcx/live_transcript_arteezys_thoughts_on_the_drama.

211 "If you have a player": Ioannis Loucas, interview with the author.

212 Evil Geniuses had to gamble: Robert Kolker," The Video Game Dream: A Pakistani Teen Gets Rich Quick In E-Sports," *Bloomberg*, July 30, 2015. www.bloomberg.com/graphics/2015-pakistani-teens-esport-dream.

213 "One less ego one more championship": See twitter.com/peterpandam/status/564734933273292800.

214 KeyArena sits in an urban park: Author was at the event.

222 "Anyone who struggles for the top will be transformed": See news.ycombinator.com/item?id=9985894.